Sex Working and the Bible

BibleWorld
Series Editors: Philip R. Davies and James G. Crossley, University of Sheffield

BibleWorld shares the fruits of modern (and postmodern) biblical scholarship not only among practitioners and students, but also with anyone interested in what academic study of the Bible means in the twenty-first century. It explores our ever-increasing knowledge and understanding of the social world that produced the biblical texts, but also analyses aspects of the Bible's role in the history of our civilization and the many perspectives – not just religious and theological, but also cultural, political and aesthetic – which drive modern biblical scholarship.

Published:

Sodomy
A History of a Christian Biblical Myth
Michael Carden

Yours Faithfully: Virtual Letters from the Bible
Edited by Philip R. Davies

Israel's History and the History of Israel
Mario Liverani

The Apostle Paul and His Letters
Edwin D. Freed

The Origins of the 'Second' Temple: Persian Imperial Policy and the Rebuilding of Jerusalem
Diana Edelman

An Introduction to the Bible (Revised edition)
John Rogerson

The Morality of Paul's Converts
Edwin D. Freed

The Mythic Mind: Essays on Cosmology and Religion in Ugaritic and Old Testament Literature
Nick Wyatt

History, Literature and Theology in the Book of Chronicles
Ehud Ben Zvi

Women Healing/Healing Women: The Genderization of Healing in Early Christianity
Elaine M. Wainwright

Jonah's World: Social Science and the Reading of Prophetic Story
Lowell K. Handy

Symposia: Dialogues Concerning the History of Biblical Interpretation
Roland Boer

Sectarianism in Early Judaism
Edited by David J. Chalcraft

The Ontology of Space in Biblical Hebrew Narrative
Luke Gärtner-Brereton

Mark and its Subalterns: A Hermeneutical Paradigm for a Postcolonial Context
David Joy

Linguistic Dating of Biblical Texts: An Introduction to Approaches and Problems
Ian Young and Robert Rezetko

Redrawing the Boundaries: The Date of Early Christian Literature
J.V.M. Sturdy
Edited by Jonathan Knight

Forthcoming:

Vive Memor Mortis
Thomas Bolin

The Bible Says So!: From Simple Answers to Insightful Understanding
Edwin D. Freed

Judaism, Jewish Identities and the Gospel Tradition
Edited by James G. Crossley

The Joy of Kierkegaard: Essays on Kierkegaard as a Biblical Reader
Hugh Pyper

From Babylon to Eternity: The Exile Remembered and Constructed in Text and Tradition
Bob Becking, Alex Cannegieter, Wilfred van der Poll and Anne-Mareike Wetter

Charismatic Killers: Reading the Hebrew Bible's Violent Rhetoric in Film
Eric Christianson

On the Origins of Judaism
Philip R. Davies

SEX WORKING AND THE BIBLE

Avaren Ipsen

Routledge
Taylor & Francis Group

LONDON AND NEW YORK

First published 2009 by Equinox, an imprint of Acumen

Published 2014 by Routledge
2 Park Square, Milton Park, Abingdon, Oxon OX14 4RN
711 Third Avenue, New York, NY 10017, USA

Routledge is an imprint of the Taylor & Francis Group, an informa business

British Library Cataloguing-in-Publication Data

A catalogue record for this book is available from the British Library.

ISBN-13 978 1 84553 332 8 (hardback)
         978 1 84553 333 5 (paperback)

Library of Congress Cataloging-in-Publication Data

Ipsen, Avaren.
  Sex working and the Bible / Avaren Ipsen.
    p. cm. — (Bibleworld)
  Includes bibliographical references and index.
  ISBN 978-1-84553-332-8 (hb) — ISBN 978-1-84553-333-5 (pb)
  1. Bible—Criticism, interpretation, etc. 2. Prostitution—Biblical
teaching. I. Title.
  BS511.3.I67 2007
  220.8'30674—dc22
                            2007019637

Typeset by S.J.I. Services, New Delhi

CONTENTS

Contents

LIST OF ILLUSTRATIONS

ACKNOWLEDGEMENTS

I dedicate this book to "Sweet" who was the first to school me about the violence that street workers encounter. Her harrowing near death experience with a serial killer of prostitutes profoundly influenced the direction of my studies. The tale she told of being treated like a criminal instead of a victim by the police politicized me to work to educate others about this injustice. If not for "Sweet" I would not have sought out the rights groups US PROStitutes Collective (US PROS) and then later, the Sex Worker Outreach Project (SWOP) to do this kind of engaged research. Doing intellectual work for a grassroots group like SWOP keeps me in line and always attuned to the practical function of knowledge production. SWOP has enabled me to remember always Marx's Feuerbach Thesis no. 11 that the point of theory is to change the world in a positive manner. Robyn Few, Carol Stuart, Shemena Campbell, Veronica Monet, and Carol Leigh: you are all Goddesses. To my pseudonymous participants: you are über-Goddesses for trusting me with your stories when you have so much to loose by speaking out: Damienne Sin, Kimberly, Gayle, Ms Shiris, and again, "Sweet".

This book is a revised version of my doctoral dissertation. I am deeply grateful to my advisor, Mary Ann Tolbert, who directed both my Masters thesis and my PhD dissertation. She has had an incredible ability to both strongly believe in my work and be my most important and incisive critic. Any flaws of this book are my own and not in any way reflective of her lack of pre-emptive critique. I am indebted to her for her patience with my long academic adolescence. My other committee members, Luise Schotroff, LeAnn Flesher, and Nantawan Boonprasat Lewis have all been incredibly supportive and curious about my developing topic in different ways. Luise was the first senior scholar who collaborated with me and always treated me as a peer. She always encouraged me to stick with affirming the erotic aspects I detected in biblical texts. LeAnn helped me to sharpen my methodological tools and Nantawan affirmed my aspirations to be a genuine liberation scholar. I was also greatly helped by my exam committee members Renate Holub and Gina Hens-Piazza. Gina has always been a big supporter of my research ideas from the very start of my graduate study. Renate has been an especially super mentor as my boss at the University of California,

Berkeley, for the past seven years, first giving me work as a reader, a graduate student instructor and now as a lecturer. Towards the end of my doctorate, Renate urged me to not give up and get a full-time job, but to finish my dissertation. I am very blessed to have so many and wonderful *Doktormütter*.

My dissertation-writing group composed of Paul Fullmer, Yong-Sung Ahn, Joe Marchal, and Sean Burke were fun and engaging sources of support: thanks guys! I will never forget the fateful day when we all met at the Mediterranean café and Paul brought me a newspaper clipping about the Sex Worker Outreach Project's (SWOP) protest of the arrest of Shannon Williams. Shannon Williams taught at my daughter's Berkeley High School Independent Studies Program and was on a leave of absence when arrested for prostitution in 2003. She turned to escorting because she was a single mom in deep debt with student loans from earning her teaching credential. Now that she had an arrest record for prostitution, she would have a difficult time getting any more teaching jobs and having a rap sheet raised the penalties higher for doing any more sex work. It became very clear to me that the law was not helping her but harming her. I soon after contacted SWOP and began a long and fruitful collaboration. I gathered about 1,000 ballot signatures for the decriminalization of prostitution in front of the school where Shannon Williams had worked, during the Tuesday afternoon Berkeley Farmer's Markets on Derby Street.

Of course, without a book contract and editors, this dissertation would not be a book. I am very grateful to Philip Davies at Equinox, who was handed an abstract of my dissertation at SBL in 2006 by Jane Schaberg, and who then tracked me down to publish it. I also want to thank Norma Beavers and Valerie Hall at Equinox for their work with the editing and logistics of publishing (especially things like how to get permissions for images and book covers etc., about which I am a total novice). Thanks for your kind patience with me!

Finally, I thank my family: Tom, Mom, Sam and Gus thank you all for your patience and pride in me. Before anyone else did, you all believed I was smart enough to go the limit and get a PhD. I am an unconventional scholar-activist-mom, and as more time passes, it has become clear to me that I am not the type of person who is supposed to get a PhD, due to my background as an ex-waitress and a "welfare kid" up from poverty. I could not have done it without the unwavering support of my people. Tom, my husband, especially had a heavy load as the main family breadwinner while I spent my energy on study, low wage part-time teaching, and "no-wage" political activism. Honey: I promise to get a job now.

Chapter 1

INTRODUCTION

> A major challenge for the future is to prepare a theology that takes this culture into account, that considers prostitution through the exegesis of the prostitute in the Bible.[1]

> If as the liberationists claim, Christ is neither male nor female in the sense that Christ represents the community of the poor, then Christ should be portrayed as a girl prostituted in Buenos Aires in a public toilet by two men. Obviously such portrayal would be considered indecent, because we are bringing to the surface the hidden face of the sexual oppression of women but for that very reason it should be seen as a true theology.[2]

> If anything I have to say, if anything I have to offer, can help any woman feel more liberated in regards to her interpretation of the Bible and/or how she reads it, then I feel that I have done my job, because I feel that in terms of dealing with women, it's incredibly oppressive.[3]

If the Bible has a liberating word for prostitutes, what might that be? In much contemporary discourse, the Bible is still used as an ideological tool to secure a sexual morality that both criminalizes prostitution and works to regulate the sexual behaviour of all "decent" women. Liberation theology claims to champion the cause of the poor and oppressed, which, theoretically, should include poor women's issues. However, when it comes to issues of sexual morality, "liberation theology is still patriarchal and as such notoriously unsuspicious of given sexual structures of thought,"

---

1. Gabriela Leite, "The Prostitute Movement in Brazil: Culture and Religiosity," in *International Review of Mission* 85:338 (1996), pp. 417–26, pp. 425–26.

2. Marcella Maria Althaus-Reid, "On Wearing Skirts Without Underwear: 'Indecent Theology Challenging the Liberation Theology of the Pueblo'. Poor Women Contesting Christ," *Feminist Theology* 20 (January 1999), pp. 39–51, p. 41.

3. "Sweet" (in Greek texts, Sweet or Γλυκερά is a typical name for a courtesan), SWOP Symposium, Berkeley, CA, 12 January 2005.

concludes liberation feminist Marcella Althaus-Reid.[4] According to the feminist theologian Rita Nakashima Brock, there is a deeply religious substratum to current prostitution law that needs to be tackled before there is hope for legal reform that is liberating to prostitutes. Brock writes that "attempts to reformulate discussions of prostitution outside religious discourse has had little success in addressing any of the problems surrounding prostitution because the religious dimension forms a substructure that needs examination."[5] Thus, prostitution as a religio-moral issue has an enormous ideological impact on the structure of public policy that affects poor women. For this reason, how prostitution is interpreted biblically and otherwise needs close examination as a women's rights issue.

It is widely thought that the Bible definitively proscribes the sexual behaviour of women and that the liberation case is hopeless when it comes to prostitutes. Biblical scholar Margaret Davies flatly asserts that the Christian Bible is of little use for the liberation of prostitutes in that "the NT excludes both male and female practicing prostitutes from the Christian community. They are treated as heinous sinners in need of repentance."[6] To counter this dismal impasse, theologian Rose Wu acknowledges that "by labeling prostitutes as 'sinners,' the voices of prostitutes are silenced" but calls upon feminist scholars to "break the silence, letting prostitutes tell their stories and interpret their experiences as an individual person as well as a corporate identity."[7] Is this oppressive sexual morality actually biblically based and, if so, in what way? Are liberation readings of prostitution in the Bible liberating to prostitutes? How would the interpretations differ if done from the standpoint of sex worker activists? This study hopes to address these questions and break out of the impasse described above.

Dorothy Smith, a feminist standpoint theorist, might characterize this situation of prostitution discourse as a "text mediated discourse" or "T-discourse." T-discourses are organized by certain ideological codes which

---

4. Althaus-Reid, "On Wearing Skirts Without Underwear," p. 42.

5. Rita Nakashima Brock, "Politicians, Pastors and Pimps: Christianity and Prostitution Policies," in Kathleen M. Sands, (ed.), *God Forbid: Religion and Sex in American Public Life* (Oxford: Oxford University Press, 2000), pp. 245–61, p. 250.

6. Margaret Davies, "On Prostitution," in M. Daniel Carroll R., David A. Clines and Phillip R. Davies (eds.), *The Bible in Human Society: Essays in Honor of John Rogerson* (Sheffield: Sheffield Academic Press, 1995), pp. 225–48, p. 242.

7. Rose Wu, "Women on the Boundary: Prostitution Contemporary and in the Bible," *Feminist Theology* 28 (2001), pp. 69–81, p. 80.

structure behaviour and thought into specific molds and patterns. The Bible, law and commentary, not to mention volumes of social scientific material are prime examples of such T-discourse, specifically focused on prostitution. According to Smith, "there are 'ideological codes' that order and organize texts across discursive sites, often having divergent audiences, and variously hooked into policy or political practice."[8] One way to break out from their power is to begin sociological investigations from the everyday lives of those for whom the discourse is a problem, to utilize these subjects as primary sources and then work backward to the institutional systems and texts that find the ideological codes necessary and useful. This strategy is to do what she calls "institutional ethnography," that is, an ethnography of oppressive institutions and their impact on poor and oppressed people.[9] Smith uses the "Standard North American Family" or SNAF as an ideological code that is often problematic for single mothers and other deviants from its norm. Smith found that this code was so pernicious it often unconsciously infected her own work that was explicitly trying to identify and problematize the code.[10]

I will utilize Marcella Althaus-Reid's concept of the binary decency/ indecency as an ideological code comparable to SNAF in how it organizes the T-discourse of prostitution. Althaus-Reid argues that the dialectic of this binary is "at the root of theological control of behaviour that is admissible for women."[11] Indecent theology is "a positive theology that aims to uncover, unmask and unclothe that false hermeneutic that considers itself 'decent' and as such, proper and befitting for women especially in sexual matters."[12] As a hermeneutic that utilizes "indecent subjects" (prostitutes) as a methodological strategy, I hope to flesh out some of the operations of this ideological code of theological in/decency from the perspective of those for whom it is a problem: prostitutes. Althaus-Reid proposes that we engage in sexual storytelling from the margins in order to "learn from the voices of women and men how the system in which we live is organized by making the unusual usual, that is, by enforcing gender constructions considered normal by legislative means, in order to disrupt and tame the different

---

8. Dorothy Smith, *Writing the Social: Critique, Theory and Investigations* (Toronto: University of Toronto Press, 1999), p. 158.

9. Dorothy Smith, *The Everyday World as Problematic: A Feminist Sociology* (Boston, MA: Northeastern University Press, 1987), p. 160.

10. Smith, *Writing the Social*, p. 170.

11. Althaus-Reid, "On Wearing Skirts Without Underwear", p. 42.

12. Althaus-Reid, "On Wearing Skirts Without Underwear", p. 39.

manifestation of sexual behaviours in society."[13] This approach can perhaps help explain how this code continues to infect the T-discourses that are purportedly oriented towards human liberation: feminist and liberation theology.

This book explores biblical prostitution and contemporary liberation readings of it to determine what the limits of those readings might be for the actual class of people in the present. In order to test liberation readings of biblical prostitution, I conduct a qualitative analysis of feminist and liberation readings of biblical prostitution by *reading with* actual sex worker activists. This study is an explicitly interdisciplinary project that combines and draws upon the fields of biblical studies, critical social theory and liberation theology as they intersect and reflect upon the issues of poverty and sexuality. The primary reason for pursuing such an interdisciplinary project is to examine and amend these contradictions and limitations in current liberation and feminist readings of biblical sexual morality. These contradictions and limitations become clearly and dramatically apparent when using biblical prostitution as the case study for sexual morality.

According to the recent analysis of Elina Vuola in her work *The Limits of Liberation*, traditional liberation theology has not gone far enough in its preferential option for the poor because it has failed to utilize poor women as subjects of theology and has avoided the issue of sexuality in analyzing poverty. She writes "issues of sexual ethics—as (not) treated in LT [Liberation Theology] up to now—are both a challenge for the supposed commitment to praxis and a critique of the actual importance of praxis for the liberation method."[14] Argentinean feminist and liberation theologian, Marcella Althaus-Reid asserts that in liberation theology "the poor, as in any old-fashioned moralizing Victorian tale, were depicted as the deserving and asexual poor."[15] The problem is that the poor are generally anything but "decent" and many of the issues poor women face are sexual, such as sexual violence, back alley abortions, and prostitution. Furthermore, when it comes to women, classical liberation theologians tend to stop short of a gendered materialist analysis and fall into age-old idealist notions of womanhood and normative heterosexuality. According to Althaus-Reid, "to challenge God is not as indecent as to challenge the sexuality of theology. Sexual

13. Althaus-Reid, "On Wearing Skirts Without Underwear", p. 49.
14. Elina Vuola, *Limits of Liberation: Feminist Theology and the Ethics of Poverty and Reproduction* (London: Sheffield Academic Press, 2002), p. 230 and 235.
15. Marcella Althaus-Reid, *Indecent Theology: Theological Perversions in Sex, Gender and Politics* (New York: Routledge, 2000), p. 30.

idealism pervades theology, including theology of liberation."[16] While liberation theologians claim to utilize a materialist approach, philosophical idealism most pertains when it comes to women. In idealist philosophy the idea, in this case the ideas of "woman" and normative sexuality are prior to any material reality. A true materialist approach looks first at the economic material reality as the matrix for ideas about women and sex, which change as the material contexts change. The church and theologians, including many liberation theologians, fail to let go of their essentialist ideas about women and family.

Liberation theologian Margaret Guider, working several decades in Brazil with the Pastoral da Mulher Marginalizada (PMM), indicates that prostitutes often have very different interpretations of the Bible than pastoral agents of the church of liberation.[17] Guider found the text of Rahab in Joshua 2 and 6 to be the sole biblical text available for a "hermeneutic of retrieval" for prostitutes. She accepts the removal of the figure of Mary Magdalene, anointing woman and other women around Jesus as prostitutes in recent feminist scholarship that has limited the texts available for analysis.[18] For example, Kathleen Corley's contention that the women around Jesus were not really prostitutes is ideologically problematic for the liberation efforts of contemporary religious Brazilian sex workers,[19] who want to see their lives reflected in the Christian story. Prostitutes' rights activist Gabriela Leite asserts: "our love for Jesus and our self-respect will help greatly our religious understanding, as will our knowledge that in the past we were very important people for Christ and for the formation of Christianity. *We want light to shine on our Christian story*."[20] This conflict of attitudes is especially poignant when it boils down to the issue of the Brazilian church's exclusion of prostitute women from the sacraments because many prostitutes do not understand why the church does not follow Jesus' example in affirmatively relating to prostitutes.[21] For

16. Althaus-Reid, *Indecent Theology*, p. 22.

17. Margaret Eletta Guider, *The Daughters of Rahab: Prostitution and the Church of Liberation in Brazil* (Minneapolis, MN: Fortress Press, 1995), pp. 96, 101, 200–201.

18. Guider, *The Daughters of Rahab*, p. 27.

19. Kathleen Corley, "Were the Women around Jesus Really Prostitutes? Women in the Context of Greco-Roman Meals," in Davis J. Lull, (ed.), *Society of Biblical Literature 1989 Seminar Papers* (Society of Biblical Literature, 1989), pp. 487–521.

20. Leite, "The Prostitute Movement in Brazil," p. 426, emphasis mine.

21. Guider, *The Daughters of Rahab*, pp. 130, 205, 211–12.

Vuola and Guider, the "anti-female and anti-sexual anthropological underpinnings" of traditional church teachings are to blame for the way sexuality is being addressed by theologians.[22] Guider notes, "the church of liberation was caught between its commitment to the oppressed as expressed in its teachings on social justice and its commitment to promote and to uphold traditional family values as expressed in its teaching on the family and human sexuality."[23] Having a "preferential option for the poor and oppressed" is all well and fine until it conflicts with church doctrines on sex.

In the realm of biblical studies, this project falls under the rubric of cultural criticism or ideological criticism, particularly as expressed by the calls made by Fernando Segovia and others for "flesh and blood," "real" or "ordinary" readers to further the twin goals of "decolonization" and "liberation."[24] The South African scholar, Gerald West, has developed an interpretation strategy of "reading with" poor and oppressed populations, which is a good example of this emerging direction in biblical studies.[25] This call resonates with the views of Gabrielle Leite, a leading Brazilian prostitutes' rights activist who says: "A major challenge for the future is to prepare a theology that takes this culture into account, that *considers prostitution through the exegesis of the prostitute in the Bible*."[26] To engage this challenge, my project seeks to do biblical interpretation *with* prostitute women who have an elaborated standpoint and politic.[27] For this reason,

22. Vuola, *Limits of Liberation*, p. 231.

23. Guider, *The Daughters of Rahab*, p. 130.

24. See Fernando Segovia "Cultural Studies and Contemporary Biblical Studies," in Fernando Segovia and M.A. Tolbert (eds.), *Reading From This Place*, vol. 2 (Minneapolis, MN: Fortress Press, 1995), pp. 5–9.

25. Gerald West, *Biblical Hermeneutics of Liberation: Modes of Reading the Bible in South African Context* (Maryknoll, NY: Orbis Books, 1991), p. 213 and in *The Academy of the Poor: Towards a Dialogical Reading of the Bible* (Sheffield: Sheffield Academic Press, 1999).

26. Leite, "The Prostitute Movement in Brazil", pp. 417–26, p. 425, emphasis mine.

27. Gerald West persuasively argues for the importance of reading with the *organized* poor in his article "Contextual Bible Study in Africa: A Resource for Reclaiming and Regaining Land, Dignity and Identity," in Gerald West and Musa Dube (eds.), *The Bible in Africa: Transactions, Trajectories and Trends* (Boston, MA: Brill, 2001), pp. 597–98. Likewise, for standpoint theorists who argue that a standpoint is different from mere perspective in that it must be attained through political struggle: see Nancy Harstock, *Money, Sex and Power: Toward a Feminist Historical Materialism* (New York: Longman Inc., 1983), p. 232.

I chose to do my biblical interpretation with a prostitutes' rights group. I hope to integrate their standpoint, rooted in existing liberation praxis, into a case study of knowledge production with marginalized women. It is a presupposition of this study that women who do sex work have important subjugated knowledge that deserves articulation and theoretical attention. This subjugated knowledge can produce interesting and vital results when undertaken within the discipline of biblical interpretation. The theoretical premises of feminist standpoint epistemology under gird and give a firm foundation for this hypothesis.

It is my hope that this attenuated option for prostitute women, or feminist standpoint method, can get beyond some impasses of traditional liberation and feminist approaches. Arguing that current feminist and liberation readings of biblical prostitution may not be liberating to prostitutes themselves, this study will offer an amendment to current feminist biblical theological hermeneutics that allows for the interpretation and praxis of prostitute women as readers of biblical texts who bring to the Bible their social theory of prostitution. Conflicts within the liberation discourses of Christianity prevent the "option for the poor" from being fully extended to poor women as theological subjects, especially with regard to sexuality. Althaus-Reid has helped to identify and name this conflict as "in/decent theology," which refuses to engage with the "indecent" as theological subjects.

By showing the conflict of readings over sex work within liberation discourse, the goal of this study is *not* to claim there is only one correct reading or that sex workers have the magic hermeneutical key to unlock the liberation door for all readers of the Bible. Conflicts of interpretation remain and contextualization continues to be important because all readings are not all things to all people. Differences will exist even among the sex workers who read the biblical texts with me. Marginalized readers can and do produce differential readings that conflict, but still remain equally valid, contingent upon for whom, when and where they are produced. The goal of this book, to provide a preferential option to sex worker readers, emphasizes sex worker liberation but other equally disfranchised readers make equally valid conflicting claims for their readings. Since sex worker standpoints are so infrequently consulted, this study attempts to begin a dialogue, which at times may seem polemical, but ultimately is a conversation without winners. The intended audiences are those interested in including prostitutes into broader analyses of oppression and to engage liberation oriented scholars in further dialogue for the purposes of creating solidarity. The scholarly standpoints of other liberation readings are critiqued in this study and perhaps, at times, under appreciated for their own unique contributions upon mainstream contexts. The orientation of this study is always on how to produce sex worker positive interpretations and so feminist and liberation readings are presented in the dialectical but focused manner in which they were reviewed in our interpretive work together. My own work is put under sex worker scrutiny in the same way I present the work of others. I found I had much to learn about the ways I myself participate in in/decency and I hope that others can benefit in the same manner.

This study draws its theoretical foundation from feminist standpoint theory or epistemology. The theory I utilize comes from the work of Dorothy Smith, Nancy Harstock, Sandra Harding and Patricia Hill Collins. Standpoint theory is a feminist descendent of Marx's historical materialism, but applied to women's reality. An operating premise of this theoretical framework is that differential experiences produce distinctive consciousnesses. For example, capitalist and proletarian subjectivity is structured differently according to their different locations within the division of labour. There also exist very pronounced divisions of labour between men and women in varied historical and cultural contexts. The division of labour produces differential consciousness and this has implications for knowledge in that, until very recent times, it is men, and elite men, who have been the producers of official knowledge. Feminist standpoint theory, by definition, accepts the existence of differential standpoints produced by differential contexts. Standpoint theory, however, does not accept all standpoints as equally valid or libratory. Likewise, most liberation scholars tend to award a higher degree of objectivity to the non-hegemonic standpoints. How to adjudicate conflicting liberation reading is an issue that is not resolved except through acceptance of multiple valid liberation readings.

If less partial knowledges are to be created, non-dominant subjectivities need to participate in knowledge production. Furthermore, the articulation of distinctive subaltern standpoints is crucial for galvanizing liberation struggles, for mapping out how oppression works, and for generating adequate strategies of resistance to oppression. Dorothy Smith asserts for feminist standpoint theory that, "Its project is to explicate the actual social relations in which people's lives are embedded and to make these visible to them/ourselves."[28] In this vein, I wish to do knowledge production with sex workers, "the most marginalized of the marginalized," according to

28. Smith, *Writing the Social*, p. 74.

liberation theologian Leonardo Boff. Such a project is an amplification of the methodological approach of liberation theology, which claims to theorize from within the experience and struggle of the poor against oppression. This liberation method will be specifically tied to the subjectivity of activist prostitute women, a subjectivity not fully taken into account by liberation theological method and praxis. For this reason, I have utilized a feminist materialist method to offset the idealist tendencies that many liberation theologians somehow fall into when it comes to women's reality. Another reason to utilize feminist method is that all of the participants consider themselves feminists even though they often have been (and continue to be) in serious conflict with other feminists over the issue of sexual labour. Most of the sex worker interpreters are card-carrying members of the National Organization of Women (NOW), which has an important history of resolutions supportive of sex worker's rights and continues to be a venue that affirms their participation.

The subjects of this project of biblical interpretation are a reading group of activist sex workers in Berkeley, California, USA, who were all involved with the effort to decriminalize prostitution in Berkeley in 2004: the Sex Worker Outreach Project (SWOP). The activists of SWOP are working to change prostitution laws that they deem harmful to themselves and all women. SWOP members gathered signatures to put a voter initiative on the 2004 Berkeley ballot to affirm the idea of state-wide decriminalization of prostitution in the state of California. The initiative lost but was of great historic significance for inserting activist prostitutes into the political landscape. The ballot initiative (a rejected city council resolution), was written by and campaigned for by actual activist prostitutes who got the chance to give an account of their politics to the local community of Berkeley as well as an international media. I worked on this voter initiative as an "embedded theologian" for the entire campaign of 2004.

After the fanfare of the 2004 US elections, SWOP went on to other projects, like my biblical interpretation project. In a series of "symposia," we read the story of Rahab (Joshua 2 and 6), the story of the two prostitutes and Solomon (1 Kgs 3:16–28), the anointing woman traditions of John and the synoptic Gospels (Jn 12:1–8/Mk 14:3–9/Mt. 26:6–13/Lk. 7:36–50) and the apocalyptic visions of the whore Babylon (Revelation 17–19). We read all the four stories together, they providing their experiences and social analysis of the institution of prostitution, I providing my prior research on representative feminist and liberation readings of each text. We explicitly tried to read each story utilizing their sub-cultural knowledge of prostitution as a way to exegete biblical prostitution, "to consider prostitution through the exegesis of the prostitute in the Bible," as Gabriela Leite urges. In this way, we were able to link the discourse of prostitution in its religious and legal dimensions to the institutions that prostitutes encounter. Together, we looked for overlaps or disjunctions between their lives and analyses and the interpretations and underlying assumptions of liberation and feminist interpreters. Within this interlude, we tried to hammer out a new interpretation that is engaged both with their experiences and with the results of biblical scholarship. We did this group reading in a succession of symposia from November 2004 to February 2005. We deliberately chose to call our interpretive work "symposia" which links back to the ancient Greek practice of having drinking dinner parties to which prostitutes are invited and asked to engage in intellectual labour. We even did foot anointing, as was done at a dinner party Jesus once attended. Women who were not able to attend a given symposium completed written questionnaires or gave me separate interviews.

Prefatory to going into the field and doing the proposed knowledge production with activist prostitutes, I completed my own initial exegetical analyses of these four passages using existing methodological tools of ideological criticism including historical, literary, liberation and feminist approaches. Thus, my own "liberation readings" of biblical prostitution also came under the empirical critical scrutiny of sex workers themselves (and were often found lacking). My year of campaign work to decriminalize prostitution with the SWOP activists should qualify my project as being sufficiently rooted into an existing liberation struggle propounded and created by sex workers. This indicates a significant departure from earlier strategies attempted by liberation and feminist scholars. My study is the first that I know of that operates with a prostitutes' rights framework and which joins itself to an existing prostitutes' struggle rather than a project that is initiated and designed by agents of the church or feminist social workers on behalf of the prostitutes. The political agency and counter-hegemonic standpoint of these women is foundational to my strategy and the basis of its innovation. Together, I hope our new interpretational work contributes to the expansion of a liberation hermeneutic that takes seriously the methods and goals of liberation theology, namely its "preferential option for the poor and oppressed," and further concretizes this option in relation to women's sexuality.

This study aims to take liberation and feminist hermeneutics to new frontiers because I believe that women who have engaged in prostitution for survival have knowledge and social analyses that are integral to the liberation of *all women*, namely on how sexual ideologies function economically, as well as religiously and morally in a patriarchal society. Feminist theologian Nantawan Boonprasat Lewis has come to similar conclusions regarding the distinctive counter-hegemonic standpoint of sex workers in Thailand and its connection to an empowering agency for the sex-workers themselves.[29] Lewis urges "an acceptance of the presence of women in prostitution and their role in solving societal problems, including the AIDS epidemic. It is an act of embracing the marginalized, who can become responsible victors in the struggle for their well-being."[30] The utilization of concrete data of the daily life (in Spanish: *vida cotidiana*) of prostitutes can lead to social analyses and biblical interpretations that directly challenge the limits of current liberation theology and biblical feminism.[31] I believe that this project has produced readings of biblical texts that will ethically inform the field of biblical studies while also empowering the liberation struggles of poor women, especially sex workers, a population which has dramatically increased in the current neo-liberal global economy where poverty and the feminization of poverty is ubiquitous.

The organization of this book will proceed as follows. Chapter 2 will delve into the methodological and political problems with extending a preferential option to prostitutes and my proposal for getting beyond these limits to liberation. The subsequent chapters 3, 4, 5, and 6 will focus upon the results and some potential consequences of including prostitutes into this option for each of the four biblical passages we have exegeted. These four chapters are each similarly structured. First, the biblical passage under study is given. Then, an account is given of some representative liberation and feminist readings that analyze each passage, including my own thoughts and motives for studying these texts. The heart of this book then ensues where the sex workers' standpoint is described and ordered

29. Nantawan Boonprasat Lewis, "Toward an Ethic of Feminist Liberation and Empowerment: A Case Study of Prostitution in Thailand," in S. Chiba, G. Hunsberger and L.E.J. Ruiz (eds.), *Christian Ethics in Ecumenical Context: Theology, Culture, and Politics in Dialogue* (Grand Rapids, MI: Eerdmans: 1995), pp. 219–30.

30. Lewis, "Toward an Ethic of Feminist Liberation and Empowerment", p. 225.

31. Vuola spells out this concept of "everyday life" very clearly in her section 3.2: "Option for the Poor as an Option for the Poor Woman," pp. 141–56. See also Maria Pilar Aquino's *Our Cry for Life: Feminist Theology from Latin America* (Maryknoll, NY: Orbis Books, 1993), p. 102, which makes a similar argument about women's everyday life.

according to the themes chosen by our SWOP readers. I then utilize some of the SWOP insights to show how a sex worker standpoint can crack open these texts in a new way, thus using my tools as a biblical scholar to back up and facilitate new readings. Every text's chapter will end with an analysis of differences between SWOP readers and the feminist and liberation readings with which we engaged and a SWOP rereading of the text via quotes strung together in a narrative format. In this way, every exegetical chapter will begin with the biblical text and then end with a sex worker standpoint for each text. Finally, in Chapter 7 I will conclude with amendments for liberation praxis and advice for those who are engaged with liberation hermeneutics around sexuality and prostitution in particular.

Chapter 2

METHODOLOGICAL AND POLITICAL ANALYSES:
A PREFERENTIAL OPTION FOR PROSTITUTES?

> The option for the poor, with all of the pastoral and theological
> consequences of that option, is one of the most important contributions
> to the life of the church universal to have emerged from the theology of
> liberation and the church on our continent. As we have observed, that
> option has its roots in biblical revelation and the history of our church.
> Still, today it presents particular, novel characteristics. This is due to
> our better understanding of the depth and complexity of the poverty
> and oppression experienced by most of humanity: due to our perception
> of the economic, social, and cultural mechanisms that produce that
> poverty; and before all else, it is due to the new light which the word of
> the Lord sheds on that poverty.[1]

Probably the concept or phrase most associated with liberation theology is
its "preferential option for the poor." The thesis of this book is that this
option has not been extended fully to prostitutes, a subcategory of the poor
and oppressed. I wish to examine why this is so and attempt to push beyond
the limits of liberation hermeneutics to include prostitutes into this option.
This chapter first examines the concept of "a preferential option for the
poor," first tracing it from its usage in the writings of Gustavo Gutierrez,
one of its major theorizers. I will continue my exploration through a
particular concrete manifestation of this "option," namely, in a pastoral
project undertaken among prostitutes during the last three decades of the
twentieth century: the Pastoral da Mulher Marginalizada (PMM) in Brazil,
as described by Margaret Guider in *The Daughters of Rahab: Prostitution
and the Church of Liberation in Brazil*. I will then contrast some themes
that come out of the analyses done in the pastoral encounters with themes
from the writings of Gabriela Leite, a (sometimes) participant in the pastoral

1. Gustavo Gutierrez, "Option for the Poor," in Jon Sobrino and Ignacio
Ellacuria (eds.), *Systematic Theology: Perspectives from Liberation Theology,
Readings from Mysterium Lyberationis* (Maryknoll, NY: Orbis Books, 1996),
p. 36.

project PMM, a former sex worker, now a sociologist and a leading prostitutes' rights organizer in Brazil. I will then outline the methodological plan for my work that would combine biblical hermeneutics and social analysis through the utilization of feminist Standpoint Theory or epistemology, functioning as a sort of "preferential option for women," who heretofore have not been fully included in most kinds of materialist analyses of poverty. I will then introduce the work I have done with a sex worker rights organization in Berkeley, California, during the 2004 election year and after, when the prostitutes of SWOP (Sex Worker Outreach Project) put a decriminalization measure on the Berkeley ballot, "Measure Q." Before moving on to our work with the biblical texts, I will give brief outlines of various legal approaches to prostitution and how decriminalization compares with these other political options pursued by governments.

Gutierrez' "Option for the Poor"

Gustavo Gutierrez succinctly makes the argument for the church's "option for the poor," in his article quoted and cited above, as well as in his classic work *A Theology of Liberation*.[2] The justifications for the "option" are multiple. Gutierrez discusses first the "new presence" or "irruption of the poor" into social consciousness during modern times. The "poor" are making themselves noticed in our era by demanding that attempts be made toward the elimination of their poverty and organizing themselves to this end. Newer, more sophisticated scientific analyses of the causes of poverty have become better known and utilized by theologians, that is, poverty has become a major topic of scientific discourse and knowledge production and these developments have been prominent features of what Gutierrez describes as the 'irruption of the poor.'[3] Gutierrez charts the church's responses to this phenomenon, which are clearly present in the official documents of the Catholic Magisterium. He begins with Vatican II, through the position taken by Latin American bishops at the Medellin conference and clearly ratified in the final document of the Puebla conference which devotes its whole fourth section to the church's "preferential option to the poor" (no. 1134–1293).

Gutierrez lays out in very strong terms the biblical foundations of this "preference" in both the Old and New/Hebrew and Greek Testaments.

---

2. Gustavo Gutierrez, *A Theology of Liberation* (Maryknoll, NY: Orbis Books, 1994).

3. Gutierrez, "Option for the Poor," p. 22.

Through the biblical witness, Gutierrez argues for varying typologies of "poverty" in order to explain the differences between "real" poverty and "spiritual" poverty. The arguments from Hebrew scripture are located mainly in *A Theology of Liberation,* chapter 13.[4] Utilizing the books of Job, the Prophets and various Torah legislations, Gutierrez asserts that "in the Bible poverty is a scandalous condition inimical to human dignity" and that "poverty contradicts the very meaning of *the Mosaic Religion.*"[5] With the Christian scriptures, he invokes multiple texts, such as the parable of the vineyard in Mt. 20:1–16 ("The last shall be first"), the Lukan (Lk 6) and Matthean (Mt. 5) *Beatitudes*, the parable of Lazarus and the Rich Man in Luke 16, the parable of the Great Banquet (Mt. 22 and Lk 14) to demonstrate the "preferential option" to be thoroughly rooted in the biblical witness and practices of Jesus.

Gutierrez contrasts the *Beatitudes* of both Matthew 5 and Luke 6 to formulate the distinction between "real" poverty and "spiritual" poverty and to show that there is no conflict between them. He does this by contrasting the situation of "material" poverty, which is an insult to God, with "spiritual poverty" which Gutierrez exegetes as an openness or "availability" to the divine will which is manifest in the actions of solidarity with the poor, a third type of poverty.[6] This distinction makes room for the discipleship of the non-poor to include themselves in the "option for the poor" through the choice of engaging in the struggle against poverty and for justice with the "real" poor. A reason for this discussion of the types of poverty is that there exists confusion about the church's stance on poverty and the poor: "Poverty is an equivocal term," thus, "we have also fallen into very vague terminology and a kind of sentimentalism which in the last analysis justifies the status quo."[7] Historically, when poverty is overly spiritualized and romanticized, concern for "real" poverty can be occluded.

Finally, Gutierrez lays out the ancient biblical roots of the notion that "the Poor Evangelize" in the letters of Paul (see 1 Cor. 1:28: "God chose what is low and despised in the world, things that are not, to reduce to nothing things that are"). He argues that the poor are to be identified with Christ, making the "option for the poor" a "Christological option" as well. Gutierrez' theology could hermeneutically privilege the social analyses of

4. Gutierrez, *A Theology of Liberation*, pp. 162–73.
5. Gutierrez, *A Theology of Liberation*, pp. 165 and 167.
6. Gutierrez, *A Theology of Liberation*, p. 172, and "Option for the Poor," pp. 22, 31.
7. Gutierrez, *A Theology of Liberation*, pp. 163, 164.

prostitutes in the PMM and SWOP but often, when prostitution is at issue, the emphasis shifts to the agency and analysis of the "spiritually poor," that is pastoral and feminist advocates. Thus, it is important to examine the degree to which the agency and subjectivity of poor women is equated with an "option for the poor" in general and what its limits might be and why. My study has a definitive preference for the "real" poor and oppressed who are prostitutes rather than the "spiritually" poor who are in solidarity with prostitutes.

Gutierrez claims that the "poor" also have to make an "option for the poor": "the word *option* does not necessarily mean that those who make it do not already belong to the world of the poor. In many cases they do. But even here it is an option; the poor themselves must make this decision, as well."[8] This stipulation perhaps relates to what Gutierrez claims about the "demands on those who receive it (free gift of the Reign of God) in the spirit of children and in community."[9] This demand could imply or constitute a sort of limitation upon the church's preferential option. The demand can permit slippage between the types of poor that leads to some confusion between the agency of the poor themselves and their churchly advocates, since the free gift must be received with the proper childlike spirit and within community. To what extent does liberation theology really give preference to the analyses, viewpoints, exegesis and political agency of the "poor" and what kinds of limits are placed around them? Does the Church of liberation carry out its "option" *for or to* the "poor" making them into indirect or direct objects of the church's benevolent actions instead of agents and evangelists of the gospel? Are there demands for doctrinal submission by the community made upon the poor that circumvent their critique?

Gutierrez for his part clearly seems to take seriously the subjectivity and agency of the "poor" while admitting its challenge: "The poor then have become active agents of their own destiny, initiating the solid process that is altering the condition of this world's poor and despoiled. The theology of liberation—an expression of the right of the poor to 'think their faith' is not the automatic result of this situation and its incarnations."[10] When it comes to women, indigenous and black populations, Gutierrez acknowledges that "we still have a long way to go in this area. Matters of culture, race, and gender will be (and have already begun to be) extremely

8. Gutierrez, "Option for the Poor," p. 26.
9. Gutierrez, "Option for the Poor," p. 22.
10. Gutierrez, "Option for the Poor," pp. 22–23.

important to liberation theology. Doubtless the most important part of this task will fall to persons who *actually belong to these respective human groups.*"[11]

However, juxtaposed to such empowering assertions there are numerous occasions when implicit in the text of Gutierrez, the protagonist role seems to fall more to the "spiritually" poor who come from the ranks of the non-poor and who do things *for or to* the poor, and, at least linguistically, efface the agency and subjecthood of actual poor persons. The issue seems a keen one for the methodology or epistemology assumed by the church of liberation. This slippage is especially pertinent when the viewpoint "from below" levels challenges to the church's role and complicity with the factors that lead to poverty. The challenge is even more acute when poor women challenge some of the most basic social teachings of the Church, such as those on sexuality. Put differently, what might be the limits on the Church's reception of the critiques of religious and cultural ideological justifications of poverty that are offered by poor women in Latin America? To address this issue I now will move on to Guider's documentation of the Pastoral da Mulher Marginalizada, in order to glimpse some of the challenges that the "preferential option for the poor" has posed to the Church of liberation in Brazil in actual practice.

Pastoral da Mulher Marginalizada (PMM)

> Among the poor, marginalized women are found, and among marginalized women, prostitutes are found. Through the teachings of Jesus, we are led to the conclusion that the poor person is Jesus. The prostitute is Jesus. Whoever does not help the prostitute does not help Jesus. Whoever claims to love the God who cannot be seen and does not love the prostitute who can be seen is a liar.[12]

During the 1970s in the aftermath of Vatican II and Medellin, the church in Brazil was inspired to extend a preferential option to some of Brazil's poorest women, those working in prostitution. It surmised that sex workers of Brazil were the most marginalized of the marginalized and that an option for Brazilian prostitute women was therefore an "option to the poor." This option was named the Pastoral da Mulher Marginalizada or PMM. Sister Margaret Guider historically contextualizes, documents and theologizes

---

11. Gutierrez, "Option for the Poor," p. 24, emphasis mine.
12. Dom Antonio Batista Fragoso, a Brazilian bishop and a founder of the PMM, as quoted in Guider, *The Daughters of Rahab*, p. 73.

the results of eight pastoral encounters between clergy, pastoral agents and prostitute women (many of whom become agents) spanning three decades in Brazil.

In a manner somewhat similar to Gustavo Gutierrez, Margaret Guider analyzes the reasons for prostitution becoming identified as a social and ecclesial problem during this particular historical moment. Prominent among many factors was the irruption of prostitute women and children into social consciousness in the wake of the "Brazilian (economic) Miracle in the 1970s, which failed to bring promised prosperity."[13] Women and children working in the sex industry were increasingly visible:

> The face of prostitution appeared everywhere, as did the prostitutes themselves. No longer were they unseen, anonymous, and unattached. Not only did they constitute a significant percentage of the female population between the ages of fifteen and thirty-five, but they were also mothers, daughters, sisters, neighbors, co-workers, laborers, teachers, nurses, and wives. The basis for distinguishing a difference between prostitutes and other women was no longer secure.[14]

Added to this new presence of prostitution was an influx of prominent immigrant clergy and missionaries concerned about the phenomenon who were willing and able to take bigger political risks than the local Church had during this era of political repression under a military regime.[15] Over time, a critical number of Brazilian bishops like Dom Fragoso, quoted above, institutionalized the pastoral project of PMM. Indeed, the prominent liberation theologian, Leonardo Boff, was a featured speaker at the sixth national encounter in 1984, where he exegeted the "attitude of Jesus" and proclaimed to the women of PMM that: "Your cause is the cause of the Gospel. You are the heart of Jesus. If we take seriously the word of Jesus— and we should take it seriously—marginalized women that believe and journey together for their own liberation and that of others, will arrive in

13. Guider, *The Daughters of Rahab*, pp. 120–22. To give an idea of the scope of the issue, in 1983 there were an estimated 4 million women and children working in prostitution in Brazil according to the estimates recounted by Guider. According to UNICEF, in 1992 there were as many as 50 million street children in Latin America as a whole, one half of the entire continent's children. The majority of these homeless children engage in some sort of survival prostitution; see Gail Pheterson, *The Prostitution Prism* (Amsterdam: Amsterdam University Press, 1996), p. 150, n.1.

14. Guider, *The Daughters of Rahab*, p. 122.

15. Guider, *The Daughters of Rahab*, pp. 84–85.

the Kingdom of the Father before me, before the bishops and before the pope."[16]

In return, when Boff was having problems with the Vatican, the prostitute women of PMM wrote a letter to Rome on his behalf to assert their solidarity with Boff.[17]

Also like Gutierrez, Guider would like to root her theology of prostitute women in biblical grounds but does not move with as much ease as Gutierrez on this unstable terrain. Noting the difficulty of retrieving liberating biblical stories of prostitution, in the light of newer researches done by first world feminist scholars, Guider abandons the traditional figure of Mary Magdalene as an exemplar of liberation for prostitute women.[18] Instead, Guider focuses her work on the biblical text of Rahab (Joshua 2 and 6): "In the world of feminist biblical scholarship, however, one of the few remaining prostitute stories approved for retrieval is that of Rahab."[19] Working from the understanding of church father St. Jerome, that Rahab's house is a model of the Church, Guider utilizes a theology of incarnation, so that the Church might begin to see itself in the mirror as Rahab.[20] Ultimately this exegesis is about the sins of the Church, not the prostitutes of the PMM, nor about the "prostitute in the Bible" as urged by Gabrielle Leite. During the course of the pastoral encounters, however, there were clearly differences of interpretation of various biblical texts, a point to which I will return at greater length.[21]

Also prominent in the analyses of Guider is the utilization of the social sciences to shed light on the causes of prostitution, particularly, social histories of prostitution.[22] Guider takes quite seriously the probability that prostitutes are carriers of important "subjugated knowledge" that can greatly

---

16. Guider, *The Daughters of Rahab*, p. 103.

17. Guider, *The Daughters of Rahab*, pp. 204–205. The complete letter is provided by Guider.

18. Guider, *The Daughters of Rahab*, p. 27. See Jane Schaberg's article for an account of how Mary Magdalene was transformed into a prostitute: "How Mary Magdalene Became a Whore," *Bible Review* (October 1992), pp. 31–52.

19. Guider, *The Daughters of Rahab*, p. 27. I would argue that this all depends upon how you read. We do not know the subjective meaning Mary Magdalene may have for millions of prostitute women. Rahab herself can easily be read as a "Pocahontas" or "La Malinche" sort of figure, an equivocal role to say the least, and not necessarily a liberative story.

20. Guider, *The Daughters of Rahab*, p. 168.

21. Guider, *The Daughters of Rahab*, p. 101.

22. Guider, *The Daughters of Rahab*, p. 9–15.

nuance traditional theories of prostitution such as sin, promiscuity, socio-biology (bad genes), psychology (incest victims, dysfunctional families), drug addiction or a strict Marxist economism, which reductively explains everything as due to the economy. She turns a critical eye to the discourse on prostitution and its various categories through time. Guider then utilizes this data to undermine the church's static definitions of prostitution as contrary to its own changing stance on the issue. The framework she adopts for understanding the contemporary figure of the prostitute is that of "sexual slavery" which is from the theory of "abolitionist" feminists.[23] Repeatedly Guider asserts the victim status of prostitute women in Brazil who she labels in the passive tense as "prostituted women." Flowing out of this characterization of prostitute as "victim" and "slave" is the political agenda of abolition, which became the official political position of the PMM.[24] The promotion of the idea of prostitute as "slave" and "victim" was done to replace the pervasive church view of prostitute as "sinner" and seductress,[25] but also can clash with the prostitutes' own view of themselves: that of agent and protagonist. In critique, Gabriela Leite writes: "as slaves they are victims and a victim is not a citizen, having no free will."[26] Considering that the traditional church conception of prostitute is that of "sinner," the move to change this conception to "victim" seems like a vast improvement. Many prostitutes *are* severely victimized. However, in the end this victim image might be counter-productive to the liberation project, which is supposed to emphasize the agency and subjecthood of the poor prostitute.

Like Gutierrez, Guider has a genuine belief in the role of prostitute women as agents of change: "In accord with the liberation methodology of accompanying the poor and oppressed to gain both voice and visibility,

23. Guider, *The Daughters of Rahab*, p. 125. This "sexual slavery" view is strongly associated with and promoted by the US feminist, Kathleen Barry, who has written the book *Female Sexual Slavery* (New York: New York University Press, 1984). Barry's more recent work *The Prostitution of Sexuality*, actually blames prostitutes who voluntarily engage in prostitution and who eschew the victim/slave label as promoting a misogynistic kind of sexuality that harms all women. Many abolitionist activists echo this view and are vehemently opposed to the prostitutes' rights agenda. During the campaign to decriminalize prostitution in Berkeley, abolitionist opponents circulated flyers that labelled me a friend of pimps and paedophiles because I sided with the sex worker rights view.
24. Guider, *The Daughters of Rahab*, p. 93.
25. Guider, *The Daughters of Rahab*, pp. 17, 111, 115.
26. Leite, "The Prostitute Movement in Brazil," p. 425.

the church of liberation encouraged marginalized women to recognize their own power, authority, and personal agency."[27] Also to her credit, Guider is stalwart in her insistence that the church must face up to its complicit role in the oppression of prostitutes and women in general, most especially through its essentialist view of women and its social teachings on sexuality.[28] Nevertheless, while Guider clearly wants to affirm the agency and subjugated knowledge of Brazilian sex workers, in key aspects of her analysis, she is in stark contradiction to the mainstream views of the international prostitutes' rights movement. She opts for the abolitionist position which favors the agency and analysis of those who seek to free the slaves and rescue the victims. This puts the subject emphasis back on the "spiritually poor" or those "in solidarity with the poor" (Gutierrez' typology), rather than on the poor themselves. Former prostitute, Gabriela Leite, has been an outspoken proponent of the citizenship rights of prostitutes in Brazil. She rejects the victim/slave subject position, she advocates for the abolition of all prostitution law (decriminalization) rather than abolition of so called "sexual slavery," and seems to root her justification of prostitute religiosity in a differing social analysis as well as a biblical hermeneutic different than that of most first world feminist biblical scholarship.[29] To the writing of Gabriela Leite I now turn.

The Prostitute Movement in Brazil

> Like most of my colleagues, I am a Christian, and like them I feel an immense vacuum concerning religiosity when faced with our culture. Prostitution is very old and as such has created its own culture, which is not respected by Christian evangelists. It is indeed a challenge to the life and mission of the Brazilian churches. *A major challenge for the future is to prepare a theology that takes this culture into account, that considers prostitution through the exegesis of the prostitute in the Bible.* Our love for Jesus and our self-respect will help greatly our religious understanding, as will our knowledge that in the past we were very

27. Guider, *The Daughters of Rahab*, p. 126.
28. Guider, *The Daughters of Rahab*, pp. 113–14, 128–37.
29. Leite's position is congruent with the positions taken by sex worker rights activists worldwide, see her and others' contributions in Gail Pheterson (ed.), *A Vindication of the Rights of Whores* (Seattle: Seal Press, 1989). For an excellent recent compilation of International platforms see Kamala Kempadoo and Jo Doezema (eds.), *Global Sex Workers: Rights, Resistance and Redefinition* (New York: Routledge, 1998).

important people for Christ and for the formation of Christianity. *We want light to shine on our Christian story.*[30]

This quote contains a very clear demand for full cultural and religious rights. Gabriela Leite loudly asserts the existence of a cultural standpoint of prostitute women that is largely unknown, neglected or ignored. I have diligently searched for a way to accommodate methodologically this demand within biblical studies. The preferential option should be enough warrant but since it has not yet been fully extended to prostitutes, much less women in general, should give one pause to search out the cause. This initial comparison of views between Leite and Guider would seem to call for a deeper commitment for liberation hermeneutics and theology to discover more about the unique standpoint of prostitutes and take seriously this data in order to claim with honesty its preferential option to the poor. The church of liberation needs to be more accountable to its own preferential option.

First, in terms of a political agenda, the two positions, abolition versus decriminalization are quite distinct. Prostitutes' rights activists frequently claim that special legislation around sex work ultimately works to penalize and re-victimize prostitutes rather than protect them. Prostitutes' rights activists assert that the elimination of prostitution law (ironically, the "abolition" of prostitution law, which they feel victimizes them by jailing them and then forcing them to work for free in prison)[31] would allow prostitutes to function as citizens and to access many of the legal rights they are usually denied, such as police protection from violence, rape and other crimes, access to health care, and the right to migrate. Slavery is already illegal in most countries, as is slave trafficking, and child abuse, so the notion of "abolition" as used by abolitionist feminists is somewhat misleading. Prostitutes' rights activists assert that only purely innocent

---

30. Leite, "The Prostitute Movement in Brazil", pp. 425–26, emphasis mine.

31. In the critical race theory of activist groups like Critical Resistance, "prison" is the new form of slavery that needs to be abolished. Thus, the black feminist prison abolitionist, Angela Davis, endorses decriminalization of prostitution, while Gloria Steinem has embraced the abolitionist point of view. In response to Ambassador John Miller, who claims to be fighting sexual slavery, Robin Head, an ex-con sex worker rights activist replied: "What in the hell does he call prison labor? Imprisoned 8 years. as a Sex Worker, forced to slave in mud fields awash in ants on horrifically abusive 'garden squads'? Then this man would have me paroled to work the rest of my life in WALMART!" They even call the prison labour the "hoe squad," according to Head.

slave/victims can access any benefit from abolition types of prostitution law, which generally advocates even more stringent penalties for those in the prostitution trade, because this innocent victim status is often very hard for prostitutes to prove.[32] What prostitutes often claim is that they would be more greatly empowered by guarantees of simple civil/human rights and rigorous enforcement of existing law that applies to all citizens, especially labour laws. Leite complains that "today's abolitionists condemn 'male vice' and advocate a feminine reform without taking into account the desires and realities of women in whose name they intend to speak."[33] With regard to the PMM, Leite comments on its covert agenda to "evangelize for normal life" as well as its abolitionist political stance, as undermining its own good intentions.[34] Leite's point clearly uncovers the ideological code of "sexual decency" for which Althaus-Reid criticizes liberation theology. For her part, Guider somewhat misrepresents the position of Leite as that of promoting the "professionalization" of prostitutes.[35] Leite, like the international prostitutes' rights agenda overall, is emphasizing the rights of prostitutes to self-organize and decide their own immediate needs and political priorities, one of which is access to health care, which is only given through formal sector employment. She would rather not wait for the "ideal society" to arrive to receive the civil and human rights such as protection from violence, police and court corruption, the right to decline a client who does not wear a condom and the prosecution of the crime of rape against prostitutes. These requests could immediately improve the lives of prostitute women. The emphasis is more upon the immediate and practical goal of reducing harm to a very large class of marginalized women. This is in sync with the recommendation of theologian Rose Wu who would like to see the feminist discussion on prostitution shift in this direction rather than staying in the rather abstract realm of arguments about whether prostitution is inherently oppressive or

---

32. Jo Doezema, "Forced to Chose: Beyond the Voluntary v. Forced Prostitution Dichotomy," in Kamala Kempadoo and Jo Doezema (eds.), *Global Sex Workers: Rights, Resistance and Redefinition* (New York: Routledge, 1998), pp. 45–46. In a legal analysis of the Trafficking Victims Protection Act, the newest anti-trafficking legislation, this innocent victim problem continues to stymie efforts to help trafficking victims. See Jennifer Chacon, "Misery and Myopia: Understanding the Failures of US Efforts to Stop Human Trafficking," *Fordham Law Review* 74: 6 (2006), pp. 2977–3040, pp. 3021–3024.

33. Leite, "The Prostitute Movement in Brazil", p. 423.

34. Leite, "The Prostitute Movement in Brazil", p. 425.

35. Guider, *The Daughters of Rahab*, pp. 98, 100, 206–207.

not.[36] In fact, Brazil has implemented an extremely successful model policy of harm reduction for abating HIV that works in respectful partnership with sex workers. When the Bush Administration imposed a worldwide litmus test in 2004 for all organizations that receive USAID money, Brazil refused to comply and missed out on 40 million dollars. The new litmus test is that any organization that receives AIDS funding must have an explicit and expressed policy opposing the decriminalization of prostitution.[37]

Another interesting difference between Leite and Guider is their use of scripture to ground their positions. Guider finds the Rahab story to be one of the few remaining useful feminist biblical paradigms for prostitute women. This contrasts with the important role that Mary Magdalene would seem to continue to play for religious prostitute women. In conceiving many of the women around Jesus as prostitute women, especially resurrection witness Mary Magdalene, prostitute women seem to find legitimation for their inclusion in the church, as well as self-esteem.[38] Guider noted the differences of biblical interpretation between the pastoral agents and the prostitute women but does not draw out the consequences of what she describes. For instance, the pastoral agents recommended to the women certain biblical figures that they thought they should identify with, such as the Samaritan woman at the well in John 4 and the Lukan Prodigal son (Luke 15). The women, in response, thought that these would actually be good stories for the pastoral agents to identify with.[39] At another occasion, seemingly empowered with Leonardo Boff's reading of the "attitude of Jesus," the prostitutes criticized the church for not following Jesus' example in relating to prostitutes.[40] This is of crucial importance considering their most important and urgent petition to the church of Brazil to not exclude them from the sacraments.[41] The church frequently refuses to baptize the children of prostitutes because of "illegitimacy" and denies prostitutes the right to be godmothers. This exclusion from the life of the church is very painful and hard to understand considering the women's own understanding of the practices of Jesus. Whose view is more biblically based? The trend in feminist biblical hermeneutics noted by Guider

---

36. Wu, "Women on the Boundary", pp. 74–75.
37. Bill Hinchberger, "Support for sex workers leaves Brazil without US cash," *The Lancet*, Vol: 366 Issue: 9489, 10–16 September 2005, pp: 883–84.
38. Leite, "The Prostitute Movement in Brazil", p. 426.
39. Guider, *The Daughters of Rahab*, p. 101.
40. Guider, *The Daughters of Rahab*, pp. 96, 200–201.
41. Guider, *The Daughters of Rahab*, pp. 130, 205, 211–12.

often seems to remove prostitutes from the vicinity of Jesus and his movement.

The extent to which the church would limit its preferential option to the poor in terms of their sexual status relates back to the problem of the church's social and sexual teachings being in direct conflict with said option when it came to gender specific forms of poverty and oppression. Guider concludes that "Despite, it's best efforts to overcome such disparity, the church of liberation was caught between its commitment to the oppressed as expressed in its teachings on social justice and its commitment to promote and uphold traditional family values as expressed in its teachings on the family and human sexuality."[42] While Gustavo Gutierrez would affirm the primacy of entrance to the Kingdom of God to tax collectors and prostitutes (Mt. 21:31), he does not mention whether it also follows that prostitutes can be included in church, and it is certainly not seen as a source of esteem for prostitute women. Rather, it is to prove God's great gratuity to even the worst of sinners, which is in a much more paternalistic framework than that urged by prostitutes.[43] Again, it seems the ideological code of sexual decency is infecting and obstructing a full hermeneutical option for prostitutes.

Indeed, throughout Margaret Guider's account of PMM there is a tension between the desire of the prostitute women for more agency and the continuation of some degree of paternalism on the part of the pastoral agents who were non-prostitutes. According to Guider, "discussion focused on whether pastoral work was being done *to, with,* or *for* prostitutes,"[44] and "the church could stand on the side of women who were victims, but it often could not support many of the strategies for liberation advanced by victims turned protagonists."[45] Oftentimes the prostitutes "questioned whether the pastoral agents truly united with the poor or merely associated with the poor, and whether the pastoral agents sided with the prostitutes or with society in general."[46] Probably this tension causes Leite to have little hope that the church will ever be able to really help poor people in general or prostitute women in particular. She concludes: "They reproduce an askew authoritarian model."[47]

42. Guider, *The Daughters of Rahab*, p. 130.
43. Gutierrez, "Option for the Poor", p. 30.
44. Guider, *The Daughters of Rahab*, p. 95.
45. Guider, *The Daughters of Rahab*, p. 133.
46. Guider, *The Daughters of Rahab*, p. 201.
47. Leite, "The Prostitute Movement in Brazil", p. 425. See also Guider, *The Daughters of Rahab*, pp. 96–97.

Not just religious dogma is interfering with a full option to prostitutes. Part of the problem may be an inheritance from the Marxist roots of liberation theology.[48] Considering the prominent role of Marxist economic analysis in liberation theology, it is not at all surprising that the church of liberation would assume that prostitution was simply a by-product of the demon of capitalism. Indeed, Marx and the biblical prophets (for example, in Micah 1 and Hosea 1–4) seem to have very compatible views of prostitution.[49] Both use the metaphor of prostitution to denounce unjust economic practices, which unfortunately maintains the deep stigmatization of prostitutes themselves. "Prostitution is only a *specific* expression of the *general* prostitution of the labourer," says Marx. Prostitution also is equated by Engels with bourgeois marriage and "work" or slavery: "the wife who differs from the ordinary courtesan only in that she does not hire out her body, like a wage-worker, on piecework, but sells it into slavery once and for all." Marx would put prostitutes into the category of the *lumpen*-proletariat (the systematically unemployed, who often resort to crime to live) along with other members of the underclass who lack revolutionary consciousness. Neither Marx nor the biblical prophets explicitly connect sexual oppression as perhaps somehow *constitutive* of economic oppression for women or related to the sexual division of labor and unaccounted for in capitalist economic surplus accumulation.[50] However, both Thanh-Dam Truong and Luise White have now theorized prostitution as a form of reproductive domestic labor that rejuvenates the workforce.[51] Indeed the analysis of the PMM often concluded that the oppression and marginalization experienced by prostitutes is really an

48. See Enrique Dussel for a good account of how liberation theology uses Marxist theory, "Theology of Liberation and Marxism," in Ignacia Ellacuria and Jon Sobrino (eds.), *Mysterium Liberationis: Fundemental Concepts of Liberation Theology* (Maryknoll, NY: Orbis Books, 1993), pp. 85–102.

49. Karl Marx, "Economic and Philosophic Manuscripts of 1944," from Robert Tucker (ed.), *The Marx-Engels Reader* (New York: W.W. Norton, 1978), pp. 83, 96 and Engels from *The Origin of Family, Private Property, and State*, p. 742.

50. See Thanh-Dam Truong, *Sex, Money, and Morality: The Political Economy of Prostitution and Tourism in Southeast Asia* (London: Zed Books, 1990), pp. 11–92. The first section of Truong's book has developed a very helpful framework for understanding prostitution in terms of a feminist Marxist materialist critique of capitalist surplus accumulation and extraction of sexual and domestic labor which she applies to Thailand.

51. Thanh-Dam Truong, *Sex, Money and Morality*, p. 91, "a source of life" and Luise White, *The Comforts of Home: Prostitution in Colonial Nairobi* (Chicago, IL: University of Chicago Press: 1990), p. 11.

exaggerated form of the lot of all women.[52] Much modern social scientific discourse also persists with a degree of disdain or objectification of prostitute women. This anti-prostitute bias then is incorporated into the theological use made of it by modern liberation theologies of many stripes, even feminist. This has important methodological ramifications that I will now discuss.

A Preferential Option for Prostitute Women?

From a different direction, feminist theologian Christine Gudorf has criticized the religious left for its misunderstanding of the "preferential option for the poor" and its romanticization of victims in her book *Victimization: Examining Christian Complicity.*[53] She insists that liberation projects that do not utilize the knowledge of the poor are destined to fail and often have negative fallout for the poor: "The failure to understand the challenge to the poor in the preferential option for the poor is the result of *abysmal ignorance of the poor on the part of the non-poor.*"[54] When plans for action developed by the non-poor fail to liberate the poor it is generally poor people who bear the consequences and get the blame as well (like when abolitionists blame prostitutes' rights activists for the failure of the abolition agenda). Therefore, "The demand of the preferential option for the poor that those who are poor commit themselves to the elimination of poverty of all types clearly demands that they work to insert themselves into the decision making processes of society, that they change social institutions so that these institutions work for the poor as they do for the non-poor."[55] Gudorf calls for the complete participation of poor people at every level of organization in anti-poverty strategies, including leadership and the development of *social analysis.*

Another benefit of such an approach to poverty is that it is less easy to co-opt by hegemonic interests. George Bush and the religious right have

52. Guider, *The Daughters of Rahab*, pp. 90, 92, 183–87, 219–21. In traditional Marxist theory, capital accumulation is a result of expropriating the extra or "surplus" labour of industrial workers by the owners of the means of production. Truong suggests another form of surplus value extraction in the sex industry.

53. Christine Gudorf, *Victimization: Examining Christian Complicity* (Philadelphia, PA: Trinity Press, 1992), p. 45 and on victim romaticization see chapter 3.

54. Gudorf, *Victimization*, p. 44. Emphasis mine.

55. Gudorf, *Victimization*, p. 45.

championed the feminist abolition cause, and they all claim to be helping prostitutes. Thus, the religious right gets to have its cake and eat it too by claiming a feminist mantle for their morality crusades. Franz Hinkelammert quite chillingly demonstrates how deftly liberation theology's preferential option for the poor can be co-opted and transformed by neo-liberal capitalist ideology into an "option for the IMF" when we uncritically accept that the IMF is helping the poor.[56] A key to averting this danger within the church of liberation is to reject paternalistic approaches to poverty. According to Hinklelammert, the only way to distinguish between a genuine preferential option for the poor and its counterfeit IMF versions is that liberation theology respects the poor as subjects whereas "the theology of the empire can only consider the poor as objects for the others, for those who are not poor."[57] Abolitionists often claim that prostitute rights activists are falsely conscious, have internalized oppression, or are mentally damaged from growing up in dysfunctional or incestuous families. In this way, they can ignore the consciousness and analysis of prostitutes and replace it with their own, as being "for their own good." Another way of looking at this claim is as self-interested paternalistic cooptation. Feminist abolitionists and other social workers currently get a lot of money from government agencies to "help" prostitutes. Laura Agustín, who has done a Foucaultian analysis of the issue, notes that "the social sector desiring to help and save women who sell sex is very large indeed...The fact that their projects are governmental exercises of power is ignored."[58] Prostitutes' rights activists for their part question the benevolence of these women who have made nice respectable middle class careers for themselves as rescuers of "enslaved women." According to Agustín, "the reformer's refusal to accept the worker's expressed desire to be left alone and to remain in the sex trade has to be recognized as convenient; after all, without subjects to rescue, she could be out of a job."[59]

56. Franz Hinkelammert, "Taking Stock of Latin American Liberation Theology," *COELI*, winter (1996), pp. 25, 27. The World Bank's website now features a page devoted to Gustavo Gutierrez' *Theology of Liberation*; the World Bank thus co-opts its critics and makes it seem like they have the same strategy of poverty elimation as Gutierrez! http://web.worldbank.org/WBSITE/ EXTERNAL/TOPICS/EXTPOVERTY/EXTPA/0,,contentMDK:20161145~ menuPK:435040~pagePK:148956~piPK:216618~theSitePK:430367,00.html

57. Hinkelammert, "Taking Stock," p. 27.

58. Laura María Agustín, "Helping Women Who Sell Sex: The Construction of Benevolent Identities," *Rhizomes* 10 (2005) paragraphs 3 and 5: http:// www.rhizomes.net/issue10/Agustín.htm.

59. Agustín, "Helping Women Who Sell Sex," paragraph 36.

It is for this reason I propose that a fruitful methodological route to take would be to utilize feminist standpoint theory or epistemology for the twin goal of doing social analysis and a liberation hermeneutics that takes seriously the subjectivity and agency of prostitute women. This approach is quite possibly congruent with Guider's call for a "theology of incarnate presence."[60] However, she does not avoid the trap of appropriating the prostitute metaphor for the church to examine its institutional sin when she states that "if and when the church commits itself to reflecting upon the problem of prostitution, it could find itself gazing into a mirror...the church has been moved to prostitute itself."[61] Her discourse stays trapped in the ideological code of decency even when criticizing the church. The prostitute metaphor as applied to the church again keeps intact the deep stigmatization experienced by prostitutes while doing very little to liberate them or to challenge sexual norms of decency. It is time to develop a social analysis and biblical hermeneutic that is truly done by and for prostitutes. For this reason, I am adapting the approach of feminist standpoint theory and instead of an abolitionist approach, I adopt a prostitutes' rights framework, which seems to be more explicitly concerned with the liberating agency of sex workers themselves.

Standpoint Theory

> A sociology from women's standpoint in the local actualities of our everyday lives must be put together quite differently from the traditional *objectifying* sociologies. Committed to exploring the society from within people's experience of it, rather than *objectifying* them or explaining their behavior, it would investigate how that society organizes and shapes the everyday world of experience. Its project is to explicate the actual social relations in which people's lives are embedded and to make these visible to them/ourselves.[62]

Standpoint epistemology has been used and developed successfully by feminist theorists to get beyond the androcentric, racial and class biases embedded in many mainstream tools of social sciences. Even within prostitution research, standpoint theory/epistemology has been utilized by literary critic Shannon Bell to compare the new writings by prostitutes to the writings of social science and literary texts about prostitutes, ancient

---

60. Guider, *The Daughters of Rahab*, pp. 154–63.
61. Guider, *The Daughters of Rahab*, p. 168.
62. Dorothy Smith, *Writing the Social*, p. 74.

and modern.[63] Standpoint theorist Sandra Harding describes the traditional Marxist social analysis as rooted in the standpoint of the genderless, but nonetheless male proletarian.[64] In contradistinction, standpoint theorist Nancy Harstock inserts gender into this Marxist "proletarian" standpoint to develop a specifically *feminist* historical materialism.[65] Historical materialism is the Marxist method of analyzing history via its changing modes of production. The mode of production is the manner in which work is organized in various historical eras. Harstock's basis for the gender specification is that there exists in every human society a gendered division of labor and this division has "consequences for epistemology."[66]

Harding characterizes three methodological features of feminist analysis as:

1. Utilizing women's experiences as new empirical and theoretical sources.
2. Committed to doing research for the explicit benefit of women.
3. Locating the researcher on the same critical plane as the overt subject matter of research rather than keeping her hidden from view.[67]

For this reason, I have made myself explicitly present in this book to disclose my social location and agenda and in order to stand alongside the SWOP interpreters as a researching subject. I blatantly use the first person singular at many points in this book.

63. Shannon Bell, *Reading, Writing, and Rewriting the Prostitute Body* (Indianapolis, IN: Indiana University Press, 1994), pp. 16–17.

64. Sandra Harding, *Whose Science? Whose Knowledge? Thinking from Women's Lives* (Ithaca, NY: Cornell University Press, 1991), p. 120. "Proletarian" in Marx means an industrial worker. While many proletarians were in fact female, in Marx' writings the implied gender of a proletarian is generally male.

65. "Historical materialism" is the method of Marx's theory of history, that material struggles between classes over provision of sustenance moves history, in contrast to Hegel's historical idealism, or theory that ideas move history.

66. Nancy Harstock, *Money, Sex and Power*, p. 232. "Division of labour" is a Marxist concept that deals with how work is organized and distributed between classes. The sexual division of labour, especially in the family, is treated as "natural" in Marx.

67. Sandra Harding, "Introduction: Is there a Feminist Method?" in Sandra Harding (ed.), *Feminism and Methodology: Social Science Issues* (Indianapolis, IN: Indiana University Press, 1987), pp. 6–9.

Feminist standpoint theory thus adapts a Marxist materialist mode of analysis to focus on the particular economic experiences and viewpoints of women, which are elided in traditional methodologies. Due to this elision, the specific ways that oppression is organized for various groups of women, especially those most marginalized, never is analyzed or described. This is especially true for those who experience multiple intersecting oppressions such as African American women. Thus, feminist Patricia Hill Collins employs a standpoint approach to get at the distinctive group standpoint of black women in America. Hill Collins uses writings of black women as primary sources and examines themes from a variety of cultural productions from blues lyrics to novels, poems to Hip-hop.[68] Hill Collins' most recent work tackles the issue of black sexual politics and the challenges posed by getting beyond a sexually conservative "politics of respectability" towards a more progressive African American sexual politics.[69] Her concept of a "politics of respectability" shares much with the concept of "sexual decency" in Marcella Althaus-Reid's critique of liberation theology. Hill Collins urges African Americans to rebel against existing black sexual political respectability espoused by powerful institutions like the Black Church.

Another important benefit of standpoint theory is that it is linked to a more empowering and effective activism by oppressed groups. Patricia Hill Collins writes: "One way of approaching power concerns the dialectical relationship linking oppression and activism...dialectical approaches emphasize the significance of knowledge in developing self-defined, group-based standpoints that, in turn, can foster the type of group solidarity necessary for resisting oppressions."[70] Latin American feminist theologian, Maria Pilar Aquino affirms that "women's perspective gives a special place to one aspect of the option for the poor: it wants to reach the questions, historical and spiritual experiences, knowledge and memory, desires, and expectations of women, not only as part of the suffering world, but primarily *as women*."[71] Unfortunately, she also admits that "we cannot say that to

68. Patricia Hill Collins, *Black Feminist Thought: Knowledge, Consciousness, and the Politics of Empowerment* (New York: Routledge, 2000), pp. 13–17.

69. Patricia Hill Collins, *Black Sexual Politics: African Americans, Gender and the New Racism* (New York: Routledge, 2004), pp. 71–75 and pp. 305–306. For the concept of the "politics of respectability" Hill Collins utilizes the work of Evelyn Brooks Higginbotham in *Righteous Discontent: The Women's Movement in the Black Baptist Church, 1880–1920* (Cambridge, MA: Harvard University Press, 1993), see Chapter 5, pp. 185–229.

70. Collins, *Black Feminist Thought*, pp. 274–75.

71. Aquino, *Our Cry for Life*, p. 113.

date liberation theology from the perspective of Latin American women has developed an analytic method capable of encompassing women's problems."[72] An adaptation of feminist standpoint theory might accommodate both the desires of prostitutes' rights activists and feminist liberation theologians. The church of liberation has a preferential option to poor women to which it is accountable, but not to privileged North American feminists, who on their part also unwittingly often display an investment in decency, perhaps for reasons of class difference. Possibly because of this commitment, it will be through the vanguard of poor and oppressed sex workers that the church as a whole could some day recognize and change its oppressive social teachings on sexuality for all women. This distinctive standpoint needs articulation and a hearing.

I combine and utilize aspects from of all four standpoint theorists above but most especially, that of Nancy Harstock's five point adaptation of Marxist proletarian standpoint for a specifically *feminist* historical materialism.[73] I shall further adapt her feminist adaptation of the proletarian standpoint and apply it to the activist prostitutes of SWOP. Harstock first argues that one of the most distinctive assertions of Marx's historical materialism is that the way humans produce their daily sustenance also determines their consciousness. Thus, we can expect that under capitalism, the consciousness of the factory worker will differ greatly from that of the factory owner. This is a result of their vastly different daily experiences within the division of labour. This difference of consciousness has consequences for knowledge. Secondly, Harstock posits that the division of labour will produce distinctive standpoints that are inversions of each other, but that of the dominant partner's will be more partial and distorted than that of the one with less investment in maintaining the unjust status quo. This goes back to the Hegelian master/slave dialectic and to the issue of who knows more, the master or the slave.[74] For example, African Americans have a different standpoint that is generally cognizant of that of the dominating European Americans, but European Americans themselves generally are ignorant of the African American standpoint because they are not required to know about it due to their position of

72. Aquino, *Our Cry for Life*, p. 116.

73. Nancy Harstock in *Money, Sex and Power*, p. 232. This same section of her book can also be found reproduced in Sandra Harding (ed.), *Feminism and Methodology*, pp. 157–80.

74. Harding, *Whose Science? Whose Knowledge?* p. 120.

power. Thirdly, this partial and perverse view of the dominant partner will structure institutions in a way that serves those in power: for example US laws on segregation and miscegenation were informed by beliefs about the racial inferiority of non-Europeans on the part of European Americans who made the laws to maintain their power. Thus, the racist standpoint of the dominant group is embedded in material institutions in a way that the subaltern standpoint is not due to the power differential. This example shows how racism is institutionalized. I want to show how "decency" is institutionalized. Fourthly, because the dominant standpoint is so entwined with institutions whose operations impact everyday life, the subordinate standpoint must be struggled for, it is not just a "perspective" or view, but is a conscious standpoint that emerges out of active struggle for better conditions of life. Thus, Harstock makes an important differentiation between a mere perspective and a standpoint, which is a consciousness derived from active struggle against domination. Simply being oppressed does not automatically grant a person critical consciousness. Finally, this standpoint has a historically liberative role because it is a less partial standpoint that can disclose the perversions or distortions of the dominant view and asks for something better. Harstock applies these five claims of historical materialism to women's standpoint developed from their generally distinctive location in the gendered division of labour, in their contributions to human sustenance and in their reproduction of human life. I will make these claims to standpoint even more specific and apply them to sex worker rights activists. Several recent theorists of prostitution claim that sex work is a form of reproductive labour in that it rejuvenates the vital energies of the labour force whether or not it leads to the production of offspring.[75] I utilize this view in my own concept of sex work, which I most simply define as the commoditization of sexual services.

The Sex Worker Standpoint of SWOP

I did biblical interpretation with a prostitutes' rights group in Berkeley, California, USA. This group pre-existed my research and has an elaborated political position and theory of prostitution that differs from the abolitionist view adopted by Guider, the PMM, and many other mainstream

---

75. Truong, *Sex, Money and Morality*, p. 91 and White, *The Comforts of Home*, p. 11.

feminists. I sought out this group, whose views are representative of the prostitutes' rights framework internationally,[76] and offered to help with their campaign to decriminalize prostitution starting in Berkeley, California. I offered to them my skills as a religion scholar and an activist in return for help with my project after the campaign was over. I became extremely intimate with the SWOP rights agenda in the work I did advocating their platform, gathering signatures, as their representative on the Commission for the Status of Women in Berkeley, speaking to the media as a supporter of measure Q, and as a liaison to the religious community of my Berkeley seminary, the Graduate Theological Union.[77] In terms of Sandra Harding's defining characteristics of a feminist standpoint approach, I endeavoured to meet all three criteria:

- I explicitly sought to have SWOP members apply their elaborated standpoint to biblical texts of prostitution.
- I wanted to do this in a way that benefited their self-defined struggle.
- I was a participant observer in their political project, trying to not objectify my friends but to maintain their status as subjects and agents of change from whom I had much to learn. In that I asked all of the SWOP readers to disclose intimate information about their lives in their interpretive work, it was only fair that I

76. There exists a growing amount of literature since the movement began in 1970s that expounds the politics of prostitutes' or sex worker rights as opposed to the abolitionist framework. A few representative examples: Claude Jaget (ed.), *Prostitutes-Our Life* (Bristol: Falling Wall Press, 1980); Gail Pheterson (ed.), *A Vindication of the Rights of Whores* (Seattle: Seal Press, 1989); Gail Pheterson, *The Prostitution Prism* (Amsterdam: Amsterdam University Press, 1996); Jill Nagle (ed.), *Whores and Other Feminists* (New York: Routledge, 1997); Wendy Chapkis, *Live Sex Acts: Women Performing Erotic Labor* (New York: Routledge, 1997); Kamala Kempadoo and Jo Doezema (eds.), *Global Sex Workers: Rights, Resistance and Redefinition* (New York: Routledge, 1998); Frederique Delacoste and Priscilla Alexander, *Sex Work: Writings by Women in the Sex Industry* (San Francisco, CA: Cleis Press, 1998, 2nd edn); International Prostitute's Collective, *Some Mother's Daughter: The Hidden Movement of Prostitute Women against Violence* (London: Crossroads Books, 1999).

77. Rita Nakashima Brock also spoke out on behalf of SWOP and Measure Q and did extensive outreach to her colleagues at our seminary. She is currently a Visiting Scholar at Starr King School for Ministry at the Graduate Theological Union in Berkeley.

Avaren Ipsen campaigning to decriminalize prostitution, Photograph courtesy of
August Schleis, the author's son

endeavour to do likewise with my own motivations and
experiences. I shall now locate all of us for the readers, starting
with myself.

My inclination for engaging in prostitution research developed over time.
For one thing, my brother's father grew up in a brothel. When my brother's
father died a few years ago, several of us from our old inner-city ghetto
neighbourhood in the late 1960s reunited during the weeklong funeral
events. During this week of reminiscence and eulogy (he was an important
black revolutionary activist in local Minneapolis politics), some of the more
forbidden aspects of our history were discussed among our ex-neighbour
women in private. Prostitution was one of the topics. It seems that, back in
the day, many of our old neighbours were approached to do "convention"
prostitution as a way of raising money for the "revolution." Convention

prostitution was described as flying out of town to various big city hotels during business or professional conventions on occasional weekends. It was supposedly quite lucrative and afforded a great measure of anonymity to the women since it was occasional, brief, and out of town. Perhaps my awareness of such downplayed historical details, such as the presence of prostitution within the 1960s revolutionary counter-culture, makes me prone to wonder about its invisible role in the success and failure of social formations to achieve more liberating conditions of life for women, especially the many women with poverty experience who populate my autobiography.

When I think about it further, many of the neighbourhood women who helped raise me were sexual outlaws of some sort—they were guilty of miscegenation, lesbianism, a wide variety of sex-work, and lots of non-marital childbearing—which has made me think there must be a *big* sexual component to class. The respectable neighbourhood church ladies certainly plugged their noses when they dealt with our kind, that is, those sexually stigmatized in some way. For example, my mother was a divorcee, guilty of miscegenation and out-of-wedlock childbirth. She also room mated with lesbian friends and worked her way through graduate school as a scantily clad cocktail waitress who occasionally modelled lingerie — considered a form of sex work by SWOP readers. When community outreach workers from the church across the street came to visit, it was very clear what they thought of my mother. They treated her as a lost cause but pleaded with her to let them "save" me, which ironically did not include watching, clothing, feeding and housing me, this was left to the sexual outlaws. Their persuasive skills were totally lacking and they did not know it because their commitment to respectability was much stronger than my mother's and most of our friends.

I again began paying attention to the issue of prostitution after starting graduate work because all at the same time I was confronted with the issue from separate sectors of my life. First was the focalization given to the issue from a group I belonged to called Wages for Housework. This is a coordinating international organization that includes a prostitute's rights cooperative called US PROS. This organization has been pushing for a policy of decriminalization of sex-work in San Francisco after years of participation on the San Francisco Task Force on Prostitution during the 1990s. US PROS also monitored the Jack Bokin trial. Jack Bokin is a serial rapist, with a pre-existing conviction record, who was convicted of the attempted murder of a prostitute. He tried to hammer her to death and then dump her body into the San Francisco bay at Pier 9. When this crime occurred, he was out on a low bail for allegedly raping yet three other prostitutes.[78] Another sector was when a close friend, "Sweet," disclosed to me some of her personal experience of devastating, near-death violence, ignored by the police authorities, when working in prostitution some years back. Even after leaving prostitution, when she worked as an advocate for prostitutes, she has experienced police harassment for simply talking to people on the streets—behaviour indistinguishable to police from illegal sexual activity. This motivated me to read the book on prostitution by feminist theologians Rita Nakashima Brock and Susan Brooks Thistlethwaite, *Casting Stones: Prostitution and Liberation in Asia and the United States.* Therein I read: "Women who attended the American Academy of Religion annual meeting in the late 1960s and early 1970s report that every evening in the hotel lobbies, prostitutes waited for their customers. As more professional women each year have joined the association and attended the meeting, the practice has either ended or become invisible."[79] Finally, my adviser, Mary Ann Tolbert, suggested the topic of biblical prostitution as something I might want to research since it involves looking at gender, class and sexual morality issues at once, which were all issues in which I had expressed an interest.

Male commentary on prostitution in the Bible contains such views as: "harlots were a regular institution of the ancient Near East, about which the Hebrews had apparently no inhibitions,"[80] or "prostitution was not considered morally wrong."[81] Such comments cause my paranoid mind to begin to wonder if all this liberal tolerance reflects a more male oriented "john" perspective that comes to overshadow the various negative and asymmetrical social consequences of being a prostitute in the biblical text. For example, prophetic metaphorical prostitutes who continually suffer the just and violent punishment of YHVH for their evil, fornicating ways or the prostitutes who were sentenced to death by burning. An example of this gendered perspective is in Gray's commentary where the moral

78. Jim Herron Zamora, "Suspect's Sex Charges Date to Mid-60s," *San Francisco Examiner*, 17 October 1997 and Athena Dorris, "The Sounds of Silence," *Alice Magazine*, January 2000.

79. Rita Nakashima Brock and Susan Brooks Thistlethwaite, *Casting Stones: Prostitution and Liberation in Asia and the United States* (Minneapolis, MN: Fortress Press, 1996), p. 171.

80. John Gray, *I & II Kings: A Commentary* (Philadelphia, PA: Westminster Press, 1970), p. 128.

81. Jerome Walsh, *1 Kings* (Collegeville, MN: Liturgical Press, 1996), p. 79.

evaluation is focused upon the behaviour of the spies who visited Rahab
"unashamedly" or upon Judah who is "not condemned". [82] But Tamar, in
Gen. 38:24, was certainly condemned: "your daughter-in-law Tamar has
played the whore; moreover she is pregnant as a result of whoredom." And
Judah said: "Bring her out and let her be burned." Levitical daughters who
become prostitutes in Lev. 21:9 are to be likewise executed: "When the
daughter of a priest profanes herself through prostitution, she profanes
her father; she shall be burned to death." The Whore Babylon of Revelation
17–19 is burned down as a city and a whore. The way I associatively imagine
all these elements together is a situation where religion scholars are trying
to decide whether it is tolerated by the Bible to hire my neighbours at
AAR/SBL conventions for the purposes of prostitution. I am too differently
located to read the texts in a manner that so dispassionately privileges
male morality with regard to prostitution, when other biblical texts suggest
that violence against prostitutes was also prevalent. Since I identify with
my family, ex-neighbors and friends, I feel under compulsion to view such
representations with a hermeneutical option for the prostitute women.
Sex work is not a remote thing that happens among other people but
rather, my people, that is, it could be me. I would like to hazard a reading
that privileges the voices of sex workers on issues of justice, sexual morality
and the gendered political economy.

The SWOP activists I worked with are a magnificent group of gifted
and beautiful women. Those who worked on my interpretation project
are: Robyn Few, Carol Leigh ("Scarlot Harlot"), Carol Stuart, Veronica Monet,
"Sweet," "Ms. Shiris," Shemena Campbell, "Gayle," "Damienne Sin," and
"Kimberlee Cline." A few men active in the prostitutes' rights movement
occasionally participated: Larry, Scarlot's boyfriend, Michael Foley and Rick,
Robyn's friends. These SWOP activists operated with varying degrees of
public disclosure over their identity. Some of these names, those in
quotation marks, are pseudonyms or stage names. Generally, only ex-
prostitutes can go fully public as activists and public figures because the
penalties are high for practicing prostitutes who are politically active. One

82. Gray, *I & II Kings*, p. 128. The violent treatment of prostitute women
within prophetic metaphorical discourse has been the subject of feminist work
that terms it "prophetic pornography." See Cheryl Exum, *Plotted Shot and Painted:
Cultural Representations of Biblical Women* (Sheffield: Sheffield Academic Press,
1996), pp. 101–28 or "pornoprophetics" in Athalya Brenner, *The Intercourse of
Knowledge: On Gendering Desire and "Sexuality" in the Hebrew Bible* (Leiden:
Brill, 1997), pp. 153–74.

sex worker rights activist visiting from another state explained how she manages to both work and do her activism: she put everything she owns in her children's names and she signed over legal custody of her children to her parents. That way she owns nothing and cannot be blackmailed with losing custody of her children. This frees her to do political activism. Only two of the women of our group were mothers, but this is a much more common scenario for prostitutes than the ratio in our group would seem to indicate.

Four out of the ten women were still working. They ranged in age from mid-20s to mid-60s—and yes, our senior activist was still working! Three of the ten had police records. Half had been or were married. There were three women who were lesbian or bisexual and one woman was transgendered. One woman was African American and another was Latina, two were Jewish, the other six were Caucasian. Three of the women had been raised in evangelical Christian contexts but only two still considered themselves Christian. Veronica, who was raised fundamentalist, commented that "right wing religious fanatics turn out more sex workers than anybody else!" Three of the women identified as pagan goddess worshipers. Over half of the women were college educated, two as far as getting Masters Degrees. They all had worked in a wide variety of venues both legal and illegal: exotic dancing, porn, escort, phone-sex, courtesan, erotic massage, in-call, out-call and brothel work. Three of the women had experience with street prostitution and only one identified primarily as a street worker. Carol Leigh and Veronica Monet are published authors and well-known public figures.[83] Another pseudonymous participant has published work in an anthology called *The New Sexual Healers: Women of the Light*.[84] Carol Stuart had been one of the founders of the St. James Infirmary, an occupational health clinic for sex workers in San Francisco and is the co-author of the equal benefits ordinance in San Francisco. Robyn Few became an international public figure after her federal arrest and conviction, which "outed" her. The SWOP campaign to decriminalize prostitution was her brainchild and project while she was serving house arrest. Seven of the SWOP women were linked to the international prostitutes' rights movement; a couple had even met Gabriela Leite, whose

83. See Carol Leigh's *Unrepentant Whore: Collected Works of Scarlot Harlot* (San Francisco, CA: Last Gasp, 2004) and *Veronica Monet's Sex Secrets of Escorts: What Men Really Want* (New York: Penguin, 2005).

84. Kenneth Ray Stubbs (ed.), *The New Sexual Healers: Women of the Light* (Larkspur, CA: Secret Garden, 1994).

call to consider "prostitution through the exegesis of the prostitute in the Bible,"[85] inspired this very book! I want the reader to know, *all* of these women I worked with are exceptionally courageous. Given the illegal context in which prostitutes' rights activists must currently work in the US, their commitment to this cause is amazing.

It is out of this background and year-long fieldwork that we at SWOP develop together our approach to biblical passages that narrate stories of prostitution. It was fascinating to even initially compare the activist prostitutes' understanding of biblical prostitution with that of religion scholars and the general public. While petition signature gathering and at political actions, I carried a sign that said, "Jesus was nice to prostitutes," (see photograph on p. 35). Many prostitutes told me that they were frequently told that this was true only if they "repented" because Jesus said "go and sin no more" in Jn 8:11. They were very empowered to learn that Jesus said this, not to a prostitute, but to the woman caught in adultery who was about to be stoned to death. Despite this biblical passage of conditional forgiveness, the sex crime of adultery has been decriminalized in most places and certainly doesn't warrant the death penalty, at least in the United States. People who approached me to comment on my sign frequently said the same: Jesus might be nice to prostitutes, but it was conditional. Deeply problematic is the idea that prostitutes are only worthy to be associated with Jesus if they leave prostitution, and therefore "repent," when this is not a viable option for so many poor women.

Another interesting issue is to what degree local prostitutes' rights activists, not just Brazilian, identify with Mary Magdalene. Do they understand Mary Magdalene as prostitute to be a disparaging or disempowering image as many first world feminists do? In response to my sign, a few people seeing it emphatically declared: "Mary Magdalene was not a prostitute!" emboldened by what they had learnt on PBS types of television shows inspired by Dan Brown's popular novel, *The Da Vinci Code*. Many sex workers feel similar to how gay people feel when "faggot" is used to insult someone. Because prostitutes identify with the prostitute, that the whore label is used to slander non-prostitutes creates very ambivalent feelings because they would prefer that their identities not be stigmatized in the first place. Like the reclamation of the term "queer" by the Lesbian/Gay/Bisexual/Transgender (LGBT) community, many prostitutes are reclaiming the title "whore." For example, Veronica Monet describes herself as an ex-prostitute and "lifelong whore" to defuse its

85. Leite, "The Prostitute Movement in Brazil," pp. 425–26.

defamatory power and to identify positively with herself and her lifework. When non-prostitutes eschew the whore label as slander, because for them that is the worst possible thing to be, they maintain the label's stigmatizing power. Prostitutes would like other women to object to the whore label because being a whore should not be an insult, not because it is a false accusation. The latter is what the "Mary Magdalene was not a prostitute" comments seem to be concerned about, salvaging her reputation. This is a concern for theological decency; it is a politics of respectability. Prostitutes wonder why Mary Magdalene cannot be a leader of the early church *and* also be a prostitute.

In contrast, a few years ago, at a local event of USPROS and the International Collective of Prostitutes, I described to Rachel West of USPROS and Nikki Adams of the English Prostitutes Collective the new Mary Magdalene being exegeted by contemporary feminist biblical scholars. This new Mary M., was not a prostitute and neither were any of the women around Jesus for that matter, but I explained that this was most probably "slander" designed to defame important early Christian women leaders. Both of those prostitutes' rights activists were a bit disappointed that their imminent ideological use of the "Magdalene" name and symbol was being deflated of its effective power. That night's event was a lecture about the historical story of a group of prostitutes' rights activists in San Francisco called the "Magdalenes" who had occupied a church at the turn of the century to protest police brutality. Considering that prostitutes' rights activists repeated this strategy in Lyon France in the 1970s which ignited church occupations all over the world, there may be some "hidden transcripts" of a prostitute culture to be discovered, of interpretation and activism rooted in the notion of friendship between Jesus and Mary Magdalene.[86] During the 1990s a prostitutes union in Tijuana formed which at one point had 250 members. They call themselves the "Las Magdalenas,"

---

86. James Scott, *Domination and the Arts of Resistance: Hidden Transcripts* (Yale University Press: New Haven, 1990). Scott has an interesting theory of consciousness among subjugated populations that contrasts with Antonio Gramsci's theory of hegemony and internalized oppression. Scott sees oppressed groups as often less constrained on the ideological level of consciousness but more constrained on the material level, by violence and other institutional mechanisms of coercion. This consciousness is kept concealed from oppressive powers that be in the form of "hidden transcripts" until the time is ripe for open resistance. It explains how a vocabulary of resistance is kept alive on the linguistic level and within group consciousness even through times of no overt activism on the part of the oppressed.

and make specific appeals to conservative Catholics to stop the police brutality against them because *Jesus was nice to prostitutes.*[87] My friend Rachel West insists that there is a long hidden historical tradition of prostitutes being involved with and funding liberation movements.[88] Prostitution historian, Nickie Roberts, claims that prostitutes were prominent in the underground resistance in Europe during World War II and that brothels were typical meeting places as well as excellent places to spy on the Nazi "johns."[89] Considering that Mary Magdalene and other women followers funded the Jesus Movement according to Lk. 8:2, this certainly sheds an interesting light on "our Christian story," as Gabriela Leite calls it. What if sex workers funded the early church? Even the Anchor Bible author of the Revelation commentary, J. Massyngbaerde Ford explored the possible missionary role of prostitutes in her article on call girls in antiquity.[90] Would that be like sacred prostitution? When the Catholic Church owns and operates a brothel, as happened during the Middle Ages, is that sacred prostitution?[91]

Sacred prostitution is the topic that most ignited the imagination of SWOP activists. One activist from Amsterdam, who responded suspiciously to my call for subjects in my research, took me to task for not addressing this topic. He as an Israeli ex-patriot, fluent in Hebrew, and he astutely wondered why I did not choose to interpret the text of Genesis 38, the story of Tamar. This is one of the few texts that seem to associate prostitution with temple prostitution by using the Hebrew words זנה/*zonah* ("prostitute") and קדשה/*qedeshah* (an adjective or substantive meaning "sacred" or "dedicated") interchangeably. I told him that I had chosen the four texts on which I had already done more mature research. I did work on the Tamar passage the first year of my Masters program before I had yet studied any Hebrew. What I did not tell him was that I wanted to avoid the issue of temple prostitution because a critical mass of scholars had been

87. Sally Hughes, "Women's Work," Freedom Review, 1 September 1995; http://www.jornada.unam.mx/2002/07/04/ls-norte.html; and Richard Marosi, "Making Nice on Vice," *Los Angeles Times*, 4 January 2005, p. A1.

88. See International Prostitute's Collective, *Some Mother's Daughter*, p. 158.

89. Nickie Roberts, *Whores in History: Prostitution in Western Society* (London: Grafton, 1992), pp. 280–81.

90. J. Massyngbaerde Ford, "The 'Call girl' in Antiquity and her Potential for Mission," in *Proceedings: Eastern Great Lakes and Midwest Biblical Societies*, Volume XII: (Grand Rapids, MI: The Societies, 1992), pp. 105–16.

91. See Vern Bullough and Bonnie Bullough, *Women and Prostitution, A Social History* (Buffalo, NY: Prometheus Books, 1987), pp. 126–29.

questioning the historical existence of the institution. Since so much of what is known as sacred prostitution was conjecture or historical reconstruction and not really directly described in any biblical passage, I thought that it would not be a good issue to focus on. I must also frankly admit it: I was too much of a coward to pursue a line of research that was becoming so far a field of mainstream scholarship. In hindsight, I think that perhaps this decision was a mistake, given the great symbolic importance the concept of sacred prostitution has for many sex workers as an enormous source of self-esteem and as a model of sex-positivity. Also, given that so many sex workers identify as pagan goddess worshippers, the sacralization of sex has great religious significance for many prostitutes. Even though I tried to avoid the topic, it always came up in most of the interpretation sessions we had. My attempt to repress sacred sex and the goddess failed. Perhaps, the trends in scholarship to deny the historical reality of temple prostitution is comparable to denying the prostitute status of Mary Magdalene and the women around Jesus and serving the ideological desires of feminists, including myself, to be "decent." Perhaps our next series of symposia will focus on temple prostitution. Everyone involved wants to continue doing these symposia; one member commented that we were a virtual think tank and that our work must continue.

Each symposium we held was structured by the discussion questions I prepared in advance (see Appendix 1). A few of the participants could not attend all the symposia so they answered the discussion questions in writing or in a separate interview. However, the group work was the definitive and most interesting mode of our work together. Agreement about story elements was not always possible, so for many of the stories there was a majority and minority position in our interpretations. Both were important to maintain, like the Jewish tradition of interpretation of schools of Rabbi Akiba (Carol Stuart) and of Shammai (Carol Leigh or "Scarlot Harlot"). Overall, the stories of prostitution that we generated, both ancient and modern, contain subjugated knowledge that I hope educates as well as informs areas of new struggle for the human dignity of women.

Excursus on Decriminalization and Measure Q

An ever-present issue on the agendas of prostitutes' rights activists concerns their ability to access the same human and civil rights protected by laws governing all other people and to not be legislated about in a special category. This equal access to the law is currently impossible due to the illegal status of most sex workers. Rights activists argue that existing laws against child abuse, slavery, assault, battery, murder, rape, blackmail, and exploitation are general laws that apply to all people and should be sufficient for addressing the negative aspects of the sex industry such as trafficking and child prostitution, which are of such dire concern to all. Therefore, law that is specially designed for prostitutes is unnecessary and actually inhibits their ability to seek legal redress. Sex workers' desperate need for equal protection before the law from violent crime is most emphasized by prostitute activists and this violence has made law reform a number one issue internationally. Decriminalization as opposed to regulation systems —including prohibition as well as legalization—is most often urged by rights activists.

What has generally energized the formation of various prostitutes' rights groups worldwide is the ongoing threat of violence against sex workers by clients, law enforcement officials, and others. In 1975, French prostitutes in Lyons instigated a strike that quickly spread throughout France, as far as England and even Australia, in response to several brutal murders that occurred in Lyons during a period of intensified police crack-down of prostitution:

> What precipitated the national strike of prostitutes in France was a situation similar to those in England with the Yorkshire Ripper and in the U.S. with the multiple murders of prostitutes in Los Angeles. A number of women had been murdered in Lyons. The police were not offering women adequate protection and they weren't solving the murders either. On top of that, police harassment had increased with higher daily and even hourly fines, and more frequent imprisonments. Prostitute women were having to spend a lot of time, energy, and money having to ward off the police and courts, and they weren't getting very far with it.[92]

When Gabriela Leite organized the first prostitutes' rally in 1987 in Brazil, police violence was at the top of the list of issues.[93] Even where prostitution is legal, but regulated, like Ecuador, "our most important struggle focused upon the extensive malpractice within the police force and on the exploitation by brothel and club owners."[94] Or in South Africa "of

92. Margaret Valentino and Mavis Johnson, "On the Game and on the Move," in Claude Jaget (ed.), *Prostitutes—Our Life* (Bristol: Falling Wall Press, 1980).

93. Leite, 'The Prostitute Movement in Brazil,' p. 418.

94. Angelita Abad, Marena Briones, Tatiana Cordero, Rosa Manzo and Marta Marchan, "The Association of Autonomous Women Workers, Ecuador, '22nd June'" in Kamala Kempadoo and Jo Doezema (eds.), *Global Sex Workers: Rights, Resistance, and Redefinition* (New York: Routledge, 1998), p. 173.

fundamental concern is the ongoing violation of human and civil rights illustrated by violence towards sex workers, dismissive attitudes of police and healthcare workers and a unique hierarchy of sex work that exists in the country."[95] Indeed, many activists make a connection between the two issues of lack of protection from violent crime and periods of intensified police harassment. With reference to a recent wave of violence in San Francisco against prostitutes which was concurrent with a police crack down in prostitution areas, Rachel West of US PROS concludes: "criminalizing sex work generates violence and abuse of prostitute women."[96] The more the justice system focuses upon prosecuting prostitutes as criminals, the more they become easy targets of violent crime. Especially targeted are women of colour, who are arrested and imprisoned at much higher rates than white women. Sex workers often fear reporting crimes against themselves because they risk arrest, and if they are immigrant, deportation. In the US, non-legal immigrants arrested for prostitution are forever unable to obtain legal residency because of "moral turpitude laws."[97] Thus, migrant prostitutes are often doubly vulnerable to exploitation and violence in countries such as the US that prohibit prostitution. In counties where prostitution is legal, repressive immigration policies often keep non-citizen sex workers unable to access legal redress or civil rights because of their migrant status.[98] In the western European countries where prostitution is currently legal, the growing majority of sex workers are non-citizen women who are nonetheless outside of the legal sex work structure.[99]

States have traditionally adopted one of three policies to deal with the issue of prostitution: prohibition, regulation, abolition, or some

95. Shane A. Petzer and Gordon M. Issacs, "SWEAT: The Development and Implementation of a Sex Worker Advocacy and Intervention Program in Post-Apartheid South Africa (with special reference to the western city of Cape Town)," in Kamala Kempadoo and Jo Doezema (eds.), *Global Sex Workers*, p. 195.

96. Angela Rowen, "Street Legal," *San Francisco Bay Guardian*, 8 July 1998, p. 22.

97. Rachel West, 27 March 1998, at St. Paulus Lutheran Church in San Francisco during a speakout and discussion called "Defending Pros and Cons: Violence, Poverty and Miscarriages of Justice."

98. Laura Agustín, "Migrants in the Mistress's House: Other Voices in the Trafficking Debate," *Social Politics* 12.1 (Spring 2005), pp. 96–117.

99. Licia Brussa, "The TAMPEP Project in Western Europe," in Kamala Kempadoo and Jo Doezema (eds.), *Global Sex Workers*, p. 247.

combination of the three.[100] A fourth option, decriminalization, is a new policy option being tried in New Zealand.[101] In all three traditional systems the rights and agency of sex workers is severely undermined. Prohibition systems make prostitutes and all aspects of the sex industry criminal. In such systems, the prostitute is seen as criminal in need of moral rehabilitation. Prostitutes, the most visible and least powerful agents within the sex industry are the main focal point of law enforcement, which keeps them "subject to blackmail, rape, and battering without recourse to legal protection."[102] This system keeps prostitutes vulnerable to corruption at every level of the legal establishment. Police informally control the sex industry under prohibition since a large part of the population still desire a sex industry to exist thus prohibition becomes arbitrarily enforced. Organized crime and pimps often get formal control of prostitution under prohibition since criminalized sex workers have need of their services and protection.

Regulation systems (legalization or contradictory systems where illegality and official tolerance systems, like mandatory health cards for entertainment workers, co-exist) [103] also tend to criminalize the majority of women who do not comply with a state's narrowly circumscribed definition of permissible prostitution. Official registration is perceived by sex workers as a permanently stigmatizing branding that traps them in work that might otherwise be a temporary, economically induced survival strategy. Official registration is also impossible for migrant sex workers. Mandatory health checks and cards violate the women's rights to and desire for regular health care and medical confidentiality and can also disable the self-protection of sex workers when clients refuse to wear condoms because "they trust in the state's control as a guarantee of the prostitute's health."[104] In legal or regulated systems, the state is a pimp: "Legalization is no better

---

100. I am drawing upon the typologies of Gabriela Leite, "The Prostitute Movement in Brazil," pp. 420–23, of Marjan Wijers "Women, Labor, and Migration: The Position of Trafficked Women and Strategies for Support," in Kamala Kempadoo and Jo Doezema (eds.), *Global Sex Workers*, pp. 72–74. Rita Nakashima Brock and Susan Thistlethwaite, *Casting Stones*, pp. 145–54, and from the bitter critiques of different prostitution law that is spread throughout all the narratives in Claude Jaget (ed.), *Prostitutes—Our Life*.

101. http://www.timbarnett.org.nz/prostitution.php

102. Brock and Thistlethwaite, *Casting Stones*, p. 154.

103. Brock and Thistlethwaite, *Casting Stones*, p. 151.

104. Leite, "The Prostitute Movement in Brazil", p. 421.

than prostitution; in some ways it is worse. The proof is that in West Germany only 12 percent of hookers have officially registered with the government, and the rest would rather live in illegality than accept the State's working conditions, wages, and control."[105]

Abolition systems of thought dominate today's discourse on prostitution, especially at the level of international law and the UN, and many state policies incorporate this view of prostitution with contradictory effects on prostitutes. In the abolitionist view, all prostitution is abuse to prostitutes; it is never voluntary and is a form of slavery, so that any policy that accepts its existence is unacceptable. For an abolitionist it is morally wrong to accept the existence of prostitution in any form. In laws that incorporate this view, the prostitute herself is not always deemed a criminal but a victim, but all activities that surround prostitution are made even more illegal, such as buying sexual services, pimping and trafficking people across state lines. This creates systems of incoherent and contradictory legislation that penalize sex workers in any case. Within this view of prostitutes as victims or slaves in need of rescue, sex workers continue to have difficulty obtaining their social and civil rights if they cannot, or refuse to, prove their victim status. This abolitionist view is the dominant feminist position in current debate especially regarding "trafficking" and the thorny issue of "forced" versus "voluntary" prostitution.[106] This way of framing the issue of prostitution is one of hot contestation by prostitutes' rights activists because it makes it very difficult for "voluntary" sex workers to fight for civil, social or labour rights. Most prostitutes' rights activists favour a policy of decriminalization, that is, repeal of prostitution law with no special legislation regarding prostitution, and the rigorous use and enforcement of existing generalized laws to deal with the crimes most

105. Margaret Valentino and Mavis Johnson, "On the Game and on the Move," in Claude Jaget (ed.), *Prostitutes—Our Life*, p. 20.

106. Kathleen Barry is the most prominent spokeswoman of the abolitionist view; see *Female Sexual Slavery* (New York: New York University Press, 1984) and *The Prostitution of Sexuality* (New York: New York University Press, 1995). For more on the abolitionist view, see also the work of Sheila Jeffreys, *The Idea of Prostitution* (Melbourne: Spinifex, 1997), and Melissa Farley, *Prostitution, Trafficking and Traumatic Stress* (Binghamton, NY: Haworth Press, 2003). See Jo Doezema for the state of the debate from a prostitutes' rights standpoint in "Forced to Choose: Beyond the Voluntary v. Forced Prostitution Dichotomy," in Kamala Kempadoo and Jo Doezema (eds.), *Global Sex Workers*, pp. 34–50. See also Agustín, "Migrants in the Mistress's House."

associated with the victimization of prostitutes (existing laws against slavery, trafficking, kidnapping, child exploitation, and so forth). Civil and health codes that apply to all other self-employed persons would of course apply to sex work as well but all criminal codes regarding consensual adult sex work would be "abolished." Full decriminalization would empower prostitutes to struggle for better conditions of life on their own terms as non-criminals. The only place that such a policy of decriminalization exists is New Zealand where the new legislation is only a few years old. Our prostitutes' activist group, SWOP, made a failed bid towards decriminalization in Berkeley, California, in 2004. The bid is otherwise known as Measure Q.

Measure Q

The sex worker activists of SWOP put a voter initiative that advocated decriminalization on the Berkeley, California, ballot in the 2004 election. Two key happenings influenced the formation of SWOP in late 2003: the prostitution arrest of a Berkeley High School Independent Studies teacher, Shannon Williams, and the conviction and sentencing of the serial killer of prostitutes, Gary Leon Ridgeway, the Green River Killer. These events galvanized San Francisco Bay Area sex worker activists to form SWOP to protest the violence they experienced due to, in their analysis, criminalization. Robyn Few, who began SWOP with several other sex workers, was herself awaiting sentencing on a federal charge of "conspiring to commit prostitution" because her name was in an arrested madam's phone book. Measure Q, originally called Angel's Initiative,[107] was Robyn's main project while serving her sentence on house arrest for this phone book crime. Beginning with the International Day to End Violence Against Sex Workers on 17 December 2003, Robyn began lobbying local city politicians in San Francisco, Oakland and Berkeley to support statewide decriminalization of prostitution. Since it was a state law than needed to be overturned, and since statewide initiatives cost millions, SWOP focused efforts on local city governments to support a commitment to ending criminalization at the California state level. San Francisco had already passed a resolution in 2000 affirming decriminalization following upon many years of study of the issue by a specially formed task force: The San Francisco

107. Named after Angel Lopez, a transgendered sex worker brutally murdered in San Francisco in 1993.

Task Force on Prostitution, called into existence in 1993.[108] This task force's final report in 1996 recommended a policy of decriminalization, a redirection of law enforcement energies towards crimes against sex workers and a redistribution of government funding towards programs to help all low income women with basic needs such as affordable childcare, housing and health care. [109] This policy was never implemented by the city of San Francisco, despite the 2000 city resolution supportive of the task force's recommendations. Robyn Few and SWOP members such as Carol Leigh and Carol Stuart, who were former members of the task force and involved with COYOTE (Call Off Your Old Tired Ethics),[110] were interested in pushing the issue forward again. This time the effort was to be across the Bay in Berkeley.

SWOP began gathering petition signatures in early 2004 asking the citizens of Berkeley to:

1. Have the City Council write a letter in support of decriminalization of prostitution at the state level and send it to elected officials.
2. Generate a semi-annual report of prostitution arrests in the city of Berkeley.
3. To make prostitution arrests in Berkeley one of the lowest priorities for law enforcement.

By May 2004, we were hopeful to get the ballot measure passed through a council resolution, without putting it on the ballot. SWOP had obtained a letter of support from the theologian and prostitution researcher, Rita Nakashima Brock, with over 50 signatories from the Graduate Theological Union in Berkeley and had the endorsement of the Berkeley chapter of the National Organization of Women (NOW). Council member Dona Spring offered to bring a version of our ballot measure to council with the stipulation that the last item be withdrawn, the low enforcement priority. Since the Berkeley Police Department had told SWOP that enforcement of

108. The 2000 resolution was called "Mitigating Violence against Prostitutes," and was sponsored by San Francisco Supervisors Tom Ammiano and Sue Bierman. The resolution was put forward by Rachel West and Lori Narne of the San Francisco prostitutes' rights organization, USPROS, who also participated on the San Francisco Task Force on Prostitution.

109. For an online copy of this report go to http://www.bayswan.org/SFTFP.html

110. One of the first US prostitutes' rights organizations, started by Margo St. James in the 1960s in San Francisco.

prostitution law was *already* a low priority, this change was an acceptable compromise. Thus on 18 May the resolution was brought to council. It was tabled pending a referral to the Commission on the Status of Women.

During the 18 May council meeting, Councilwoman Betty Olds offered a spot on this Commission to any SWOP member who was a Berkeley resident. Soon after, I volunteered to serve SWOP on the Berkeley Commission on the Status of Women. Before I was even sworn in, the Commission rejected the resolution as written and requested more information on the issue. By the time I joined the commission in July, every session until the November election was devoted to deliberating Measure Q. One of the fiercest opponents of Measure Q was Councilwoman Linda Maio. Maio also appointed someone to the Commission to fight me, a resident who lived near the red light area of San Pablo Avenue, Carol Whitman, who was very opposed to the idea of decriminalization. She quit the Commission the day after the November election. The monthly Commission meetings become a venue for people on all sides of the issue to come and speak their minds. Mainly, it was angry residents who feared that prostitution would increase in Berkeley with the passage of Measure Q and that their property values and quality of life would decline and, on the other side, sex worker activists giving accounts of police harassment and how convictions affected their futures. At one meeting, my friend and a Berkeley resident who lived near the red light district, Shemena Campbell, came and spoke about surviving by prostitution in order to become a University of California, Berkeley graduate, only because she had evaded arrest. Many residents were unkind and unable to believe that she was smart enough to go to University of California at Berkeley but was still selling sex. One unsympathetic man said he worked in low paying jobs when he came to Berkeley with no money, why could not she? It was clear that many residents of the red light area had much to learn from the sex workers about women and the economy. That dialogue occurred directly between sex workers and residents and was a very positive thing and very much a goal for SWOP.

Both supporters and opponents organized other debates on Measure Q. San Francisco anti-prostitution activist, Melissa Farley, held a daylong anti-decriminalization conference at the Julia Morgan Theatre on 30 August 2004. Abolitionist opponents from all over the country came to Berkeley to advise our council members on the key feminist arguments against prostitution decriminalization. I myself arranged two events. One was a debate at University of California at Berkeley on 26 September and the other was a roundtable discussion on 26 October at the Starr King School for Ministry, the Unitarian seminary at the Graduate Theological Union. It was very difficult getting together both sides for a debate because the abolitionists generally refused to participate in any event where the other side was invited to speak. They specifically organized their entire 30 August conference to exclude any pro-decriminalization voices. For this reason, SWOP picketed their August event. A SWOP member and Berkeley alum, Susan Lopez-Embury, who was not known to the local abolitionists because she had been away at the London School of Economics getting her Master's degree, assisted me with the University of California debate. The only reason Melissa Farley and Norma Hotaling agreed to be at the debate was that they did not know SWOP members orchestrated it.

The East Bay chapter of NOW also held a debate on 4 October at a Lutheran Church and had invited opposing sides to attend. At this event, Councilwoman Linda Maio was a speaker, and made the statement that "the heart is hardening against sex workers because of Measure Q." Maio thought that prostitutes were making things worse for themselves by demanding rights and that it would make the public less sympathetic to their victimization. As a biblical scholar familiar with the Exodus narrative, I thought this was an ironic thing for Maio to say. It was the wicked Egyptian pharaoh, the oppressive government leader, whose "heart was hardened, and he would not listen to them" in the Exodus story at 7:12 when Moses began petitioning for the release of the Hebrews from their slavery in Egypt. Now, here in Berkeley when local sex workers were asking for their rights, the people's "heart was hardening" and they would not listen, especially Linda Maio, just as in the repeated refrain of the Exodus narrative (7:12; 8:15, 19,32; 9:7,12,35;10:27, 14:4, 8, 17). Pharaoh and his army's hearts were hardened all the way to the Red Sea. And indeed the sea did not part for sex workers in the November 2004 election either.

Endorsers lined up on both sides. Among those supporting Measure Q were State Senator John Burton, former San Francisco District Attorney Terrence Hallinan, black feminist intellectual, Angela Davis, and the Green Party. Prominent among those opposed were former State Assemblywoman Dion Aroner, Mayor Bates, Ms. Magazine founder, Gloria Steinem, and the Wellstone Democratic Club. Enormous pressure was brought upon our prominent local politicians to rescind their endorsements. Former Berkeley Councilwoman Ying Lee and Alameda County Supervisor, Keith Carson, withdrew their endorsements after pressure from Linda Maio and Abolitionists. At a large debate at University of California at Berkeley between Robyn Few and Norma Hotaling, Melissa Farley's group circulated fliers that impugned the reputations of Senator John Burton, District

Attorney Terrence Hallinan, Alameda County Supervisor Nate Miley and myself, asking why "responsible" people such as ourselves were trying to help paedophiles abuse women and children. None of us relented to the pressure to rescind our endorsements.[111] However, it took a group of four women from SWOP an hour of intense talking to keep Supervisor Miley's support after abolitionist Sheila Jefferys contacted him all the way from Australia urging his withdrawal.

Opposition to decriminalization was fierce and was intensified by fear-based rhetoric from international abolitionist feminists, in addition to the usual neighbourhood residents complaining of the nuisance accompanied by street prostitution. While street prostitution only accounts for a very small proportion of all sex work (10–15 percent), opponents of Measure Q collapsed all prostitution with street prostitution and claimed repeatedly that decriminalization would amount to condoning more street prostitution and drug abuse in the poor neighbourhoods. However, in its very preamble, Measure Q only pertained to adult private consensual sexual commerce: "Shall the City of Berkeley affirm the importance of privacy and autonomy, express its disapproval of laws that prohibit consensual adult sexual behavior, and encourage the legislators of the State of California to repeal such laws?" Decriminalizing prostitution would never make public sex legal. For her part, Councilwoman Linda Maio championed mandatory diversion programs for women arrested in prostitution, in order to force them "to get help." For women who do not have a drug addiction, there is no assistance. For women who cannot make enough money to support their families in low wage work, there is no assistance. In addition, not all treatment models agree that coerced treatment for addiction even works.

What sex workers advocate is a "harm reduction" model of service delivery that aims to create places of safety for marginalized populations and then asks them what they need to survive instead of assuming that the state already knows. Under the conservative Bush Administration "harm reduction" came into disfavour despite a highly successful track record in reducing HIV infection rates among marginalized groups. In 2003, a litmus test was inserted into the reauthorization of the 2000 Trafficking Victims Protection Act (TVPA). The litmus test made all organizations receiving any USAID monies agree to take an anti-prostitution oath. Thus U.S. non-profits and international NGOs alike were required to be against

---

111. Ann Harrison, "The Pimps are coming! Opponents of Berkeley's Prostitution Measure use alarmist rhetoric," *San Francisco Bay Guardian*, October 2004, http://www.sfbg.com/39/04/news_prostitution.html

decriminalization or legalization to get any public funding to help prostitutes. "Harm reduction" as an approach for dealing with high-risk populations (for HIV infection), such as prostitutes, was effectively defunded. Anti-prostitution activists like Melissa Farley and Norma Hotaling, who previously were on the record as in favour of decriminalization (of prostitutes, never johns or pimps), turned into opponents of decriminalization. Prostitutes' rights activists feel that this change of politics was in order to keep their government funding which, for Hotaling's organization, Standing Against Global Exploitation (SAGE), works with the criminal justice system to get many of its clients who would otherwise go to jail.

When Measure Q made the ballot in June, SWOP paid for a poll to see how much support existed for the measure. It was about 50/50. By November, public opinion in Berkeley changed to only 36 percent of the population in favour of decriminalization. Reasons for the failure were due to fears fuelled about the increase of street prostitution, even though, in fact, Berkeley was not decriminalizing prostitution with this mainly symbolic measure. Fear mongering about pimps abusing heroin addicted underage prostitutes having sex on people's front lawns and littering the streets with condoms dominated the discourse in Berkeley even though clearly, the prohibition model that had been in place for nearly one hundred years, was failing to stop this very scenario of street prostitution, which was an expensive failure for tax payers. Even some left activists critical of the prison industrial complex, who generally favoured less police and less jail time for poverty crime, such as Van Jones of the Ella Baker Center for Human Rights, came out opposed to Measure Q. The message that jailing poor women for having consensual sex for money was not "helping" was utterly lost on many progressives who would otherwise seem to be natural allies. The fact that most of the women who go to jail for prostitution and/or are deported are black and non-citizen immigrants makes prostitution law not just a class issue but also a race issue. The low earning power of minority women in the US means that women of colour and immigrant women are overrepresented in the sex industry. They are more likely to be jailed and so this is a kind of economic violence.[112]

112. María Isasi-Díaz, "Economic Violence Against Minority Women in the USA," in Mary John Mananzan, Mercy Amba Oduyoye, Elsa Tamez, J. Shannon Clarkson, Mary C. Grey, Letty Russell (eds.), *Women Resisting Violence: Spirituality for Life* (Maryknoll, NY: Orbis Books, 1996), pp. 89–99.

While Measure Q failed at the polls by a 3 to 1 margin, it was an enormous success in reinvigorating the prostitutes' rights movement in the United States. It was the first piece of legislation written, petitioned and lobbied for by actual sex worker activists. Says Robyn Few, "Measure Q allowed us to speak out as political actors and demand better working conditions. We, as sex workers, are part of the political landscape."[113] This was the original goal of the resolutions we tried get through city councils, to start having politicians thinking about sex workers as *constituents*, not criminals. Repeatedly, neighbourhood groups refused to think of sex workers as their neighbours and co-citizens. Every neighbourhood meeting featured residents claiming that the prostitutes that worked in their areas were from "somewhere else," imported into Berkeley by the carload, by equally foreign or black pimps.[114] Being able to engage neighbours in dialogue was probably the most important part of the process of creating non-punitive community based solutions to poverty crime in the red light areas. Furthermore, Measure Q inspired many sex workers in other parts of the US and the world to organize similarly. A national convention of over 150 sex workers and allies convened in Las Vegas in July 2006 to strategize how to fight the trends towards increased criminalization occurring worldwide during the Bush regime. In 2007, the state of Hawaii introduced senate and assembly bills to decriminalize prostitution. One of its proponents, Tracy Ryan, spoke at a Berkeley Commission on the Status of Women meeting. Another proponent, Pam Vessels is a UCC pastor. Measure Q was part of the rebirth of the sex workers rights movement in the new millennium.

113. Kai Ma, "Taking Sides on Prostitution," *In the Fray*, 7 Feb 2005, p. 11.
114. I find there is a racist subtext to the pimp dominated rhetoric in that pimps are generally depicted as non-white in most cultural productions.

Chapter 3

RAHAB'S DEAL

Joshua 2 (NRSV)

2 Then Joshua son of Nun sent two men secretly from Shittim as spies, saying, "Go, view the land, especially Jericho." So they went, and entered the house of a prostitute whose name was Rahab, and spent the night there. [2] The king of Jericho was told, "Some Israelites have come here tonight to search out the land." [3] Then the king of Jericho sent orders to Rahab, "Bring out the men who have come to you, who entered your house, for they have come only to search out the whole land." [4] But the woman took the two men and hid them. Then she said, "True, the men came to me, but I did not know where they came from. [5] And when it was time to close the gate at dark, the men went out. Where the men went I do not know. Pursue them quickly, for you can overtake them." [6] She had, however, brought them up to the roof and hidden them with the stalks of flax that she had laid out on the roof. [7] So the men pursued them on the way to the Jordan as far as the fords. As soon as the pursuers had gone out, the gate was shut.

[8] Before they went to sleep, she came up to them on the roof [9] and said to the men: "I know that the LORD has given you the land, and that dread of you has fallen on us, and that all the inhabitants of the land melt in fear before you. [10] For we have heard how the LORD dried up the water of the Red Sea before you when you came out of Egypt, and what you did to the two kings of the Amorites that were beyond the Jordan, to Sihon and Og, whom you utterly destroyed. [11] As soon as we heard it, our hearts melted, and there was no courage left in any of us because of you. The LORD your God is indeed God in heaven above and on earth below. [12] Now then, since I have dealt kindly with you, swear to me by the LORD that you in turn will deal kindly with my family. Give me a sign of good faith [13] that you will spare my father and mother, my brothers and sisters, and all who belong to them, and deliver our lives from death." [14] The men said to her, "Our life for yours! If you do not tell this business of ours, then we will deal kindly and faithfully with you when the LORD gives us the land."

[15] Then she let them down by a rope through the window, for her house was on the outer side of the city wall and she resided within the

wall itself. [16] She said to them, "Go toward the hill country, so that the pursuers may not come upon you. Hide yourselves there three days, until the pursuers have returned; then afterward you may go your way." [17] The men said to her, "We will be released from this oath that you have made us swear to you [18] if we invade the land and you do not tie this crimson cord in the window through which you let us down, and you do not gather into your house your father and mother, your brothers, and all your family. [19] If any of you go out of the doors of your house into the street, they shall be responsible for their own death, and we shall be innocent; but if a hand is laid upon any who are with you in the house, we shall bear the responsibility for their death. [20] But if you tell this business of ours, then we shall be released from this oath that you made us swear to you." [21] She said, "According to your words, so be it." She sent them away and they departed. Then she tied the crimson cord in the window.

[22] They departed and went into the hill country and stayed there three days, until the pursuers returned. The pursuers had searched all along the way and found nothing. [23] Then the two men came down again from the hill country. They crossed over, came to Joshua son of Nun, and told him all that had happened to them. [24] They said to Joshua, "Truly the LORD has given all the land into our hands; moreover all the inhabitants of the land melt in fear before us."

Joshua 6:22–25 (NRSV)

6 [22] Joshua said to the two men who had spied out the land, "Go into the prostitute's house, and bring the woman out of it and all who belong to her, as you swore to her." [23] So the young men who had been spies went in and brought Rahab out, along with her father, her mother, her brothers, and all who belonged to her—they brought all her kindred out—and set them outside the camp of Israel. [24] They burned down the city, and everything in it; only the silver and gold, and the vessels of bronze and iron, they put into the treasury of the house of the LORD. [25] But Rahab the prostitute, with her family and all who belonged to her, Joshua spared. Her family has lived in Israel ever since. For she hid the messengers whom Joshua sent to spy out Jericho.[1]

Scholar Standpoints

Given the prominence of Rahab in the liberation praxis and reading of Margaret Guider, I chose to interpret this story from a sex worker standpoint at the earliest stages of my research. The biggest challenge to a liberative reading of this story, contra Guider, appeared from a postcolonial feminist

---

1. *The Holy Bible: New Revised Standard Version* (Nashville, TN: Thomas Nelson, 1996 [1989]).

perspective that I first encountered while at the first Society of Biblical Literature (SBL) meeting I ever attended. Laura Donaldson briefly asserted the view of Rahab as a "Pocahontas" figure during a session on Ruth in a Semiotics and Exegesis Section in San Francisco in November of 1997. Musa Dube, another participant in this session, later also took on the figure of Rahab in a similar manner in her book *Postcolonial Feminist Interpretation of the Bible*.[2] Yet another participant in that fateful SBL session was Athalya Brenner who published a reading of Rahab that is the closest to that of our SWOP interpreters.[3] I began my own initial research on the topic of prostitution while attending a seminar at the Pacific School of Religion on the origins of Israel with Norman Gottwald the following spring of 1998. Rahab of Jericho became a focal point of my attention due to the conflicting critical readings that Gottwald and Donaldson proposed. The image Gottwald had given me of Rahab was as part of the Hebrew underground resistance movement struggling for the overthrow of the oppressive Canaanite political economy. Donaldson, from a Native American post-colonial view, interpreted Rahab (or Ruth) in terms of a foreign religio-military conquest of native women. Seeing Rahab as a paradigmatic Israelite working towards the establishment of a more humane social system had great liberative potential but seemed stymied by its overtly triumphalist literary context. Thus, I began wrestling with these varying readings while juggling differing literary layers, with differing reconstructions of history seen refracted in the text, and all the time wondering if and how historical and literary approaches might interface.

I also began to research the phenomenon of prostitution through history. Here follows the initial view I had worked with while first working on the Rahab story: prostitution is the exchange of sex for money or any other consideration. Though an institution of multifaceted causation and variation, it is highly correlated to conditions of great economic and gender inequality, which are often enforced through violence and rationalized by various ideologies, especially the double standard of sexual morality for men and women. A common ideological strategy involves focalizing upon the moral status of the prostitute alone in analyses of the institution, to the exclusion of all the other, perhaps more significant social factors that tend

---

2. Musa Dube, *Postcolonial Feminist Interpretation of the Bible* (St. Louis, MO: Chalice Press, 2000).

3. Athalya Brenner, "I am Rahab, the Broad," in *I am....Biblical Women Tell Their Own Stories* (Minneapolis, MN: Fortress Press, 2005), pp. 82–98, Brenner's Rahab is rich, not the more typical sex worker from the underclass.

to support the existence of prostitution. Such factors include the socialization of men into a hyper-masculinity of dominance over and entitlement to female bodies, and the general economic aspect of male access to female sexuality, be it through marriage or on a fee for service basis (prostitution), which tends to put most male/female sexual behaviour on to a continuum of sexual commodity fetishism. Most particularly, warfare and major shifts in economic modes of production that produce poverty, urbanization, and social dislocation also contribute to the proliferation of prostitution.[4] I have changed my definition a bit since then to see prostitution as a form of domestic labour, which garners a living wage, but the above analysis still mostly holds.[5] I follow Luise White's definition of prostitution,

> Prostitutes' work is reproductive...in fact, they sell that part of themselves...of male labor power and family formations. Prostitutes perform tasks that frequently include conversation, cooked food, and bathwater that restore, flatter and revive male energies: prostitutes sell sexual intercourse in a relationship, whether abrupt or deferential... Thus, prostitution exists in a direct relationship to wage labor and is domestic labor; it is illegal marriage.[6]

I then encountered during my initial research the heated politics of prostitution and the conflicting political strategies of abolitionists who analyze prostitution mostly in terms of patriarchy and whose primary goal is the elimination of all prostitution, and the rights based approaches to sex work that wishes to assert and strengthen the agency of sex workers. I had impulses towards both of these approaches but subsequently opted for

---

4. I here utilize the analysis of Rita Nakashima Brock and Susan Brooks Thistlethwaite, *Casting Stones:* pp. 15–18. Other writers that repeatedly make these connections: Cynthia Enloe, *Bananas, Beaches & Bases: Making Feminist Sense of International Politics* (Berkeley: University of California Press, 1990); Margaret Eletta Guider, *The Daughters of Rahab*; Saundra Polluck Sturdevant and Brenda Stoltzfus, *Let the Good Times Roll: Prostitution and the U.S. Military in Asia* (New York: New York Press, 1992); Sheila Jeffreys, *The Idea of Prostitution*; and Vern and Bonnie Bullough, *Women and Prostitution.*

5. For other scholars who define prostitution in terms of sex as a source of life (bodily pleasure and procreation), see Thanh-Dam Truong, *Sex, Money, and Morality: The Political Economy of Prostitution and Tourism in Southeast Asia* (London: Zed Books, 1990), p. 82 and Luise White, *The Comforts of Home: Prostitution in Colonial Nairobi* (Chicago, IL: University of Chicago Press, 1990), p. 11.

6. White, *The Comforts of Home*, p. 11.

the latter, rights based view. This has led me to focus less on my own initial moral outrage towards men as "johns." This meant that I was much more oriented then to the issue of whether Israel ever eliminated prostitution when they took over Canaan, in order to find anything liberating about Rahab's story. I am now more inclined towards the pragmatic task of empowering prostitutes, wherever they may be located, to improve their conditions of life, however they define this task, be it by forming a union or escaping violence or going to college or changing the laws. This shift hermeneutically meant that I focus on the agency of Rahab in securing her own survival to find the liberation theme. Back in the beginning of my research, I shared with abolitionist feminists a deep anger over the moral of status of men who buy sex but over time and more relationships with sex workers, I was taught to redirect my attention to the macroeconomic level.

The story of Rahab begins with Joshua's directive in Josh. 2:1 to his spies "'Go, view the land, especially Jericho.' So they went, and entered the house of a prostitute whose name was Rahab, and spent the night there." The vast majority of biblical commentators on Rahab tend focus on her identity as a prostitute as something that needs comment, judgment or apology. Concomitant with this type of attention is the normalization of the possible "john" status of the Israelite spies or the normalcy of their relations with a prostitute and their presence in her house, often thought of as an inn or a brothel. Feminist Phyllis Bird states that the spies "have chosen the natural place to begin the reconnaissance of the land."[7] That a bar, brothel or inn is said to be a "natural" location for military men is a major way that our attention gets diverted away from prostitution as a male social practice and rerouted back to the social identity of Rahab. Robert Boling's Anchor Bible commentary both successfully highlights and reinscribes the normalcy of the contiguous relationship between military men and brothels:

> It has been pointed out that going to Rahab's establishment was not necessarily a deviation from orders, for "the inn and the brothel have been found in one establishment often in the history of mankind," and where better to get information than a bar?...It remains true that the visit to her house was the sum total of the men's reconnaissance activity. Probably the narrator intends to titillate by reminding readers of an *immemorial symbiosis between military service and bawdyhouse*. It is reliably reported that at the height of the 1948 warfare, morale in the

7. Phyllis Bird, *Missing Persons and Mistaken Identities: Women and Gender in Ancient Israel* (Minneapolis, MN: Fortress Press, 1997), p. 211.

desperately besieged Jewish quarter of Jerusalem was considerably bolstered by the arrival of a barber and a prostitute.[8]

Within the tangled confusion of originary and literary Israel, I have been thinking through the interface of history, story and ideology but always oriented towards liberation readings of Rahab. Liberation readings use a variety of tools both literary and historical and there exist a number of liberation readings with vastly different conclusions. I initially focused on Gottwald's revolutionary model of Israelite origins as opposed to a foreign conquest type of historical referent.[9] Gottwald's theory of Israelite origins is that a coalition of disaffected indigenous groups within Canaan joined a group of ex-slaves from Egypt and took over the territory now called Israel. This coalition may have included prostitutes in addition to oppressed peasants, metal workers, pastoral nomads and mercenaries.[10] This model theorizes a kind of peasant revolt against the ruling elites during a period of weakened hegemony. The "conquest model" is what is explicitly narrated in Joshua, that the Israelites entered the Promised Land from the outside and conquered the territory by eradicating the former indigenous inhabitants. With the "peasant revolt model" it is possible that, underlying a later theological cover up, there was an originally liberative outcome for Rahab, and prostitutes generally, realized in historical Israel because they were one of the disaffected groups rebelling. This reading is hampered by being more historical than literary. Most ordinary readers outside of biblical studies operate with the text as it is. The text as it stands is one of conquest and annihilation of the original inhabitants of Jericho characterized as the evil foreign "other." Feminist liberation readers who read the text in its final canonical form and have important critiques of the Rahab story are Musa Dube, Rita Nakashima Brock, Susan Brooks Thistlethwaite, Gail Corrington Streete and Phyllis Bird.[11] Feminist and liberation readers who read with a

8. Robert Boling, *Joshua* (Garden City, NY: Anchor Bible; Doubleday, 1980), p. 145, emphasis mine.

9. Norman Gottwald, *Tribes of Yahweh: A Sociology of the Religion of Liberated Israel, 1250–1050 BCE* (Maryknoll, NY: Orbis Books, 1979). See Part V or pp. 191–219 for his discussion of these different models.

10. Gottwald, for an overview of allied groups see pp. 474–92; see pp. 556–58 for prostitutes, pp. 584–87 for the indigenous peasants, pp. 577–79 for metal workers, and for the mercenaries/bandits called *apiru* (which may be the term from which the name "Hebrew" is derived), see pp. 401–409.

11. Phyllis Bird, "The End of the Male Cult Prostitute: A Literary-Histoical and Sociological Analysis of Hebrew *qadesh-qedeshim*," in *Supplements to Vetus Testamentum* 66 (1997), pp. 37–80, p. 214 or in "The Harlot as Heroine:

final form text but still see it as a liberative story are Danna Fewell, David
Gunn, Robert Polzin, and of course, Margaret Guider. This divergence of
interpretations suggests the possibility that a liberative reading might be
possible within the bounds of the existing narrative context of Joshua, that
is, a literary reading.

In any configuration, the nature of Rahab's deal or exchange is
ambiguous. Where or what is Rahab's אתנן־זונה/*ethnan zonah*, her "harlot's
hire" or pay, so despised by prophets and Deuteronomic law (Mic. 1:7,
Hos. 2:14 and 9:1, Ezek. 16:31, 34, 41, Deut. 23:18 but expropriated in Isa.
23:17,18)? Was her fee to survive alive with her family? To be integrated as
a prostitute or as the "whore tribe" in Israel? Was her survival her fee for
services, sex and subterfuge all included? Maybe this is an etiological story
to explain the presence of sacred prostitution in Israel. Alternatively, could
this be a story of the integration of a prostitute into Israel that aimed at the
amelioration of exploitive economies and exchanges? Is Rahab's deal
understandable, acceptable or moral? Or, was she a collaborator, a Quisling
sell-out, motivated by fear? Even worse, is Rahab a puppet or parrot, a shill
used by the writers of the conquest to legitimate their domination?

Such are the obstacles to a liberative reading of the Rahab story. There
is also the frequent structural contiguity between militarism and
prostitution pointed out by Boling. Rita Nakashima Brock and Susan Brooks
Thistlethwaite do not positively utilize the Rahab story in their theological
exploration of prostitution, probably for these reasons:

> Sex industries around military bases are ubiquitous. Since prehistoric
> times soldiers have used women sexually, through rape, kidnapping,
> and slave brothels that followed armies...Rahab of Jericho may have
> been such a prostitute, which would explain her friendliness toward the
> Hebrew soldiers.[12]

> One ancient and powerful image of the prostitute is her function as a
> threshold into foreignness and strangers, for example in the biblical
> stories of Rahab at Jericho and Gomer in the book of Hosea.[13]

Narrative Art and Social Presupposition in Three Old Testament Texts." *Semeia*
46 (1989), pp. 119–39. Gail Corrington Streete has a reading of Rahab congruent
with Bird's, arguing that the text works with, rather than upsets, prostitute
stereotypes, in *The Strange Woman: Power and Sex in the Bible* (Louisville, KY:
Westminster John Knox Press, 1997), pp. 47–48. See also the article by Judith
McKinlay, "Rahab: A Hero/ine?" *Biblical Interpretation* 7:1 (1999), pp. 45–57.

12. Brock and Thistlethwaite, *Casting Stones*, p. 6 and n.10, p. 338.
13. Brock and Thistlethwaite, *Casting Stones*, pp. 55–56.

> The sexual exploitation of women by soldiers is an expected fact of
> military life in every society that has an organized militia. It "comes with
> the territory."[14]

This "immemorial symbiosis between military service and bawdy house"
noted by Boling is problematic for a liberationist reading of the Rahab story
in the contemporary world, a reading which gives a preferential option to
prostitute women, which is my primary interpretive aim. At the turn of
the twenty-first century, militarism and the sexual exploitation of women
(through rape, slavery, and economic neo-colonial occupation) remain
tenaciously enmeshed and globally ubiquitous.[15] Were the Hebrew (or
apiru) mercenaries or rebel guerrillas of Gottwald's reading any different
than most other military men throughout history? Any liberative reading
of this story would surely require a confrontation with the military "john"
aspect of the Israelite spies' behaviour. This obstacle is closely linked to the
postcolonial critiques of this story by Musa Dube, Laura Donaldson, and
others.

Another, related, stumbling block is the "pagan confessor" or "foreigner's
credo" aspect of the Rahab story which raises potential problems for an
anti-(post)colonial consciousness.[16] It is common for interpreters to point
out the theological and literary bent of the Deuteronomistic historian in
the composition of Rahab's speech to the spies in Josh. 2:9–11:

> I know that the LORD has given you the land, and that dread of you has
> fallen on us, and that all the inhabitants of the land melt in fear before
> you. [10] For we have heard how the LORD dried up the water of the Red
> Sea before you when you came out of Egypt, and what you did to the
> two kings of the Amorites that were beyond the Jordan, to Sihon and
> Og, whom you utterly destroyed. [11] As soon as we heard it, our hearts
> melted, and there was no courage left in any of us because of you. The
> LORD your God is indeed God in heaven above and on earth below.[17]

This D style recital of history and the emphasis on fear and melting
hearts found suspiciously on the lips of a foreign woman is another

14. Brock and Thistlethwaite, *Casting Stones*, p. 71.

15. Brock and Thistlethwaite, *Casting Stones*, p. 109.

16. Phyllis Bird uses the classification "pagan confessor", see *Missing Persons
and Mistaken Identities*, p. 215. Frank Moore Cross uses the phrase "foreigner's
credo" in "A Response to Zachovitch's 'Successful Failure of Israelite Intelligence'"
in Susan Niditch (ed.), *Text and Tradition: The Hebrew Bible and Folklore* (Atlanta,
GA: Scholar's Press, 1990), p. 100.

17. *The Holy Bible: New Revised Standard Version* (Nashville, TN: Thomas
Nelson, 1996, 1989).

reason that Rahab can easily be interpreted as a kind of Pocahontas or La Malinche figure, a colonist's fantasy woman who sexually welcomes the invaders. Judith McKinlay points out that Rahab ironically speaks the Deuteronomistic language of Holy War but that "if Rahab has been reading Deuteronomy, the spies obviously were not, or they would have remembered that Deut. 7.2 and 20.16–18 categorically forbid any such arrangements. In Holy War there were to be no survivors at all."[18] Musa Dube has utilized the figure of Rahab to critique this kind of conquest ideology.[19] Dube argues that Rahab is not a real person but a parrot for the conquerors' ideology of conquest. Cynthia Enloe, a feminist political scientist, creates a scenario for a common ideological function of this story type:

> A school teacher plans a lesson around the life of Pocahontas, the brave Powhantan "princess" who saved Captain John Smith from execution at Jamestown and so cleared the way for English colonization of America. The students come away from the lesson believing the convenient myth that local women are likely to be charmed by their own people's conquerors.[20]

Brock and Thistlethwaite also make a connection between colonialism, racism and the Pocahontas story type in Hollywood film:

> Every romantic tale of Asian women depicts her falling in love with a Western man, making herself sexually available, and rejecting her own native, "inferior" men (depicted as coldly violent or not virile enough). The latest in this media parade of distortions is the Disney movie Pocahontas. Sexual metaphors and realities abound in the history of colonization, especially as military actions.[21]

The Rahab story of Joshua 2 and 6 is especially susceptible to a Pocahontas reading within the frameworks of the canonical Deuteronomic redaction level, in which most literary readings are done, and within a triumphalist conception of Israelite origins. A liberative reading of the Rahab story has to come to terms with such damaging representations of the "other" and ideological strategies that co-opt the voice of the "other" to legitimate domination and naturalize violence or threats of violence. For this reason Musa Dube reads Rahab as a parrot or ventriloquist dummy who speaks in

18. Judith McKinlay, *Reframing Her: Biblical Women in Post-Colonial Focus* (Sheffield: Sheffield Phoenix Press, 2004), p. 41.

19. She calls this approach her "Rahab Reading Prism," see Musa Dube, *Postcolonial Feminist Interpretation*, pp. 76–83.

20. Enloe, *Bananas, Beaches, & Bases*, p. 1.

21. Brock and Thistlewaite, *Casting Stones*, p. 179.

a voice not her own but constructed out of the colonist's fantasy.[22] An example of this naturalization of violence is when scholars collapse the extraordinary "faith" of Rahab with "obedience and submission" to YHVH and his military host in utter acceptance of the Deuteronomic ideology.[23]

With all of this said, it is a rocky road for me back to a reconstruction of egalitarian pre-monarchic Israel. Within a peasant revolt conception of early Israel, Rahab is seen as one of the many social types of outcasts who may have been incorporated into the alternative social system of Israel. Insomuch as Israel's new economic system would be composed of allied extended families engaged in self-sufficient agriculture, theoretically the need for prostitution would be decreased.[24] This, combined with Yahwistic religion as a servomechanism that eschewed sexual commodity fetishism and rejected the divinization of sexuality would tend to reinforce the suppression of prostitution in Israel.[25] Carol Meyers' work in *Discovering Eve*, fills out this conception of pre-monarchic Israel more specifically in terms of what it might mean for women. This picture is accomplished especially through the utilization of cross-cultural data on women's roles in certain types of free agrarian economies. In a political economy that is overwhelmingly domestic, non-statist, and labour intensive, the importance of women as workers and reproducers would tend to be highly valued. This would be so despite patriarchal assertions or institutions that might seem contrary to this egalitarian reality.[26]

In terms of the Rahab story, many historical critical scholars have made it their task to strip off the later redactional layers to get back to the earliest phase of the story.[27] Gene Tucker's historical critical treatment of the Rahab story first strips off the Deuteronomic elements, particularly located in

22. Musa Dube, *Postcolonial Feminist Interpretation*, p. 78.
23. See K.M. Campbell, "Rahab's Covenant: A Short Note on Joshua ii 9–11," *Vetus Testamentum* 22 (1972), p. 244. This equation of faith with military submission is quite pronounced in this short note.
24. Gottwald, *The Tribes of Yahweh*, pp. 556–58.
25. Gottwald, *The Tribes of Yahweh*, p. 695.
26. Carol Meyers, *Discovering Eve: Ancient Israelite Women in Context* (Oxford: Oxford University Press, 1988), pp. 40–45.
27. I have utilized the commentaries of Boling, Soggin, and Gray. Gene Tucker's article was particularly helpful for understanding the rationale behind separating different story strands: "The Rahab Saga (Joshua 2): Some Form Critical and Traditio-Historical Observations" in James M. Efrid (ed.), *The Use of the Old Testament in the New and Other Essays: Studies in Honor of William Franklin Stinespring* (Durham, NC: Duke University Press, 1972), pp. 66–86.

Rahab's recital of the Deuternomistic level mini-creed of YHVH's saving acts in Josh. 2:9–11. Therefore, the "foreigner's credo" aspect of the story could be eliminated by stripping away the later accretions and going back to the earliest version. Scholars have noticed that two versions of the story may have been joined together before splitting again in its present locations in Joshua 2 and 6. These two versions were united by the etiological conclusion of the story in Josh. 6:25: "Rahab the prostitute, with her family and all who belonged to her, Joshua spared. Her family has lived in Israel ever since." This etiological conclusion probably sought to explain the origin of the Rahab group within Israel. The existence of two versions is predicated on the confusion between the story elements that presuppose an armed conflict leading to the conquest of Jericho and the contradictory liturgical account of the conquest in Joshua 6. Here the conquest is due to the miraculous act of YHVH who brought down the walls of Jericho alone (which is where Rahab's house was located and conflicts with the story elements where her house is spared).

At a pre-pre-Deuteronomic level the exact content and function of the story is quite speculative. It is here that scholars have imagined a different, more vital role for Rahab's collaboration with the Israelites. She may have given the signal for attack to the invading forces and functioned as a fifth column within Jericho.[28] It is within this speculative space that Phyllis Bird tried and failed to imagine the possibilities of a story where "a connection is to be seen in class affinity or class interest" and where a parallel could be drawn "between the low or outcaste estate of the harlot of Jericho and the low and outcaste estate of the band of escaped slaves beyond the

---

28. Tucker, "The Rahab Saga," p. 84 in James M. Efrid (ed.), *The Use of the Old Testament*; Gottwald, *The Tribes of Yahweh*, p. 557; and J. Alberto Soggin, *Joshua* (Philadelphia, PA: Westminster Press, 1972), pp. 38 and 83. Murray Newman, "Rahab and the Conquest," in James T. Butler, Edgar W. Conrad, Ben C. Ollenburger (eds.), *Understanding the Word: Essays in Honor of Bernhard W. Anderson*, (Sheffield: JSOT Press, 1985), pp. 167–184, also sees this greater role for Rahab at the earliest level but believes that there were two oral phases rather than two traditions conjoined. The earliest phase would be the story as told by the Rahab people which emphasized the heroic deeds of Rahab. Newman sees the function of this original phase as "security clearance" legend to protect the Rahab group from overzealous Yahweh worshipers (p. 174). The next oral phase involves the reworking of the legend, especially through insertion of Josh. 2:17–21, to emphasize more the role of the spies and to upgrade their image, p. 175.

Jordan."[29] Is there any redaction layer where the behaviour of the spies is not sexually exploitive of Rahab? One is hard pressed to detect in any level of the text cues that would neutralize the sexual impropriety of the spies' visit to Rahab's house. A definition of prostitution that shifts attention back from the morality of prostitutes onto the behaviour of men might be helpful for understanding the problem of male exploitation of feminist concern in the Rahab story of Joshua 2 and 6. According to abolitionist feminist, Sheila Jeffreys, prostitution means:

> Male sexual behavior characterized by three elements variously combined: barter, promiscuity, emotional indifference. Any man is a prostitution abuser who, for the purposes of his sexual satisfaction, habitually or intermittently reduces another human being to a sexual object by the use of money or other mercenary considerations.[30]

Thus, the behaviour of the spies is ambiguous at best when it comes to judging their treatment of Rahab as clients. Did they barter sex for her life and that of her family? If the morality of those Israelites is questionable and Rahab is a heroine for joining the cause of the Israelites, is not her heroism cancelled too?

Phyllis Bird does not bother with a redaction history of the Rahab story because it does not change the major crux of her argument that sexual innuendo pervades the whole story.[31] The suggestive language of intercourse/entry in the Hebrew verb בא together with the suggestive use of the verb שכב pervade the whole first section of the story and cannot be sifted out by anyone doing redaction analysis. It is her view that the story hinges on the negative social stereotyping of prostitutes. Readings that focus on Rahab's profession—that is, was she a "sacred prostitute" or why does the story not censure her profession?—miss the mark according to Bird. It is in the reversal of expectations of stereotypical "whore behaviour" that the story plays with.[32] However, Bird is also focused on Rahab and her behaviour as constitutive of the institution of prostitution. The behaviour of the men is still invisible and normalized in her reading. With the exception of Daniel Hawk, Fewell and Gunn, few scholars squarely face the

---

29. These are quotes of Phyllis Bird's *Missing Persons and Mistaken Identities*, pp. 212 and 216, who seems to have in mind the peasant revolt theory but doesn't cite anyone specifically. Bird finds such ideas theologically appealing but lacking a firm textual basis in any layer.

30. Jeffreys, *The Idea of Prostitution*, p. 4.

31. Bird, *Missing Persons and Mistaken Identities*, pp. 208, 210, 212.

32. Bird, *Missing Persons and Mistaken Identities*, p. 215.

morally questionable behaviour or location of the Israelite spies.[33] Only post-colonial feminists question the legitimacy of the Israelite invasion and the archetypical treatment of conquered women as war spoil, which are both discernable in the Joshua narrative.

A few older commentators of the Rahab story have often seen a possible etiological story explaining the continuance of Canaanite "sacred prostitution" in Israel. Many modern day sex workers strongly identify with the notion of sacred prostitution. However, the theory of Canaanite cultic prostitution has come under severe scrutiny in recent decades by a number of scholars who wonder if this alleged institution was not, in fact, the invention of prophetic polemic and metaphorical language or driven by the specious and late testimony of the Greek historian Herodotus. Bird concludes that the Hebrew קְדֵשָׁה/*qedesah* is simply a title for female temple personnel that gets contaminated by association with the popular prophetic harlot metaphor. Thus the idea that it denotes an actual "temple prostitute" is a false inference; it is just a metaphorical insult.[34] In dissent, John Burns

---

33. L. Daniel Hawk, "Strange Houseguests: Rahab, Lot, and the Dynamics of Deliverance," in Danna Nolan Fewell (ed.), Reading *Between Texts: Intertextuality and the Hebrew Bible* (Louisville, KY: Westminster/John Knox Press, 1992), pp. 89–97. Working with the many structural and phrasalogical similarities between the Rahab and Lot narratives, Hawk sees the spies in very ominous light: they are comparable to Lot. Danna Fewell and David Gunn, *Gender, Power, & Promise: The Subject of the Bible's First Story* (Nashville, TN: Abingdon Press, 1993), p. 117.

34. Bird, *Missing Persons and Mistaken Identities*, p. 234. See also, Mayer Gruber, "Hebrew *Qedesah* and her Canaanite and Akkadian Cognates," *Ugarit-Forschungen* Band 18 (1986), pp. 133–48, Eugene Fisher, "Cultic Prostitution in the Ancient Near East? A Reassessment," *BTB* 6 (1976), pp. 223–36. These later two articles also find the evidence for an actual institution of cultic prostitution among Israelite and non-Israelite neighbors to be lacking. A scholar who dissents from the view that the sexual role of cult functionaries is a mirage or mere invention of prophetic polemic is John Barclay Burns, "*qades* and *qadesa*: Did they Live off Immoral Earnings?" *Proceedings: Eastern Great Lakes and Midwest Biblical Societies* 15 (1995), pp. 157–68. For studies outside of biblical scholarship see the work of Martha Roth, "The Priestess and the Tavern: LH 110," in Barbara Bock, Eva Cancik-Kirschbaum and Thomas Richter (eds.), *Munuscula Mesopotamica: Festschrift fur Johannes Renger* (Munster: Ugarit-Verlag, 1999), pp. 445–64; and Mary Beard and John Henderson, "With This Body, I Thee Worship, Sacred Prostitution in Antiquity," in Maria Wyke (ed.), *Gender and the Body in the Ancient Mediterranean* (Oxford: Blackwell Publishers, 1998), pp. 56–79; and Julia Assante, "The kar.kid/*harimtu*, Prostitute or Single Woman? A Reconsideration of the Evidence," in *Ugarit-Forschungen* Band 30

would like to maintain the connection between prostitution and religious institutions insomuch as they may have profited from the sale of sex, at least indirectly, if they did not directly organize it as a religious institution. Also in response to the changing consensus, Karel Van Der Toorn wonders if the sexual association attaching to illegitimate religious practice was a side effect of festival revelry that goes out of control, like modern day "fraternity parties" where sexual inhibitions break down.[35] Indeed, this is also how he interprets the mass rape of the women of Shiloh in Judges 21! This reading makes invisible the differing social consequences of illicit sexual behavior for men and women in societies that live by a sexual double standard and totally effaces the militaristic context of civil war in which the story is located—not to mention the fact that many women have been raped at frat parties. What is helpful about the work of Van Der Toorn and Burns is the maintenance of a connection between exploitive sexual practices and illegitimate religious worship that could be rooted in an overall exploitive political economy. Thus the prostitute metaphor of the Hebrew prophets may perhaps not be at all arbitrary, or merely a shocking metaphor to disturb the conscience of men, but rather, it may have a connection to a socio-economic reality. Religion is also very much implicated in the perpetuation of sexual ideologies harmful to women and has a strong relationship to maintaining the institution of prostitution.

The picture that is forming is that perhaps the existence of sexual exploitation of women—as war "booty," as rape victims as an expected consequence of war, as in the survival of common not "sacred" prostitution insomuch as men continue to purchase it—in greater or lesser degrees, remained a constant in male Israelite social practice, just as it remains normative and invisible to many biblical commentators. It may not be at all accidental that a metaphorical connection is made by latter Hebrew prophets between prostitution, exploitive economics, foreign policy and idolatry—understood as commodity fetishism and profiteering by the religious establishment. These are certainly all related in today's global economy. Recent analyses of the economic function of prostitution, particularly those rooted in the life stories of migrating prostitutes could

(1998), (Munster: Ugarit-Verlag, 1999), pp. 31–96. See also articles by Bird, Roth and Budin in Christopher Faraone and Laura McClure (eds.), *Prostitutes and Courtesans in the Ancient World* (Madison, WI: University of Wisconsin Press, 2006).

35. Karel Van Der Toorn, p. 203 in "Female Prostitution and the Payment of Vows in Ancient Israel," *JBL* 108 (1989), pp. 193–205.

greatly animate these interconnections made by the prophets. Alienation of land, changes in land use, colonization, urbanization, militarization, migration, all of these factors tend to bring about great increases in the sale of female sexual labour in male supremacist societies.

Unless I am simply an unwitting captive to the negative party line of the "Deuteronomic template" of Judg. 2:10–23,[36] it seems that in addition to the spies, Samson (Judg. 16:1) and Jephtah's father Gilead (Judg. 11:1) are both guilty of continued sexual commodity fetishism, unless these are Deuteronomic fabrications designed to slander the non-statist leaders of early Israel. It matters not whether it is done to foreign women or Israelite women since the existence of the institution really hinges on male behaviour, most especially in male dominant societies. Not only that, but the continuous intermittent warfare and oppressions imposed by various groups (Canaanites, Midianites, Moabites, Ammonites etc.,) depicted in Judges would make tenuous and vulnerable the alternative social system being attempted by an egalitarian pre-monarchic Israel. The continued necessity of militarization coupled with the ongoing threat or allure of external oppressive economies would have to put the women of Israel at risk for sexual violence and exploitation. The dynamics of this situation even in pre-monarchic Israel disturbs the static picture of agrarian life for "everywoman Eve" presented by Carol Meyers, just as it did in feudal Europe and just as it does now in the 2/3rd's world.[37] Perhaps it is time to recall Althaus-Reid's critique of peasant romanticism within liberation theology and apply it to scholarship on premonarchic Israel.

It is at this point that the Deuteronomic level begins to look more appealing to me, although I am back in triumphalist conquest territory. If I am unable to eliminate exploitive prostitution out of early Israel, a Deuteronomic critique of the fragile morality of Israel almost feels preferable. The literary treatment of Rahab within the Deuteronomic corpus by Robert Polzin, the similar narrative reading of Fewell and Gunn and the theological treatment of Rahab by Margaret Guider all have similar or complementary conclusions about the significance of the Rahab text in its final form. All use Rahab as a mirror of Israel or as a figure who blurs the boundaries of inside and outside the people of God. Fewell and Gunn argue that

36. David Penchansky, "Up for Grabs: A Tentative Proposal for Doing Ideological Criticism," *Semeia* 51-I (1990), pp. 35–41. The "Deuteronomic Template" coerces readers to understand Israelite oppression as punishment for their sins.

37. Meyers, *Discovering Eve*, pp. 122–38.

Rahab as an "outsider who becomes and insider," is "confusing Israel's self-identification."[38]

Polzin who does extensive analysis of the text situates and interprets the Rahab story within its larger context in the Deuteronomic history, which spans Deuteronomy to 2 Kings.[39] Polzin identifies two contradictory voices within the corpus, one the voice of "authoritarian dogmatism" the other is the prevailing voice of "critical traditionalism."[40] This interplay of voices produces a very complex and nuanced portrayal of the situation at Rahab's house. Polzin concludes that Rahab in Joshua, along with several other "exceptional outsiders" are incorporated as types of Israel into a sustained reflection on what it means to be an Israelite in a covenant with God.[41] In his reading insider and outsider to the land are held in creative tension in terms of moral merit, each qualifying the other. Fewell and Gunn likewise see the overt triumphalism of the text as subverted by the blurring of the boundaries between insider and outsider. Joshua and the spies are culpable, according to the voice of "authoritarian dogmatism," for their failure to believe in the repeated promises of God by the fact of conducting a reconnaissance mission at all.[42] In addition to this act is their violation of the ban of total annihilation (*herem*) by making pact with a Canaanite prostitute.[43] The countervailing voice is provided by Deuteronomy 9–10, which Polzin views as the law that the Rahab story is attempting to work out with all its attendant contradictions. According to the literary analysis of Polzin, Rahab *is* Israel. When the spies come to Rahab's house, they hear the Deuteronomic declaration of faith coming out of the mouth of the Canaanite prostitute (Josh. 2:9–11), the credo which they should already know and not need to hear from a foreign prostitute. This irony puts them to shame and slightly neutralizes the triumphalism of their "conquest." Enhancing this would be a greater recognition of the spies' culpability as possible prostitution abusers, something Polzin does not address. The Pocahontas problem is not eliminated in Polzin's interpretation.

---

38. Fewell and Gunn, *Gender, Power & Promise*, p. 121.
39. Robert Polzin, *Moses and the Deuteronomist: A Literary Study of the Deuteronomic History* (New York: Seabury Press, 1980), 1, p. 18.
40. Polzin, *Moses and the Deuteronomist*, p. 84.
41. Polzin, *Moses and the Deuteronomist*, pp. 144–45.
42. Polzin, *Moses and the Deuteronomist*, p. 86.
43. Polzin, *Moses and the Deuteronomist*, p. 87.

Similar to Polzin's reading is the use Margaret Guider makes of St. Jerome's interpretation of Rahab as a metaphor of the Church. In *The Daughters of Rahab*, Guider recounts the Catholic Church's stance towards prostitution, including the church of liberation in Brazil. Her conclusion calls for a theology of embodiment that incorporates the subjugated knowledge of prostitutes in order to enhance its creative agency and to force the church into recognition of its own identity as a "prostitute."[44] This view echoes the Hebrew prophets who call out the people of Israel for prostituting themselves or selling out to foreign superpowers. Guider's book chronicles the project of the Brazilian church of liberation's efforts to extend a hermeneutical option for prostituted women in Brazil during the last three decades. She notes that while the Catholic Magisterium has been able to support an economic critique of society, contextual analysis done with prostitutes tended to indict the Church's own teaching on sexuality as highly complicitous with their oppression. This realization the church has not yet been able to absorb.[45] Guider would like the church to make such a realization by recognizing itself incarnated as a prostitute so that it can acknowledge its own sins. This perpetuates the idea of the prostitute as the pre-eminent symbol of the sinner, something that prostitutes' rights activists critique as a form of projection and scapegoating. This is not quite the same as seeing the prostitute as an incarnation of the crucified Christ, something recommended by Marcella Althaus-Reid. Such an incarnational view would be a fuller form of identification subversive of the in/decency binary.

While it is certainly helpful for all of society to reflect on the many ways it resembles prostitutes, perhaps it is time to confront the issue by focusing more upon the actual liberation of prostitutes on their own terms. Prostitutes often get re-objectified when they are used as ciphers for fallen humanity and other more powerful actors are ignored for their important role in the perpetuation of a prostitution economy. What seems to be needed are more "exceptional insider" john stories, about men who come to empathize with the situation of prostitutes and decide to work in common cause with prostitutes to change the exploitive economy.[46] Alternatively, how about an emphasis on narratives of families who have been "saved" by the earnings of their prostituted family members: sex workers who sacrifice

44. Guider, *The Daughters of Rahab*, pp. 27, 168.
45. Guider, *The Daughters of Rahab*, pp. 133–34.
46. I actually got to meet several such "exceptional insider" men on the Measure Q campaign.

their bodies for the lives of their loved ones. Certainly, such sacrifice is as beautiful and as ugly as death on a cross or the willingness to sacrifice children like Issac or Jephtah's daughter. The most common story in the 2/3rds world right now is that of the dutiful daughter who engages in prostitution for the sake of her parents, siblings or children, to save their land, to provide money for education, and to bring in foreign currency to pay off the foreign debt.[47] This accords well with the aspects of the Rahab story that depicts her saving her family and the linen on the roof as an indication of agricultural or textile labour that does not pay the bills in an exploitive economy that underpays domestic labour.[48]

Prostitutes also know all too well that "john" behaviour pervades all male populations, not just the military. Even a cursory review of current literature on the topic shows that prostitution is something that has been perpetuated by lower class men working on banana plantations,[49] peace activists in Okinawa,[50] by U.N. peacekeepers in Bosnia,[51] by Peace Corp volunteers in Korea,[52] by the clergy attending the Council of Constance in 15th century Switzerland,[53] and by religion scholars attending their annual conventions.[54] Therefore, a reading where the Israelites soldiers are allied with prostitutes for mutual liberation might seem to strain the limits of verisimilitude, desirable as that might be. Or, perhaps I am too focused on whether or not the men are heroic when I should be looking at Rahab. It is at this impasse in which I, myself, have gotten stuck, that the sex workers of SWOP helped lead me to a different kind of reading—one that I would have never ever conceived of on my own.

---

47. Saundra Sturdevant and Brenda Stoltzfus, *Let the Good Times Roll: Prostitution and the US Military in Asia* (New York: New York Press, 1992), pp. 318–21 and Brock and Thistlethwaite, *Casting Stones*, pp. 61–63.

48. Prostitution and textile production have been repeatedly linked throughout history: See Edward Cohen, "Free and Unfree Sexual Work: An Economic Analysis of Athenian Prostitution," in Christopher Faraone, and Laura McClure (eds.), *Prostitutes and Courtesans in the Ancient World* (Madison, WI: University of Wisconsin Press, 2006), pp. 95–124.

49. Enloe, *Bananas, Beaches & Bases*, pp. 140–41.

50. Brock and Thistlethwaite, *Casting Stones*, p. 81.

51. Jeffreys, *The Idea of Prostitution*, p. 300.

52. Sturdevant and Stoltzfus, *Let the Good Times Roll*, p. 170.

53. Bullough and Bullough, *Women and Prostitution*, p. 129.

54. Brock and Thistlethwaite, *Casting Stones*, p. 171.

Sex Worker Standpoint on Rahab

Every biblical interpretation session I conducted with SWOP began first with the reading of the text and then brainstorming about life parallels that the sex workers share with the biblical story. Subsequent to this, I introduced for discussion the above listed representative liberation readings and feminist interpretive issues. A number of themes that emerged are congruent with concerns that liberation and feminist scholars have raised. Probably the issue that produced the most conversation was explaining Rahab's action. Why would she side with the invading Israelites? Is she a traitor to her own people? Two readings were produced to address these basic questions. The first or majority reading went with the grain of the text, while the dissenting minority position of Scarlot Harlot, the "Unrepentant Whore," went against the grain.[55]

Majority SWOP Reading

Flowing from this issue of Rahab's motivation and tightly interconnected were the issues of defining what is a prostitute, her status in the community, typical relations of a prostitute with clients and the authorities of the state, that is to say the king, the police and military men. Most of these intersecting issues congealed into a very coherent reading of Rahab that was operating at the level of the story in its narrative context. That is a reading that takes the narrative at its face value and need not reconstruct a different version that might have existed in earlier history, like Gottwald's.

The modern day parallels lent to a unique reading of Rahab as a heroic survivor who struggled for better conditions of life for herself and those she loved. Although this reading would be furthered by the Gottwaldian theory of peasant revolt, it still needed to contend with the post-colonial critiques of Third World feminist scholars. Some of the more straight forward liberation interpretations viewing Rahab as a heroine were dismissed out of hand as being insulting to prostitutes, such as those that see Rahab as a metaphor or mirror of imperfect Israel, the repentant sinner, or the erring church. Interpretations that can see only negative prostitute stereotypes in the text were also rejected. "Goddamn it, why do *we* have to be bad?" was Robyn Few's immediate response. Carol Stuart chimed in: "Why do *we* have to be the pariah? But you see, I think this story tells us we're not pariahs, I think this story says 'you are not the pariah if you do

---

55. Leigh, Carol, *Unrepentant Whore: Collected Works of Scarlot Harlot* (San Francisco, CA: Last Gasp, 2004).

this,' I think this story is saying…'you're a saint.'" Finally: "Rahab is the mirror of our sins and her house is the church? So, Rahab is a sell-out? She's not no sell-out! Bull. She got damn good sense!" Sweet affirms. So, the reading of Margaret Guider, Saint Jerome, Robert Polzin, of Rahab as mirror, or Bird's Rahab who does what is contrary to typical whore behaviour were immediately rejected as not liberating to prostitutes because they maintain the whore stigma as a key to interpretation. "Forget the metaphors, forget the metaphors. She is a whore. She gave up her people, so she could gain, whatever financial gain, which was for her family, her family's survival. OK? That is absolutely the definition of prostitution" asserted Carol Stuart. Veronica Monet also shades in this view: "Prostitutes are often in a position to help others and/or look after family members. Unlike many other women who must be cared for, most prostitutes are self-sufficient and moneyed."

The above definition of prostitution, as sacrifice for one's own survival and the survival of one's family is basic to this SWOP reading. This sacrifice, in and of itself, is seen as heroic. Robyn sums it up: "Prostitution is a job that a lot of women get into because they are starving, because they have to feed their families and take care of it." Before one can understand why Rahab would side with the invading Israelites, it is necessary to understand why most women become prostitutes in the first place. It is then furthermore important to keep in mind that most communities generally *do* treat prostitutes as pariahs, despite their self-sacrificing behaviour, even in our own decolonizing times, and personally blame prostitutes for the effects of economies that are bad for women. This theme of selling sex to save one's family is primary and pervasive but so is the stigma attached to this decision. "Well, because she was a prostitute, her people probably persecuted her so they really weren't *her people* in the first place…so how can they be her people if they look down upon her, or she was "less-than" because of the means by which she had to take care of her family. Those were not her people." In this quote, Sweet provides a way to understand the motivation Rahab may have had in opting for the Israelite cause via her imagined status in the community. Just the fact that she was a prostitute at the outset explains the tenuousness of her own citizenship status in Jericho. "I am sure her best friends fit into her house, OK? So we're *not* talking about a woman who loves her city and the people around her," Robyn insisted. Everyone could agree that Rahab most likely was not treated well by her own city, and this furthermore is shown by how easily she abandons it. Sweet also adds: "that further legitimates to me the fact that she was probably already a prostitute, therefore rejected by her people, therefore had nothing to loose by giving them up, but had everything to gain by saving her family." Veronica Monet agreed: "Rahab was no doubt vilified by the fellow inhabitants of Jericho but she was exalted by the Israelite God. Seems like the conquerors would enjoy elevating someone that was despised by their enemies."

Flowing from the status of the prostitute in the community are typical prostitute dealings with law enforcement. These dealings frequently involve being squeezed for information or blackmailed for sexual favours. This police informant angle can also help to explain why Rahab might be less than happy to help the police of Jericho. Robyn fills in the scenario like this:

> Right after the men came to her house the cops came and they asked, they wanted to know, who, 'who are those guys,' because everyone had seen them go to Rahab's and everyone knows Rahab because they all go to her too! You know how it is. Everyone knows who *you* are because you been seeing 'em all even though no one should ever, ever know that but you. You've got all the secret sleepers because you sleep with everybody. So it's: 'hey, who are those guys at your house?'

Likewise, it happens on the streets of the San Francisco Bay Area, according to Robyn: "Girls walking the streets constantly and cops pull over saying "hey what do you know?" and if they tell 'em they can continue walking the streets that night." It can also involve demands for sexual favours and involve ways of operating that can cause great harm to the street worker. Says Sweet, "They would pick you up and have you suck they dick…and not only that, not only do they force you into being an informant, they will tell the person that you informed on that you did it, and leave you to be killed, and in harm's way. Cuz your life don't really mean nothing because you're just a lowly ass prostitute."

Prostitutes' rights activists' demand for decriminalization flows out of such experiences of police abuse and complicity with violence against prostitutes. The police authorities are typically seen as a big part of the problem and certainly no source of benevolent help from harm. To prove this assertion, Norma Jean Almodovar, a prostitutes' rights activist in Los Angeles, has an extensive website documenting instances of such abuse, as reported in local newspapers.[56] Almodovar used to be a cop herself for 10 years, so she ought to know a lot about such scenarios.[57] Thus, the cops coming to Rahab and demanding information might be indicative of a

56. http://www.iswface.org/library1.html. See Section no. 8, Category: Prostitutes and Law Enforcement/Government Agents.
57. Norma Jean Almodovar, *Cop to Call Girl* (New York: Avon, 1993).

pattern of police harassment and possible coercion to be a snitch. This most certainly would be an unpleasant experience for Rahab whose livelihood would depend on taking care of her clients, thus causing a double bind.

Many scenarios were entertained by the SWOP group, including imagining an invasion of Berkeley by either allies or the Bush Administration cracking down on internal enemies with the FBI or Homeland Security. Robyn ethically posed Rahab's situation in this way:

> I'm sorry but I would have a hard time selling out Berkeley...there is no way in hell. Unless I hated everyone around me and I hated everything that was going on and I was angry and mad and heard all these fantastic stories about these poor people who were being persecuted yet all these fabulous things were happening to them by someone who had come down to help out the poor and the downtrodden...the lowest of the low, right? And she is surrounded by these fat rich pigs who are eating up everything and coming in and treating her like shit, ya know? OK, so she is hating all the people around her, she is despising her world and the people who live in it and she is willing to have them annihilated and she'll bring in her friends. Come on you guys, I don't know, for me it's a hard ethical question...can you watch your city destroyed cuz you hate them, hate them that bad, this must have been a lot of hate.

The life parallel that was most telling was that experienced by Robyn herself who had been arrested by US Attorney General John Ashcroft (who signed her warrant) on federal charges. It was the result of another sex worker going to the FBI with information about a suspected terrorist. Instead of being appreciated for her patriotism, she and everyone in her phone book were arrested, including Robyn, on federal charges for "conspiracy to commit prostitution." Sex workers generally avoid going to the police authorities to report crimes committed against themselves or others for this very good reason: it is self-incriminating and often culminates in their own arrest. Robyn compares the woman who went to the FBI in contrast to Rahab:

> That woman went out of fear to save her community that she thought was going to die. Here she was in the same situation. She's in a room sitting and some man knocks on the door and she doesn't know him but once he gets in there she starts to realize that this could be a man that could destroy her entire state. There is a possibility of starting a war in her country and she is afraid so she goes to the police, she makes a decision to *not* keep that quiet, to *not* cut some kind of deal to be safe but to go to the police and save her community. And instead of being a hero, which she should have been, she was ignored...well she wasn't ignored though cuz *we* were put in jail.

Carol has a harsher view of the situation: "She goes to the FBI because she is scared of this guy who shows up at her door, OK and then what happens is *you* get arrested, so how is she a hero? She isn't a goddamn hero, she's a goddamn sycophant!" In this view, since as a prostitute she is not really a full citizen entitled to police protection, she should have known better, she should have expected to be dismissed or arrested. Sweet sums it up: "You're not valued, you're not important. So, therefore even though you could be giving information that could be saving the nation from a tragic terrorist attack, you're just a lowly prostitute. Why should anything you say have any significance?" Why would a prostitute in such a situation be expected to be loyal to a city or country that does not treat her as fully human? The SWOP readers for the most part do not believe that the people of Jericho are Rahab's people; therefore, it is not traitorous for her to side with the invaders, who might happen to be her clients.

Attitudes to clients varied in the group even though many SWOP women saw the clients in the story negatively, or, in general, saw sex work as often due to a lack of resources and social supports for poor women. Clients in the story are generally thought of as those who used Rahab's services *before* the arrival of the spies, not necessarily the spies themselves. Here is Robyn's take on the situation:

> I keep thinking the kings who are living up there fat while everyone else is starving and all the poor women have to feed their kids in any way they can, have to be prostitutes and screw all these men that they hate OK? They hate these men and they're screwing them cuz they have to. And this is the point she is thinking this is her one payback and she can walk away scot free and she can save everyone she loves, which is not that many people in that city.

Sweet strongly correlates selling sex with lacking resources and therefore a sacrifice that might not be necessary if communities would only choose to better care for all their citizens:

> its a sacrifice cuz you're willing to give up what is supposed to be most precious to you which is your personal body and share it with these different fucking slobs in order to get your basic needs met. So in that way it legitimates that argument. However there are people who are perfectly happy to do it, so what do you say about that?

Echoing this last sentence is Gayle, who worked more on the high end of the industry and felt very positive about the clients for whom she provides erotic services. Gayle thought of the situation at Rahab's house in this way: "the soldiers had sex with the prostitutes, because that is what happens, you protect the prostitutes, that's their business. It's not demeaning to them. They're not going to kill these women unless someone is deranged."

At other times it is the spies who are clients but who are viewed as allies in a peasant revolt a la Norman Gottwald. Carol characterizes the invaders as "Nice Jewish Guys" with the "cut schmeckels" who escaped oppression in Egypt via a red marking on their doors, who in turn offered salvation to Rahab via a red cord in the window. "She already knew, we already painted our front doors red and that's how we got there, that's how we got out of Egypt." The "Nice Jewish Guys" help promote the prostitutes and integrated them into their revolution, because they were likewise revolting against their status. Due to their common cause, it doesn't matter that the spies are clients because by writing this story they are trying to teach the other Hebrews to be nice to prostitutes, as in "we have to educate these people and tell them that whores are not all bad." Carol who, like Scarlot, is Jewish, likes to point out that now that Andrea Dworkin died, there are no prominent Jewish anti-sex feminists. She thinks Jewish culture is much less erotophobic, which to her, is the special penchant of Christianity. Robyn Few sees the situation in light of the failed Berkeley ballot initiative for decriminalization, "Measure Q":

> Back in those days, the 'winning team' was bunch of losers who, they were the weirdoes, they were the underdogs. You guys are forgetting what's really happening, we're talking about the big.....we're the losers, just like the Berkeley measure Q. You have to realize that the government's bad people...poor measure Q people, and there's a whole bunch of *other* measure Q people out there who just come to your house and they show up and they say 'hey look.'...and she knew that and she said 'hell, I am going to help, bring this war on.' She started the revolution!

Minority Opinion of SWOP

The dissenting opinion of Scarlot Harlot urged the group to question the rhetorical strategy of the text and brought a very healthy scepticism to the discussion. Scarlot had a pronounced hermeneutic of suspicion about the writer(s), the characterization of God and the winners of the story in whose interests the story was written. Scarlot also advocated for an extremely novel liberation reading that rendered Rahab a Goddess. Her attitude was, if we attempt to read this in a way liberating to prostitutes, why not go all the way? Nevertheless, most of the group still preferred to see Rahab on a more ordinary human level because that was where her story most resonated with their own. In the end, the majority view prevailed and Scarlot was grudgingly won over.

Scarlot's minority opinion was influenced by her knowledge of another mythical Rahab in Job, Psalms, and Isaiah, a primeval spirit or serpent of chaos. She tried to conflate this other Rahab with Rahab of Jericho to have her be more powerful, a dragon Goddess who controls access to the city. Despite the negativity attached to this other Rahab persona, Scarlot sought to invert this negativity to create a powerful counter deity to YWWH. Scarlot did not like the character of God in Joshua: "It's problematic to not start with a critique of God." Furthermore, God is characterized in the text as "some kind of shyster, Mafioso type", which made it difficult to view the actions of Joshua and his army in a positive way. "I don't believe that God is going to send in these fabulous people when he has such a bad reputation and he is such a bully and he messed up all the nice Goddess worshipping pagans," says Scarlot. God's character made Scarlot question if the text were not trying to teach prostitutes how to be a "good whore" or as she put it:

I have a different feeling. My feeling and it really starts with the basis of resenting the people who are coming around to the house and they are supposed to be so powerful and with god and stuff. Because I feel that the story in a way has the purpose to tell people how to be a good prostitute. And for me I see it as a chance thing. But she probably didn't like the community and I guess there I believe there was a point in that story. But it was kinda like chance and she had no other choice and they are trying to make her look like some good girl to follow God.

In contrast, Scarlot felt that to create a true liberation reading, Goddesses needed to be added to the story:

Well I think to put this together in a way that is positive from my perspective, um, I don't know what liberation theology does with all this, but I remember seeing a book about Jewish Goddesses. I'm thinking it could all be more positive if there were Jewish Goddesses and whore Goddesses, being major players, so I wouldn't really bother reanalyzing this unless I was restructuring the power of the deity and restructuring for that kind of interpretation, to have a good kind of theology that would work for prostitutes. I'm thinking any kind of restructuring of this theology that is going to have a male deity and not a female deity also is going to be problematic to any kind of reconstruction to create, like liberation theology that would be positive, that you were looking for like Gabriela was talking about or whatever, would be to integrate the Goddess and to create that out of the mythology. An interpretation that gets past this kind of old patriarchal religion thing, that's what I'd like. Like, an interpretation, say, I like the whole, like, including other interpretations of Rahab, like broadening her out, so that suddenly she is not this prostitute in the story but that is only one aspect of her, and that she is these other Rahabs and prostitutes so that she is a superwoman

like Buffy or something....and that, not like she is a beast, but that she
is a Goddess. She is the Goddess, the whore Goddess, the dragon. She
is the one in charge and she lets them through, basically because she is
the keeper of the gates.

The chief objection to this reading was brought up by Carol and Robyn
that it is easier to identify with Rahab as a regular prostitute than as a
Goddess: "Can't she just be a regular person, I mean she is a regular person
who made it...like my mom and your mom, or my sister or my aunt?" It is
ordinary women who are selling sex and making life and death decisions
like Rahab's. Sweet also pointed out other aspects of the story that conflict
with a Goddess reading.

> Well I'm a very self-assured, assertive, ya know, OK-in-my-skin woman.
> I feel that Rahab is much more the same way than some power swinging
> Goddess because if that was the case then she would have bartered for
> more than just the lives of her family. So I see her more as someone like
> you or I, doing what she had to do to survive. If she was divine she didn't
> need they help in the first place! So it doesn't fit 'cuz if they had to
> appease her, why not ask for more? She is saying "Please! Just spare the
> lives of me and my family. Family means everything, all we have is each
> other, this is who I struggle everyday to take care of, they are everything
> to me, give me the lives of my family." Now if they was wiping out the
> city they could have gave her all kinds of stuff, if she had any real power.

Meanwhile, the counter critique of the majority reading of Rahab as an
ordinary woman was very aware that, despite Rahab being a hero in
tradition, this did not really translate into better treatment of prostitutes.
Scarlot points out that "to even say this Marxist analysis of this thing, to
twist it around and say 'OK it is really a story about underprivileged people
fighting back; it is not a story about the capitalists winning everything and
the dominating forces winning...' that's in denial about how it's being used
at least." While we may be able to assert that the point of the story was to
change people's attitude about prostitutes, the effect has not been very
noticeable. According to Veronica, the narrative "forces the reader to see
the prostitute as a heroine, as blessed and protected by God. This should
cause the reader to be more tolerant of real life whores but it does not. Too
bad, as I think that was the original intention." Norma Jean Almodovar, the
author of a website on police abuse of prostitutes as informants, wrote to
me about the hazards of reading Rahab as a hero:

> In the sense that Rahab was a heroine to Bible aficionados, I think it is a
> good thing—but also contradictory—since in today's world, she would
> be in jail just for being a prostitute—jailed by the same Bible reading

gang that makes her a hero for the Jews! But that's usually what happens—first, a prostitute is called upon to help cops/ military/ Jewish scouts—then once the situation has resolved itself, the prostitute is still the outlaw—and off she goes to jail—or gets murdered—for her efforts!

Rahab was viewed by most readers as a heroine whether or not the Joshua group were "good guys," because she was seen more as a savvy survivor. It is imaginable that there was a kind of political alliance between the invading Israelites and the other outcast people of the region, including prostitutes. However, it is not necessary for Rahab's heroism that she side with the "right" group but only that she and her family survive. That she managed this survival by her own wits is most important to the sex worker interpreters. Sweet likes to emphasize the intelligence of Rahab:

> If she was a victim only and operating out of false consciousness, why was she the only one who was the only person out of that city who was able to survive, and not just able to secure her own survival but the survival of her entire family? I think their underestimating her intelligence was their biggest downfall. I think she was smarter than all the mother-fuckers, the king, the spies; very, very wise woman!

"Those are not her people!"

Launching off from Sweet's assertion that the people of Jericho were not Rahab's "people," it might be worthwhile to compare Rahab's treason to other more conventional biblical heroes to see if perhaps there is a gender, class or sexual double standard being invoked against Rahab because she is a prostitute. Abraham, Moses, the Egyptian midwives and Pharoah's daughter all behave in ways that could be similarly construed, as traitorous to their people. It begs the question, who are one's people? Is it a person's family, their city, their tribe, their region, their social strata? Or is it those with whom one makes common cause to survive, and if conditions permit, work for full human flourishing and attain the peace (*shalom*, that is to say, well being) of God?

In Gen. 12:1–2 Abraham was instructed by God to "go from your country and your kindred and your father's house to the land that I will show you. I will make you a great nation, and I will bless you, and make your name great so that you will be a blessing." I begin by comparing Rahab to Abraham since that is also a comparison made by the New Testament author of James at 2:25. Hebrews 11:31 also lists Rabab as an exemplar of faith, along with Abraham, Moses and other ancestral heroes. The faith and actions of these figures are defined in the same manner as Rahab's in Joshua: for

believing in a better future and leaving their people. James compares
Abraham to Rahab for his works in 2:21 "when he offered his son Issac on
the altar." James 2:25, in direct comparison to Abraham's act, praise Rahab:
"Likewise, was not Rahab the prostitute also justified by works when she
welcomed the messengers and sent them out by another road?" In Hebrews,
faith is the topic of the whole of chapter 11 as "the assurance of things
hoped for, the conviction of things not seen (Heb. 11:1)." Hebrews gives the
most attention to Abraham and Moses as exemplars of faith although Rahab
is mentioned at 11:31 as the narrative moves to Canaan from Eygpt: "by
faith Rahab the prostitute did not perish with those who were disobedient
[or unbelieving], because she received the spies in peace." Rahab's action
was reckoned as rooted in a faith comparable to Abraham's.

Moses' story is also one of rejecting the people who raised him and the
status of being a member of the royal household. Hebrews 11:24–25 says
"by faith Moses, when he was grown up, refused to be called a son of
Pharoah's daughter, choosing rather to share the ill-treatment of the people
of God." When Moses was rescued from the Nile river it was by Pharoah's
daughter who raised him as her own child. She directly defied the decree of
her father that "every boy that is born to the Hebrews you shall throw into
the Nile" (Exod. 1:22) because she recognized that that "this must be one of
the Hebrew's children" (Exod. 2:6). She followed in the lead of the Egyptian
midwives who delivered the Hebrew babies, "feared God", and refused to
comply with the genocidal command of the Pharaoh. Thus, "God dealt
well with the midwives…because they feared God, he gave them families"
(Exod. 1:22). These women were possible Egyptian role models for Moses,
who, though a Hebrew by birth was recognized as an "Egyptian" by the
daughters of Reuel (Exod. 2:19). Moses leaves his people, both Egyptian
and Hebrew, when he resides as an "alien"[58] in a foreign land, which is why
he named his son "Gershom."

The New Testament text of Acts 7 has a recital of history by the martyr
Stephen which also recounts the behavior of Moses and Abraham. Herein,
Abraham is also extolled for leaving his country and relatives to follow the
path that God had made for him (Acts 7:2–4). Stephen's speech focuses
especially on Moses, a rejected prophet and liberator of Israel, who was
raised in Pharaoh's household "when he was abandoned, Pharoah's daughter
adopted him and brought him up as her own son" (Acts 7:21). Who were
Moses' people?

---

58. *Ger* means "alien" in Hebrew.

Since it is the Christian New Testament texts that are using such arguments about exemplars of faith and works, I think it is also pertinent to ask, who were Jesus's people? Jesus for his part advocated a notion of fictive kinship among those working for the reign of God in many Gospel texts. In Mk 3:33 Jesus asks "Who are my mother and my brothers?" and he looked at those who sat around him and said, "Here are my mother and my brothers! Whoever does the will of God is my brother, sister and mother." In some cases it would appear that oppressive fathers are to be excluded (replaced with persecutions?) when Jesus responds to Peter in Mk 10: 28–31 about leaving everything to follow Jesus:

> Truly I tell you, there is no one who has left house or brothers or sisters or mother or father or children or fields, for my sake and the sake of the good news, who will not receive a hundredfold now in this age— houses, brothers and sisters, mothers and children, and fields with persecutions—and in the age to come eternal life. But many who are first will be last, and the last will be first.

Prostitutes could definitely be an example of the last who become first. In Mt. 21:31–32, Jesus says to the religious leaders that the "tax collectors and the prostitutes are going into the kingdom of God ahead of you. For John came to you in the way of righteousness and you did not believe him, but the tax collectors and the prostitutes believed him: and even after you saw it you did not change your minds and believe him." Like Rahab, they may be less invested in the existing status quo and motivated to act toward a different reality such as, "the assurance of things hoped for, the conviction of things not seen" as described by Heb. 11:1.

Rahab's motivation to help the invading Hebrews happens on the other side of the Red Sea. The invasion of the Promised Land is the dark side of the Exodus story where the liberation blueprint of the Israelites might seem questionable to the indigenous inhabitants of Canaan. Native American and Palestinian interpreters have poignantly argued this critique of the non-liberative underbelly of the Exodus narrative.[59] That the Israelites behaved as oppressively to the native inhabitants of Canaan as they were themselves oppressed by the Egyptians, including the practice of genocide, puts a big question mark on their liberation paradigm. However, it may be the very fact that Rahab is depicted as a prostitute that her status

59. These critiques of Exodus are in R.S. Sugirtharajah (ed.), *Voices from the Margin: Interpreting the Bible in the Third World* (Maryknoll, NY: Orbis Books, 1991) see Robert Allen Warrior, "A Native American Perspective: Canaanites, Cowboys, and Indians," pp. 287–95 and Naim Stifan Ateek, "A Palestinian Perspective: the Bible and Liberation," pp. 280–86.

as a traitor or as a realistic person is questioned. What SWOP readers argue is that Rahab's behavior does not lack verisimilitude as a rational act and that her actions do not automatically qualify her as a pawn or parrot of a colonizing ideology.[60] The negative stereotype of the prostitute is that "they can be bought" because they lack any inner moral conviction or loyalty, thus they cannot really qualify as full-fledged political actors.[61] Others, from Marx to Melissa Farley, assert that prostitutes are falsely conscious anyhow. Thus, this negative stereotyping may have an impact on the evaluation of Rahab as heroine who has the capacity to make her own alliances and figure out the best way to survive. Until we begin to question the integrity of Abraham and Moses in the same way, perhaps we should give Rahab the benefit of doubt and assume she knew her own mind when she allied with the spies.

Analysis of Differences between Biblical Scholars and SWOP Activists

The biggest key to the differences with the post colonialist interpreters was that the prostitutes insisted on maintaining Rahab's prostitute identity and endeavoured to do it in a positive manner. Musa Dube, Laura Donaldson, and Judith McKinlay all interpret Rahab as a colonized territory or as a lifeless ventriloquist dummy, but not as a real prostitute. Prostitution is a major post-colonial issue. Therefore, this story element really needs to be part of such an interpretation. Sex workers emphasize that it needs to be examined from the experience of those who undergo the experience, not from the experience of women who are utterly horrified by the idea of being abused in this way but have not actually undergone the experience. This horror on the part of non-prostitutes is something that often gets in the way of approaches that are more pragmatic to the issue. It also contributes to a sense of being beyond the pale or utterly damaged goods, which forgets the fact that, for instance, many feminist theologians come from backgrounds of domestic sexual abuse but are still considered credible scholars, authentic in their own identity.

60. R. Maldonado, makes a comparable argument about Ruth's behaviour, in defence of La Malinche, a Mexican Pocahontas figure in "Reading Malinche Reading Ruth: Towards a Hermeneutics of Betrayal," *Semeia* 72 (1995), pp. 91–109.

61. See McKinlay, *Reframing Her*, p. 46 and Bird, *Missing Persons and Mistaken Identities*, p. 214. Prostitutes insist that it is their sexual services that are purchased, not themselves, or their integrity.

Not only do SWOP readers insist on Rahab's prostitute identity, they also consistently read her as an agent, always an agent, despite whatever constraints impinge on her decisions. Rahab chose to do sex work to make a living to help her family. She chose to join the Hebrews. Her life choices make sense to other sex workers. Until prostitutes receive equal civil and human rights under the law, it is not reasonable to ask them to have unquestioning allegiance to any government. Prostitutes cannot be given the duties of citizenship without the privileges of citizenship. The moral agency of sex workers is complicated by this lack of rights but it still does not mean that prostitutes are amoral or total victims. Sacrifice for family, even when it is a sacrifice that many respectable people cannot imagine opting for, needs to be recognized even if an utterly different kind of economy that does not require such sacrifice is desirable and needs to be envisioned.

Another interesting difference is that the heroism of Rahab is not necessarily hinged on her allegiance to the Hebrew cause. Nor does this cause need to be justified for Rahab to be an intelligent and heroic survivor. Rahab is primarily a heroic figure because she is loyal to her family and sacrifices for them in a way unimaginable to those with privilege and resources. This resolves my own quandary about the spies' sexual propriety and/or possible exploitation of Rahab. The clients as prostitution abusers was not problematic to creating a pro-sexworker interpretation for SWOP readers. This is more of a concern for non-prostitutes. SWOP interpreters do not single out johns as villains because the whole hypocritical moral-economic sexual hierarchy is to blame, not just patriarchy. Besides, many prostitutes find sex work preferable to other kinds of labour.

Finally, SWOP readers do not like their identities co-opted to label or denounce others. Even if prostitutes agree with the critique, it is still unacceptable to metaphorically label as whore the church, the proletariat, the sinner, the police, a bad president, or erring Israel. The conventional inference is that a prostitute/harlot/ho/whore is the paradigmatic sinner, sell-out, mercenarily motivated, or pimped. Instead, sex worker rights activists work towards a positive identity as prostitute or ex-prostitute.

SWOP Retelling the Story of Rahab, a Collage of Quotes

As a conclusion to the section on Rahab, we retell the story from a sex workers' perspective by threading quotes by the following speakers: Avaren, Robyn, Carol, Sweet, Gayle, Scarlot, Veronica, Norma Jean.

The Hebrews, an escaped band of slaves from Egypt, wander in the desert for forty years. While there, they gather to themselves all the disaffected populations who had been exploited in Canaan and forced to live as outsiders in unoccupied places. They lived by banditry and occasionally were hired as mercenaries. At the end of this long period of homelessness they decide it is time to go in and take over the land of Canaan. Preliminary to this, Joshua the leader of the Israelite coalition and successor to Moses, sends spies into the border town of Jericho to check out the situation. The spies go to the house of Rahab, the prostitute. O.K. Here she is this prostitute that opens the door, just like we all do, to anybody. Because whoever has the money gets in, right? So she opens the door to these guys and all of a sudden she comes in and they tell her who they are. And she has heard of them, she knows who they are. So all of a sudden she is in total fear, that they are going to destroy her and her entire village, that's what's going to happen, that's what they tell her, 'we've come to see what's going on.' Just think about what this is. Imagine we're sitting in our house in Berkeley and we get a phone call from these two guys and we say 'Alright come on in.' They've got $500.00 or $250.00, so they come on over, they knock on the door. Alright, we have had a good time, they're sitting around, and they say, 'We really came, ya know, we were sent, to scope out the city because we're going to kick some ass here.' She already knew: those guys with cut schmeckels. They were circumcised and the rest of her clients weren't. She heard all these fantastic stories about these poor people who were being persecuted yet all these fabulous things were happening to them by someone who had come down to help out the poor and the downtrodden...the lowest of the low, right? And she is surrounded by these fat rich pigs who are eating up everything and coming in and treating her like shit, ya know? OK so she's hating all the people around her, she is despising her world and the people who live in it and she is willing to have them annihilated. She didn't *love* these people. She sold out easily out of fear that they would all be killed, but also that she was given a chance. Oh come on you guys! I'm sorry but I would have a hard time selling out Berkeley.

Well, because she was a prostitute, her people probably persecuted her so they really weren't her people in the first place. She was a woman who knew what was valuable to her and she chose that over people who thought little of them or what she valued and the lengths she went to make sure that all was well. What higher calling is there than to take care of and love your family? What higher calling is there than that...to sacrifice all for your family? I don't know about anyone else but if I do nothing else right in life I want to be a good mother, and a good daughter. She is saying 'Please! Just spare the lives of me and my family. Family means everything all we have is each other, this is who I struggle everyday to take care of, they are everything to me, give me the lives of my family.' They asked her to join their revolution and told her to put out a red cord in the window so that they would know to pass over her house. They explained to Rahab the significance of the red: 'We already painted our front doors red and that's how we got here, that's how we got out of Egypt.' She was told, hang the crimson cord out, because she was a true believer because she believed that if she didn't hang that rope out and have all those people in her house that day she was going to die, so trust me, she had a choice. She could have said, 'Oh you guys are full of it, nothing is going to happen to me, you are not going to come and do this stuff.' But instead she believed that they were and that these were the right guys to come in and do this. We don't know if Rahab was previously sympathetic to this, philosophy, the Israelite philosophy. I think she was doing what she needed to do to protect herself so she wouldn't be harmed. Maybe she thought 'I'm looking at better opportunities for my next generation to give them opportunities that I was never allotted because of this label that I have been given before I even stepped, breathed life on this earth because of either my gender or my color'...we have to assume Rahab is an intelligent woman who decided to count up the cost. The truth is, back in those days, the 'winning team' was bunch of losers who, they were the weirdos, they were the underdogs...we're the losers, just like the Berkeley Measure Q. You have to realize that the government's bad people Poor Measure Q people, and there's a whole bunch of *other* Measure Q people out there who just come to your house and they show up and they say, 'Hey look.'...And she knew that and she said 'hell, I am going to help, bring this war on.' She started the revolution!

The other Hebrews back at the camp were potentially the first audience of the story, like an audience of 'we have to educate these people and tell them that whores are not all bad.' We were speaking to our own here, right? Writing to our own community? We're not writing to the Christians, Christianity did not exist. They were trying to write and educate their own, like, 'look you guys, we're into whores!' Nice Jewish guys and they, they really try to promote the prostitutes here and I'll go for that, like you know, the nice Jewish guys and they like the prostitutes and they are writing her as a hero and she is the mother of blah bla...Right, I don't like it personally but yeah I can see where people would like that. I don't like it cuz of the whole male deity thing. It just offends me deeply, the singular male deity, but I would just go for the nice Jewish guys who promote the prostitutes. So give 'em a pat on the back, be a good prostitute, they're good nice Jewish guys. Rahab was no doubt vilified by the fellow inhabitants of Jericho but she was exalted by the Israelite God. Seems like the conquerors would enjoy elevating someone that was despised by their enemies.

The military uses prostitutes...they're going after the prostitutes to have free sex, I mean sorry, to have sex. Perhaps they will want it for free, if they are the invading force, but they are not going to get rid of the prostitutes, they are going to save them! And say: 'you can come over to our camp and we'll give you a very nice house and get out of the way while we mow down the city.' After Joshua, whatever, is there, they burn the city, they go back to their camp to celebrate, what they didn't add, which I am sure happened is the soldiers had sex with the prostitutes, because that is what happens, you protect the prostitutes, that's their business. It's not demeaning to them. They're not going to kill these women unless someone is deranged. And then they celebrated by having sex with these women who probably gave it to them for free for sparing their lives. We couldn't have had that in the Bible though, Oh, no. In today's world, she would be in jail just for being a prostitute—jailed by the same Bible reading gang that makes her a hero for the Jews! But that's usually what happens—first, a prostitute is called upon to help cops/military/Jewish scouts—then once the situation has resolved itself, the prostitute is still the outlaw—and off she goes to jail—or gets murdered—for her efforts!

Chapter 4

SOLOMON AND THE TWO PROSTITUTES

1 Kgs 3:16–28 (NRSV)

[16] Later, two women who were prostitutes came to the king and stood before him. [17] *The one* woman said, 'Please, my lord, this woman and I live in the same house; and I gave birth while she was in the house. [18] Then on the third day after I gave birth, this woman also gave birth. We were together; there was no one else with us in the house, only the two of us were in the house. [19] Then this woman's son died in the night, because she lay on him. [20] She got up in the middle of the night and took my son from beside me while your servant slept. She laid him at her breast, and laid her dead son at my breast. [21] When I rose in the morning to nurse my son, I saw that he was dead; but when I looked at him closely in the morning, clearly it was not the son I had borne.' [22] But *the other* woman said, 'No, the living son is mine, and the dead son is yours.' *The first* said, 'No, the dead son is yours, and the living son is mine.' So they argued before the king. [23] Then the king said, '*The one* says, "This is my son that is alive, and your son is dead"; while *the other* says, 'Not so! Your son is dead, and my son is the living one.'" [24] So the king said, 'Bring me a sword,' and they brought a sword before the king. [25] The king said, 'Divide the living boy in two; then give half to the one, and half to the other.' [26] But the woman whose son was alive said to the king—because compassion for her son burned within her—'Please, my lord, give her the living boy; certainly do not kill him!' *The other* said, 'It shall be neither mine nor yours; divide it.' [27] Then the king responded: 'Give *the first* woman the living boy; do not kill him. She is his mother.' [28] All Israel heard of the judgment that the king had rendered; and they stood in awe of the king, because they perceived that the wisdom of God was in him, to execute justice.[1]

1. *The Holy Bible: New Revised Standard Version* (Nashville, TN: Thomas Nelson, 1996, [1989]).

Scholar Standpoints

I initially chose to work on the text of I Kgs 3:16–28 as a "prostitution" text because it is a story that involves two sex workers interacting with the legal system of their time. Law reform is the number one concern for sex worker rights activists worldwide, so this text provides an opportunity to engage with many of the complicated issues surrounding the legal status of the contemporary sex worker while assessing a biblical depiction of justice for a marginalized group. Thus, this chapter began many years back as my book's pilot project in attempting to "read with"[2] prostitute women by intercalating their writings or life texts with a biblical text. I initially attempted an intertextual reading since I had not established a formal reading group and had to rely on sex worker rights' written texts to interact with the biblical and scholarly texts.[3] I wished to discover, following the suggestion of Timothy Beal, "how might the established boundaries (or 'critical consensus') of intertextual relationships—and the strategies of containment which maintain them—be transgressed in order to discover new relationships and prioritize other voices?"[4] To produce a reading that really privileges the non-hegemonic views of prostitutes' rights activists, I naturally revisited the text again in my book with my group of ten "flesh and blood" readers to give an even fuller preferential hermeneutical option to prostitutes via standpoint theory.

While the story of Solomon's Judgment in I Kgs 3:16–28 is almost universally known, in popular consciousness, the professional occupation of the women in the story is generally absent. This absence is often true of biblical criticism as well. Stuart Lasine's work exemplifies how this elision works: "Far from inviting us to explain the women's behaviour in terms of their profession and low station, the fact that the women are harlots is

---

2. For an explanation of this "reading with" concept see notes 25 and 27 on page 6 of this book or in West's *Biblical Hermeneutics of Liberation*, p. 213 and "Contextual Bible Study in Africa" pp. 597–98.

3. I did a modest interpretation session with two friends who had been sex workers. One of these friends, "Sweet," also participated in the subsequent SWOP symposia.

4. Timothy Beal, "Ideology and Intertextuality: Surplus of Meaning and Controlling the Means of Production," in Danna Nolan Fewell (ed.), *Reading Between Texts*, p. 36. In the recent intertextuality issue of *Semeia* 69/70 (1995) Timothy Beal, Tod Linafelt and many others engage in such transgressive intertexual readings following upon a much broader definition of permissible textual relationships than has been traditionally allowed within the discipline of Biblical Studies.

designed to focus our attention precisely on the fact that their distinguishing characteristic is motherhood."[5] One of my academic colleagues advised me to be sure to *prove* to my audience that the mothers were prostitutes by emphasizing that the Hebrew text really, truly, actually, says נשׁים־זנות/*nashim zonot* or "prostitute women" in 1 Kgs 3:16. Otherwise, readers might think I was doing a creative interpretation and adding this story element on my own. The prostitution aspect is usually downplayed by being portrayed as a naturalized component of ancient Israelite society or effaced by emphasizing the women as mothers so that a comforting certitude of maternal nature can be discerned. According to Carole Fontaine, "The *zonôt* of 1 Kings 3 are functional 'widows,'" that is types of poor or dispossessed mothers who had to appeal to authority figures on their own behalf. [6] In another article by Annelies van Heijst, the "good" mother's renunciation of her maternity claim is theologized in as an example of women's wisdom that avoids divided thinking. [7] The story is read from a mother's perspective, but not a prostitute mother's perspective. Another way the prostitution aspect is downplayed is by focusing upon the story as mainly about Solomon's virtuoso display of wisdom. The significance of the story as one about and/or ideologically impacting prostitutes is not usually in the spotlight. How does this ancient judicial scenario play out in today's context of prostitution politics? New insights can be discerned through juxtapositioning the biblical text with current sex worker experiences of the justice system. There are many analogies and similarities between the justice seeking prostitutes in 1 Kgs 3:16–28 and stories of modern day prostitute women who are demanding justice and protesting the coercion and violence they experience.

The text of Solomon and the prostitute women is located at the beginning of the narrative that recounts the reign of Solomon in 1 Kgs

5. Stuart Lasine, "The Riddle of Solomon's Judgment and the Riddle of Human Nature in the Hebrew Bible," *JSOT* 45 (1989), pp. 61–86, p. 70.

6. Carole Fontaine, "The Bearing of Wisdom on the Shape of 2 Samuel 11–12 and 1 Kings 3," in Athalya Brenner (ed.), *A Feminist's Companion to Samuel and Kings* (Sheffield: Sheffield Academic Press, 1994), pp. 143–67, p. 155.

7. Annelies van Heijst "Beyond Divided Thinking: Solomon's Judgment and the Wisdom-traditions of Women," *Louvain Studies* 19 (1994), pp. 99–117. The contrasting view of Phyllis Bird ("Harlot as Heroine: Narrative Art and Social Presupposition in Three Old Testament Texts," *Semeia* 46 [1989], pp. 119–39) that the negative social stereotyping of prostitutes is integral to the story is a point more helpful to my purposes of highlighting prostitution in this story.

3–10. Because of the numerable contradictions and indeterminacies in the account of the career of Solomon there exists no easy-to-utilize scholarly consensus regarding the text's date, author, audience or ideology. Indeed, Stuart Lasine uses this chunk of narrative in a recent article as a premiere example of "textual indeterminacy."[8] Often at stake in current scholarship is the nature of Solomon's reign and whether or not it is a positive portrait of his political economy. Other scholars wonder if perhaps there is Deuteronomistic "lampooning" at work in the Solomon narrative.[9] Lasine reviews differing possible historical contexts for the Solomon narrative and concludes that the diverging positive and negative evaluations of Solomon's rule by biblical scholars are created by the indeterminate text itself. In exception, however, when it comes to the story of Solomon's judgment, Lasine sees a more determinate textual ideology, given the folk origins of the story, which can supposedly transcend placement or historical situation. Lasine categorizes the story of 1 Kgs 3:16–28 as a popular folk-riddle and its ideology is seen by him to be an example of "strain ideology" that is trying to resolve social uncertainty about deceit and truth telling in unstable times. The riddle is resolved by Solomon's insight into maternal nature, characterized by either self-sacrifice or envy. He exempts this story from the overall general indeterminacy of 1 Kgs 3–11 for which he argues.

Lasine's exemption of this story from the overall general indeterminacy of 1 Kgs 3–11 is linked to previous work on this particular story and his debate with Hugh Pyper regarding the effects of intertexts on the tale.[10] It is out of this debate that I became first interested in this narrative. For me, the key question comes from Hugh Pyper: "what are two prostitutes doing in the court of Israel's wisest king?"[11] This question crystallized my own emerging question regarding the role of prostitution in the overall political economy of Solomon. This role is especially interesting in light of the possibility that biblical widows needing justice, economic or otherwise, may be among the very types of women who might resort to prostitution to survive economically.

8. Stuart Lasine, "The King of Desire: Indeterminacy, Audience, and the Solomon Narrative," *Semeia* 71 (1995), pp. 105–106.

9. Edward Newing, "Rhetorical Art of the Deuteronomist: Lampooning Solomon in First Kings," *Old Testament Essays* 7 (1994), pp. 247–60.

10. Lasine, "The Riddle of Solomon's Judgment," pp. 61–86; "The Ups and Downs of Monarchical Justice: Solomon and Jehoram in an Intertextual World," *JSOT* 59 (1993), pp. 37–53; Hugh Pyper, "Judging the Wisdom of Solomon: The Two-Way Effect of Intertextuality," *JSOT* 59 (1993), pp. 25–36.

11. Pyper, "Judging the Wisdom of Solomon," p. 31.

Other characterizations of the folk story genre would allow much greater plasticity of application and contextual meaning. For example, Burke Long asserts "because it is a question of folk story, we must be open to the obscurity of origin and a multiplicity of setting and occasions on which such a story might have been told."[12] Scholars who categorize this story as popular folk tale/story/riddle usually mention its many parallels in other cultures, none of which seem to include prostitutes as the protagonists, but more often, widows of one husband.[13] It might be possible that the widows were transformed into prostitutes for ironic effect to make a mockery of Solomon's political economy and courtly wisdom. The prostitution aspect could be an invisible trace of a Deuteronomistic moustache drawn upon a more respectable widow petitioner story.[14] Since it is possible to read the larger overall narrative as a negative or even simply indeterminate portrait of Solomon's reign, perhaps one should not be too quick to exempt this story aspect from consideration as ironic or a parody. Given that Solomon prays for an understanding mind to govern this "great people" (1 Kgs 3:9) in the preceding passage, is it not at least a little interesting that the only narrated example of his judicial practice is done for prostitutes? This switch from widows to prostitutes is particularly significant in light of the possibility that biblical widows may be among the very types of women who might resort to prostitution to survive economically. A similar switch occurs in the story of the widow Tamar in Genesis 38. The story of the widow Ruth can be understood as about widows utilizing a sexual strategy to get their needs met.

Since one of the primary undecidable sites of debate in the Solomon narrative regards the nature of his political economy, it is into this

12. Burke O. Long, *1 Kings: With an Introduction to Historical Literature* (Grand Rapids, MI: Eerdmans, 1984), p. 70.

13. H. Gressmann, "Das Solomonische Urteil," *Deutsche Runschau* 130 (1907), pp. 212–28. I actually utilized Theodor Gaster's sampling of parallels in *Myth, Legend, and Custom in the Old Testament* (Gloucester: Peter Smith, 1981, II), pp. 491–94.

14. G.H. Jones, in *I and 2 Kings* (Grand Rapids, MI: Eerdmans, 1984, I), p. 131, outlines the issue of the date of incorporation of this folk unit as being related to varying judgments about why there seem to be no traces of Deuteronomistic elaboration in the episode. Some scholars see this as a clue to its post-Deuteronomistic, post-Chronistic date of insertion. Others see the unit as being attached to Solomonic traditions in pre-Deuteronomistic time (therefore already in the source "Book of the Acts of Solomon" mentioned in 1 Kgs 11:41, see Jones, *1 and 2 Kings*, p. 58 and escaping Deuteronomistic tampering because the story conformed to an accepted image of "Solomon's charisma."

unresolved space that I wish to contextualize the institution of prostitution as a part of any political economy and gendered division of labor. In a move away from theories of prostitution that are rooted in personal morality or medical pathology that is to say promiscuity, nymphomania, genetics, post-traumatic stress, incest, or the uncontrollable male sex drive, more recent attention has been given to the role of prostitution within gendered economies, especially in economies of gross inequity, maldistribution, or crisis; that is a feminist materialist analysis. Conditions or factors that are often correlated with the proliferation of prostitution are often connected to changes or disruptions in economic modes of production such as land consolidation and loss, urbanization, migration, debt-bondage, colonialism, nationalism, warfare and militarism, and uneven economic development that results in great disparities of wealth.[15] Combined with these correlates are various gendered divisions of labour, especially the role of unpaid domestic and reproductive labour done by women which subsidizes the wages of paid workers and therefore the economy as a whole, or, which commands a very low price in the waged sector. For example, in the Philippines of the 1980s "as the price of sugar has declined on the international market and large landowners have pushed more and more Filipinos into landless poverty, more young women have come to make a living by servicing the social and sexual needs of American military men."[16] The importance of understanding this larger context is so great that Filipino feminists refuse to discuss prostitution without reference to the issues of land reform, demilitarization, nationalism, and migration.[17] Prostitution has also been analyzed as a hegemonic means of controlling or appeasing indigenous male labourers in situations of colonialism and neo-colonialism where pre-existing familial patterns of organization are destroyed or disabled when populations are coerced into slave wage labour.[18] In a good

15. I am dangerously summarizing a number of contextual findings. A number of recent studies give these factors in various combinations for a wide variety of geographical locales and historical contexts: Kamala Kempadoo and Jo Doezema (eds.), *Global Sex Workers*; Cynthia Enloe, *Bananas, Beaches, & Bases;* Saundra Polluck Sturdevant and Brenda Stoltzfus, *Let the Good Times Roll;* Thanh-Dam Truong, *Sex, Money, and Morality;* Luise White, *The Comforts of Home;* Vern and Bonnie Bullough, *Women and Prostitution.*

16. Enloe, *Bananas, Beaches, & Bases*, p. 86.

17. Enloe, *Bananas, Beaches, & Bases*, p. 39.

18. Enloe describes this in terms of the United Fruit Company in Central America, that she describes as a "plantation economy" of which brothels are an intentional part, pp. 140–42. Luise White describes the deliberate use of the

example of these linkages, Maria Mies, a feminist political economist, gives the International Monetary Fund (IMF) and the World Bank (WB) the nickname of "International of Pimps."[19] This nickname is due to the role of international development agencies in the growth of sex tourism worldwide in the new International Division of Labor or IDL: "The most blatant manifestation of the new IDL with the neo-patriarchal or sexist division of labour is sex-tourism."[20]

David Jobling offers an example of a Marxist oriented approach to the Solomonic narrative that would be reconfigured by including prostitution into the economic mode of production. He has done a deconstructive ideological reading of the narrative account of Solomon's reign in 1 Kgs 3–11 which he designates a "golden age" story.[21] Due to the fact that what is being depicted is an ideally functioning political economy that does not in actuality continue to exist, such a golden age representation may well contain elements of the "real economy" that serve to undermine the "ideal economy" being presented. The elements of internal "reality economics" appearing in the Solomonic text noted by Jobling are: the creation of a state apparatus for the imposition of tribute to provision the royal court and the new policy of forced labour in 1 Kings 4, 5 and 9. In terms of external economic relations, the unfavorable trade deals made with Hiram of Tyre (1 Kgs 5:7–12, 7:13–14, 9:10–14) where Solomon imports luxury goods and skilled labour in exchange for domestic staple goods suggests to Jobling a situation where Solomon is the weaker trading partner. What interests me the most about Jobling's work here is how prostitution could be listed as a possible intruding element of "real economics" that undermines the economic utopia of the golden age. In fact, Jobling sees the isotopy of "sexuality" as absent from most of the Solomonic narrative until the very end in 1 Kings 11 where it emerges (the 1,000 wives and concubines who lead astray) and displaces "real economics" as the primary cause of Solomon's downfall. This is interesting given the fact that prostitution could be

institution of prostitution by colonials in Nairobi during the first part of this century. Prostitution provided colonials an economical solution to housing shortages for labourers and helped to replenish their labour power by providing access to commodified domestic and sexual labour after forced land seizures, in "Prostitution, Identity, and Class Consciousness in Nairobi during World War II," *Signs* 2:1 (1985), pp. 255–73.

19. Maria Mies, *Patriarchy and Accumulation on a World Scale: Women in the International Division of Labor* (New York: Zed Books, 1998), pp. 137–42.

20. Mies, *Patriarchy and Accumulation on a World Scale*, p. 137.

21. David Jobling, "'Forced Labor': Solomon's Golden Age and the Question of Literary Representation," *Semeia* 54 (1992), pp. 57–76.

included in both his categories of sexuality and economics that contribute to the unsustainability of the golden age utopian economy.

Within the categories of analysis used by Jobling, the presence of prostitution in Solomon's reign counts neither as sexuality nor economics. This corresponds with its frequent absence in most economic theory overall. However, when you read the prostitute episode of 1 Kgs 3:16–28 in conjunction with some of its modern day co-variables, many of them are also found in the Solomon narrative. In addition to the "reality economics" discussed by Jobling (forced labour, tribute/tax, trade imbalance), there are contradictory reports of militarism, an overall context of colonialism, and massive accumulation of wealth on the part of Solomon. In 1 Kgs 4:24–25 and 5:4 the text reports of no warfare and general peace during Solomon's reign. On the other hand, there are many military adversaries of Solomon who are listed in 1 Kgs 11:14–25, one of whom, Rezon of Aram-Damascus, made trouble for Solomon continually (1 Kgs 11:25). The overall story of Solomon as an inheritor of recently conquered territories and peoples- including Jebus/Jerusalem (1 Kings 4:20–21 and 9:20–22) is suggestive of a colonial situation where some sectors of the population benefited from the labour of those deemed non-Israelite. This could be the situation of the two prostitute women who already have a house in Jerusalem, even though Solomon, YHVH, and pharaoh's daughter do not. In addition, the first prostitute's testimony that "*ain zar*" was in the women's house, is usually rendered "no stranger" or "no client" but can also mean "no foreigner." This could be a slight glimpse of the situation from the women's perspective, if they were Jebusite. The dominant theme of Solomon's great accumulation of wealth runs throughout the Solomonic narrative, especially at 1 Kings 10, and also expressed by his monumental building projects of the temple in chapter 6 of 1 Kings and his palace in chapter 7. When reading the modern and ancient texts together, the presence of prostitution in Solomon's economy takes on a negative valence that possibly shows the negative impact his policies had on women. Women working as prostitutes within a context of colonialism, coerced labour, heavy taxation, militarism, trade imbalances, and disparities of wealth makes it questionable that this is a golden age economy for women. Prostitution is a very big business today, providing many governments with lots of taxable or fineable revenue. Solomon could be interpreted as taking symbolic control of the sex industry by exerting his sword wielding justice in the interests of consolidating his power. This sort of use of prostitutes as political pawns is exactly the sort of situation that many prostitutes today struggle against in their efforts to achieve justice. So far, what I have been trying to do is make visible and denaturalize the presence of prostitution in the narrative depiction of Solomon's political economy through juxtaposition with some modern theorizing that contextualizes the role of prostitution in economies that are unfavorable to women.

Sex Worker Standpoint on Solomon and the Two Prostitutes

Contemporary prostitutes have to deal with the criminal justice system as "criminals" and as "unfit mothers." When SWOP activists read this story, two levels of justice are operative for contemporary sex workers: the risky, corrupt justice system that exists and the desire for authentic justice and relief from violence that drives prostitutes to organize politically. In the corrupt court system that exists, prostitutes experience violence in addition to the daily violence associated with their jobs. This violence is bolstered by the sad truth that perpetrators of crimes against sex workers generally receive immunity from persecution for their crimes. Prostitutes are commonly seen as "getting what they deserve" when they are assaulted, raped, murdered, coerced or blackmailed. It was very clear from the onset that this story of Solomon is a negative depiction of justice for prostitutes or mothers in general, because Solomon uses the threat of violence to dispense justice. The SWOP readers were divided over how to interpret the significance of the women's prostitute identity and whether or not it was possible to be in solidarity with both of the prostitute mothers. Therefore, again, we had a majority and minority reading of Solomon's riddle.

The threat of violence and access to equal protection before the law co-exist in this biblical story in a disturbing mix that is both true and false to the experiences of contemporary sex workers. In the Solomon story, the crime committed against one of the prostitutes is by another prostitute. One prostitute has stolen the child of another prostitute after accidentally killing her own child, or, one prostitute, whose own child has died, is abusing the legal system in order to steal the child of the other prostitute. Or, perhaps one of the women is so bereft she is in utter denial about the death of her child and wants to replace it with the other woman's child. While conflict, rivalry, or violence does occur among prostitutes, this is not where the major threat of crime and violence usually comes from, and where such rivalry does occur, it is seen as a consequence of vertical violence from those who wield coercive power over the lives of prostitute women. The story portrays the Solomonic court as the intervening hero who can protect the prostitutes from one another. Police and social workers are also depicted likewise today in anti-prostitution politics. However, the more realistic threat of coercive state violence is also represented in the Solomonic judgment story. It is this element of violent abusive treatment by the legal establishment that has the most verisimilitude for prostitutes. Solomon threatens to sever the living child with a sword and the threat is real enough that one woman thereby withdraws her justice claim. Ironically enough, it is at this point that one of the prostitutes realizes that the judge is more of a threat than her co-worker. That the mother has to give up her claim to justice in order to receive justice severely undermines this story's ability to represent ideal justice even for "a pair of disreputable prostitutes." This kind of justice is a performative contradiction.[22] This contradiction combined with Solomon's violent legal methods make it doubtful that other prostitutes would willingly return to his law court. To the extent that this story exemplifies the Solomonic justice system as a whole, it has implications for all Israel. Perhaps the people of Israel are not "in awe from the presence of the king," but literally "scared off from the presence of the king" in the concluding verse in 1 Kgs 3:28. The Hebrew supports either translation: ויראו מפני המלך.

Majority SWOP Reading

A consistent feature of both the majority and minority readings of SWOP is that Solomon's court is a toxic justice system for prostitutes. This assessment is because it is a place of violence toward sex workers, an experience that is still a very common one for prostitutes today. Scarlot is emphatic about emphasizing the violence: "Yeah, it was a bluff. It's still abusive and it's still sick...to turn around and say you wanna push the heroism of a prostitute in a story that really should be focused on this violence...I still say that the overriding situation in this is that it is ridiculous that this king is going to cut the baby in half!" Even Carol Stuart, who denies the significance of the prostitute identity could agree about this characterization of Solomon: "When I first heard this story, I was horrified at Solomon, who is this creature with the sword?" However, in the majority reading the prostitute identity is lifted up and analyzed as significant. An attempt is made to be in sympathy with the "other mother" not just the one who the story deems as the real mother who gave up her

---

22. See Terry Eagleton's discussion of performative contradictions in *Ideology: An Introduction* (New York: Verso, 1991), p. 26, as language that means one thing but does something contrary to its meaning, somewhat like prostitution law in general.

claim to save the child. We agreed that we did not know who the real mother in fact was and whether the real mother was the one awarded the child. The text is ambiguous on this point of true biological identity but clearly wishes to show us who is the most *deserving* mother. The good prostitute mother is pitted against the bad prostitute mother, and we might be suspicious therefore of how they are depicted. The majority reading, this time, goes against the grain a bit. The division of women as good and bad mothers is something that SWOP readers resisted to forge a better reading. The key themes that go into this interpretation are: prostitutes as mothers, their bad experiences with the judicial system, and if/how to empathize with the "other mother."

Prostitute Mothers

Prostitutes as mothers seeking justice is an important theme in the SWOP majority reading just as it is important within a prostitutes' rights theory framework overall. Motherhood is a common theme for women in prostitution, and it exits in the Solomon narrative. "Pros are women from all walks of life but above all single mothers...through prostitution we provide the welfare the state won't provide for us and our children, for student husbands and elderly parents."[23] The Solomon story seems to make the motherhood of these prostitutes a consequence of prostitution. This gives a false impression that the prostitutes are mothers because they are promiscuous and immoral people. The contrary is true to life for most sex workers, they are mothers first, or daughters or wives, and very often, the sex work itself is a kind of self-sacrifice made by mothers in order to survive economically. Years back when discussing this story with me, Rachel West of US PROS said, "Emphasize that prostitutes are mothers trying to support their children." The prostitutes' rights movement began in Lyons, France, in 1975 when over a hundred prostitutes occupied a church sanctuary. They hung a banner outside the church of St. Nizier that read: "Our children don't want their mothers to go to prison." The first paragraph of their "Letter to the Public" and to Giscard d'Estaing, President of France, stated: "We are mothers talking to you. Women trying to bring up their children alone as best we can, and today are scared of losing them. Yes we are prostitutes, but if we are prostitutes, it is not because we are depraved; it is the way we have found to deal with the problems in our lives."[24] A recent

23. Margaret Valentino and Mavis Johnson, "On the Game and on the Move," p. 28.

24. Claude Jaget, "Hookers in the House of the Lord," in *Prostitutes—Our Life*, p. 46.

survey of migrant sex workers in the Dominican Republic confirms this profile of the typical prostitute as a mother:

> Seven or more out of 10 are mothers who work in different locations than where they live, 51 percent of whom do not receive financial assistance from the biological fathers of their children. Twenty percent have an additional income to sex work. Contrary to the myths about causes of sex work, less than 10 percent of these women are victims of abuses or maltreatment by their parents...The age when they began sex work for money is the most consistent finding in the studies, motivated principally by economic needs beginning, on average between the ages of 18 and 20, approximately three to four years after their first sexual contact and for the most, after having had one to three children.[25]

Our SWOP interpretation session of the Solomon story followed on the Rahab reading, so the situations of the prostitutes in both stories were comparable to our readers. Robyn Few exclaimed: "Martyrs; Martyrdom! Women are martyrs. We have Rahab who gives up her whole town to save her family. And now we're talking about another woman who will give up her own fucking child. Martyrs!" Scarlot agreed that this story was, in fact, constructing how good mothers should behave, "they want mother's to be totally selfless." A mother who behaved in the expected manner will perhaps get what she wants but a rebellious mother would be totally shunned. This strong expectation that mothers be self-sacrificing caused Sweet to wonder if perhaps the first mother knew this and played the game the right way and won: "if she is knowledgeable about how justice is being doled out up to that point, who is to say she is not being manipulative of what the likely outcome would be?"

Corrupt Courts

Many mainline biblical scholars see in the Solomon judgment story a situation where the two prostitutes have equal access to the law. Walsh sees the king "attending to justice even in a case involving the least important of his people."[26] Nelson extols this example of "God's justice that is fair to all, even to a pair of disreputable prostitutes."[27] Given that equal protection is what so many modern day sex workers struggle for, this kind of reading has an immediate seductive appeal that needs further examination because

---

25. Kamala Kempadoo, "COIN and MODEMU in the Dominican Republic," in Kempadoo, Kamala and Jo Doezema (eds.), *Global Sex Workers*, p. 262.

26. J.T. Walsh, *1 Kings* (Collegeville, MN: Liturgical Press, 1996), p. 80.

27. Richard Nelson, *First and Second Kings* (Atlanta, GA: John Knox Press, 1987), p. 39.

it is at this surface level of appeal that ideology often is most potent. Because the effects of state policies upon prostitute women are often negative whether prohibitive or tolerant, we cannot simply assume that this equal access is depicting a liberating justice system for sex workers. It is therefore important to be careful about what we label justice or liberation. Also given the conflicting legislative evidence in other parts of the Hebrew Bible it is difficult to determine which, if any, of the above types of state policies regarding prostitution is most reflected in the Solomon story. Lev. 21:7 and 14 prohibits priests from marrying prostitutes, defiled or divorced women and a priest's daughter who becomes a prostitute is to be burned to death in 21:9. Furthermore Lev. 19:29 prohibits Israel from prostituting its daughters. However, other biblical texts narrate the buying and selling of sex without moral censure, for example when Judah or Samson or the spies in Jericho go to see a prostitute in Gen. 38:15–18 or Judg. 16:1, Josh. 2:1. According to Judg. 11:1, the hero Jephthah's mother was a prostitute. For these reasons, Elaine Goodfriend summarizes that "Israelite society's attitude toward prostitution was decidedly negative; yet despite legislation intended to outlaw this institution…the prostitute seems to be tolerated."[28] The sort of "tolerance" of prostitution that the Solomon story seems to imply needs to be qualified by the experiences of sex workers today who claim that "tolerance is always discriminatory"[29] or who ask "doesn't the problem lie in this hypocritical 'tolerance'—one of the problems at least?"[30]

The extent to which the Solomon judgment story realistically reproduces the abusive experiences that prostitutes commonly encounter in the legal establishment indicates that the story assumes a twisted material reality that continues to accept the violence of the state against poor women and that expects the obedient acquiescence of mothers for the sake of their children. Veronica summed it up aptly: "he is allowed to even suggest murdering a baby without being a bad guy but if she calls his bluff she is an

28. Elaine Goodfriend, "Prostitution," *Anchor Bible Dictionary* (New York: Doubleday, 1992, V), p. 505.

29. Leite, "The Prostitute Movement in Brazil," p. 421.

30. Claude Jaget, "Hookers in the House of the Lord," in Claude Jaget (ed.), *Prostitutes—Our Life*, p. 38—here is the full context preceding the question: "linked to the problem of the "tolerance" of prostitution, which in fact is what exists, and which allows huge profits to be made from prostitution, either by the State (with the system in force in Lyons) or by a few individuals (in the German system, for example); all thanks to the work of young women who are exploited by society without any respect for them."

31. See Terry Eagleton's discussion in *Ideology: An Introduction,* of "naturalization" as an ideological strategy, p. 59.

evil mother." Since most readers can understand this story positively as an example of justice, "even to a pair of disreputable prostitutes" shows how naturalized such abuse of prostitutes is for many people.[31] Most current prostitution law operates with a similar assumption that even if prostitutes are victims they do not know what is best for themselves and need to be coerced into rehabilitation by the state. This maintains an emphasis on mental pathology as the main cause of prostitution, not political economy.

Would a pair of prostitutes even go to Solomon's court, especially to a judge known for violence, mused Robyn: "they went before him with this argument, they took the argument to him. So there was that much trust. I mean, I don't know that I would take my argument to an invading conqueror that I didn't trust. So this one woman who needed justice, they went there, somehow they went before him with this argument." Kimberlee's first response was "why aren't they going straight to jail for reporting themselves as prostitutes?" Veronica was stunned by the fact that the prostitutes were even allowed to be mothers because in today's world prostitutes have their children taken away: "our government, operates as the husband and takes the children away if you're a prostitute. So I actually thought this is a bit of a more progressive culture, isn't it, because the baby gets to stay with its mom, the prostitute was allowed to keep her child. Now, I don't know if maybe they felt that they had a social system where they could say well you're the child of a prostitute or you're a bastard child so therefore were not worried about prostitutes having children because their children will never become part of accepted society." Another SWOP reader, Shemena, had experienced custody battles from the point of view of the child being fought over. Shemena's mother fought to keep custody of her children despite the courts declaration of her unfitness due to being schizophrenic. For this reason Shemena cheered for the rebellious mom in the story who refused to give up her claim even though this insistence on justice was considered harmful to the child. The experience gave Shemena the ability to see the other mother in a sympathetic light. Another real life parallel that helped everyone to frame the situation of the mothers was the example of San Francisco's rights activist Daisy Anarchy.

Daisy Anarchy has been in a years long custody battle to get back her child. She also has controversial strategies of activism with which not all SWOP readers agree but nonetheless almost everyone had to admit she was a sister in the struggle for sex worker rights. Robyn insisted: "what about the Daisy Anarchy mothers? Daisy Anarchy is a resistance fighter! OK come on, there is a fight, it is a fight for justice."

Solidarity with Both Mothers

The initial "reading with" I did of this passage was some years ago with Sweet and another woman. They drew this conclusion about the situation in Solomon's court: "It is like a no win situation. So it is trying to figure out the best way to work in the situation that is already bad." In the collaborative reading we did then and later with SWOP we spent much time trying to empathize with the mother who agreed to the splitting of the baby. Lasine' theory of maternal envy was seen by many as misogynistic and anti-prostitute. With the examples of real life rebellious prostitute's rights activists such as Daisy Anarchy, and the martyrdom of the mother and her seven sons in 4 Maccabees (she endured torture and the torture and death of her seven sons rather than go apostate), we tried our best to honour both of the prostitute mothers in the Solomon story. It was very difficult because it conflicted with one of the primary definitions of a prostitute as one who sacrifices for her family. Not all could agree about the relevance of analyzing the mothers as prostitutes nor could most identify with the response of the second mother. Everyone could agree that Solomon was not the hero and his courtroom was unjust. In the majority reading we came to see two prostitute mothers offering two kinds of responses to an inherently unjust, abusive situation. They were forced to respond in the presence of the unjust judge's violence. The one mother withdrew her claim in the face of violence towards the child, which is the most understandable response. The other mother gets enraged at his violent scare tactic and decides to call his bluff. Fed up with a system of justice that continually requires mothers to sacrifice, sacrifice, sacrifice, she realizes at this moment that her submission to violence is based upon her rationalization that things will get worse if she protests and/or that the violence will go away if she submits. So she angrily rejects the subject position of self-sacrificing mother and decides to give Solomon back his violence by calling his bluff. The difficulties we had in creating this scenario mostly had to do with how much the narrative context and our world needed to change to allow for this understanding of the women's responses. Very, very few mothers would do this. A rebellious response is still hard to think plausible, recognize, much less valorize, "that's the worst possible crime against society—'poor things' are fine as long as they let themselves be pitied, but not when they rebel. In rebelling, they violently exposed the hidden, what's 'not said,' what's 'not seen.'" [32]

Solidarity with both mothers was explored in our subsequent SWOP group readings but not unanimously. One hinge of the dispute was over

32. Claude Jaget, "It's a Man's World," *Prostitutes—Our Life*, p. 186.

the significance of the prostitute identity in the text. Most of our readers agreed that the women were named as prostitutes for a reason and that we needed to explore that emphasis since popular understanding totally omitted the mothers' identity as prostitutes. Veronica asserted a good explanation echoed by many:

> The reason, in my opinion, that they have to be prostitutes is really clear, because of the fact that you were either with your father or you were with your husband and if you were with your father or your husband you wouldn't even be allowed an audience with the king. You would be back at the home and your father or your husband would speak for you and put the moral quandary before the king. You'd be at home, you wouldn't get to talk anyway.

The identification of the women as prostitutes was to explain why they lived together and why no man represented their petition to the king. For Carol Stuart, "all women that are not invisible are whores." Since any woman outside the family structure would be seen as a prostitute we shouldn't give it too much weight, thought Carol. "So they are whores! They live together, maybe they are lesbians. Substitute doctor in there or lawyer, nazi smazi from prostitute; why is it even relevant?"

Kimberlee wondered with some feminist scholars if perhaps the text needed the mothers to be prostitutes because of the common assumption that prostitutes are immoral: "they had to be of ill moral character to be willing to go and steal another woman's baby and replace it with (a dead one)." The illogical character of the prevalent stereotype is illustrated by Kimberlee:

> When I was coming back from Taiwan I was waiting at the airport for my flight and there was this Marine who was on layover from Okinawa on his way back to the states and I told him I was there, ya know, for the whore culture festival and everything and he was like 'well isn't being a prostitute kinda immoral?' and I said, 'listen, did you just sign a four year contract to kill people? So don't tell me giving people happiness is wrong when you have a responsibility to kill brown people, not just anyone, specifically brown people, that is what *your* job is!'

Assumptions about the immorality of prostitutes are a commonplace. There is a popular assumption, including in the Bible, that a prostitute's word has questionable or no truth-value. As in the case of the San Francisco woman, Erica Baldwin, who was nearly hammered to death by serial rapist Jack Bokin, not believing the word of prostitutes can have death dealing consequences. Baldwin was attacked while Jack Bokin was out of jail on low bail for allegedly raping two other prostitute women and had a history of sexual violence.[33] His subsequent trial, which I monitored with USPROS, dwelled excessively on the credibility of the victims as truth tellers. The Green River Killer, Gary Leon Ridgeway, who murdered as many as 70 prostitutes over two decades in the Seattle area, had actually been identified very early on by a prostitute.[34] Failure to believe prostitutes has the consequence that violent criminals get away or are acquitted. Another assumption, though not explicit, is that by a threat of violence one can elicit truth.[35] A threat of violence can just as easily elicit an answer desperately calculated to appease the violent person. The failure of Solomon to use other methods of inquiry to discover the truth is sometimes noted by scholars. Solomon could have cross-examined the women, looked for other unknown witnesses, character witnesses, or he could have looked for physical evidence such as the babies' navels.[36] But as Phyllis Bird concludes, "he does not attempt to discern the truth thru interrogation—a hopeless approach with habitual liars."[37] Claudia Camp reads this assumption as well with the help of wisdom writing that characterizes harlot speech as deceitful: "female sexuality that exists outside of male control functions as a metaphor for deceitful speech, and the character of the 'harlot' thus poses the ultimate test of kingly wisdom."[38] Due to this problem of being unable to solve the dilemma of one prostitute's word against the other's, Solomon is rarely criticized for his violent judicial scare tactics, which are excused as or assumed to be a trick, ruse, trap, or bluff. But since Solomon is the only person in the story wielding the actual power to sever the child in two, the common criticism of the mother who says "let him be neither mine nor

33. Jim Herron Zamora, "Suspect's Sex Charges Date to Mid-'60s," *San Francisco Examiner*, 17 October 1997 and Athena Douris, "The Sounds of Silence," *Alice Magazine*, January 2000.

34. Sheriff David Reichert, *Chasing the Devil: My Twenty Year Quest to Capture the Green River Killer* (New York: Little, Brown and Co., 2004), p. 131. A pimp also identified the killer in 1983 but this wasn't followed up on by police, p. 103.

35. Gina Hens-Piazza, *Of Methods, Monarchs, and Meanings: A Sociorhetorical Approach to Exegesis* (Macon, GA: Mercer University Press: 1996), p. 147. Stuart Lasine in the "Riddle of Solomon's Judgement and the Riddle of Human Nature in the Hebrew Bible," *JSOT* 45 (1989), pp. 61–86, pp. 63–66.

36. If the babies were born several days apart, the degree of healing where the umbilical cord was severed would indicate relative age.

37. Phyllis Bird, "Harlot as Heroine: Narrative Art and Social Presupposition in Three Old Testament Texts," *Semeia* 46 (1989), pp. 119–39, p. 133.

38. Claudia Camp, "1 and 2 Kings" in C.A. Newsom and Sharon Ringe (eds.), *The Women's Bible Commentary* (Louisville, KY: Westminster/John Knox Press, 1992), p. 100.

hers, sever," may be misplaced. Scholars who point out the violent, justice-betraying behavior of Solomon's sword, as a travesty of his life-protecting role, get closest to validating the experience of today's prostitute women who seek justice.[39] According to Gina Hens Piazza, Solomon's sword "blackmails motherhood."[40] For sex workers currently demanding justice, the violence of the legal system is the main problem they wish to rectify. Many re-experience violence when coerced into well-meaning but ill-conceived "rehabilitation" programs instead of jail time. The institutional threat of loosing custody is frequently used to blackmail the motherhood of prostitutes, and poor women in general, to coerce certain behaviours demanded by the state.

The scholarly feminist reading of biblical prostitution that accepts as a presupposition of the text that prostitutes are liars was ultimately rejected as harmful by SWOP members. This stereotype is extremely dangerous to the health of prostitutes and needs to not be reinforced in any way. When I raised the issue, Carol Stuart immediately reacted strongly: "That's awful, that's awful. No, that's horseshit. Is this, Melissa Farley? Horseshit!" When I explain that the biblical scholars don't say this *is true* but note that the text of Proverbs does depict prostitutes as deceitful, Veronica still wants to know: "do the feminists think that that is a true assessment of prostitutes? And do they find fault with that supposition, is my question?" Melissa Farley is a local abolitionist feminist who does not find fault with that presupposition and vehemently denies the truth value of SWOP rights activists' words. Farley argues that all prostitution is inherently abusive and thus implies that sex worker rights activists must have a false consciousness if they deny their victim status and demand rights rather than rescue.[41] Feminist biblical scholars perhaps need to be more explicit

39. Hens-Piazza, *Of Methods, Monarchs, and Meanings*, p. 145, "a sword courts an ambiguous meaning" and Lasine, in "The Riddle of Solomon's Judgment," p. 66 and p. 79 n.6, discusses the possible travesty of the sword symbolism, but forgives all because Solomon is "just pretending."

40. Hens-Piazza, *Of Methods, Monarchs, and Meanings*, p. 153.

41. Prostitutes' rights activists have also complained about Farley's research methodology which they say has often distorted the views of sex workers who participate in her studies, in other words, they claim that her research is unethical. One activist reports that "Melissa interviewed prostitutes that our friends in South Africa—SWEAT—helped recruit and Melissa was dishonest in what she told the outreach project and when the findings came out (they were told she did participatory research and they would be able to comment on her analysis, but were not given that opportunity) they felt like she totally misstated what they had said."

about what theory of prostitution they operate with since it is such a controversial issue among feminists. Many seem to operate with an implicit anti-prostitution framework without knowing how contested this stance is by sex worker activists.

A materialist reading, like that of David Jobling's is favored by SWOP readers, but which includes prostitution as part of the economy and gendered division of labor. Since he does not do this kind of gender analysis on the role of sexual commerce in comparable political economies, I have provided it (pp. 96–98) as a background with which to understand why prostitution might exist in Solomon's golden age economy and in our own. I have done this with writings from a sex workers rights framework which gives more detail to the common assertion that "prostitution is a job that a lot of women get into because they are starving, because they have to feed their families and take care of it," as Robyn puts it. Or, according to Gayle: "What else can they do to make money and to support their family? Usually they are single mothers and they have kids and they are women of color. So what are they gonna do except a regular job pays em $10 an hour cuz they don't have the education. *That* is the crime." To be rehabilitated back into the previous situation of non-living wages which so many mothers are rejecting by entering the sex industry, is understandably ridiculous to SWOP readers. It is unfortunately a consequence of viewing prostitution as a moral problem and not a political economy problem. The economic contextualization of prostitution is something rights activists want to keep front and centre in all theorizing and policy making about prostitution. Liberation readings however need to incorporate gender into their theories and not as an add-on to existing male oriented theory but as constitutive of all poverty. In a forthcoming

See Melissa Farley's website at http://www.prostitutionresearch.com and a book she recently edited, *Prostitution, Trafficking, and Traumatic Stress* (New York: Haworth Press, 2003), for the theory of prostitution that currently is influencing lawmakers worldwide to create more stringent legal penalties for the sex industry. For example, in the US the new "end demand" amendments of the 2005 HR 972 or reauthorization of TVPA or Trafficking Victims Protection Act. For more information from a sex worker rights perspective go to: http://www.bestpracticespolicy.org/policyupdate.html. Many other countries such as Finland, UK, South Korea are currently enacting or proposing similar increases in criminalization. Rights activists are opposed to more criminalization and find it harmful to prostitutes and even to the task of combating trafficking and child prostitution which are already illegal for other reasons, that is to say child abuse and slavery are different crimes.

section, I take up the task of analyzing the emerging monarchy as an economy that is bad for women.

Minority SWOP Reading

The minority reading interestingly enough incorporates the traditional reading that deems the prostitute identity of the mothers as not significant, and therefore, there is no need to be in sympathy with the bad mother because she is just crazy. In this reading the fact that the mothers are prostitutes is irrelevant. A good mother, prostitute or not, will always choose to save her child, period. This finding is consistent with the primary SWOP definition of a prostitute as one who sacrifices to sustain her family. Carol Stuart was the main voice of the minority opinion. Her staunch insistence that the "other mother" is just a "crazy person" is consistent with what she originally defines as a prostitute back in the Rahab reading: "She is a whore. She gave up her people, so she could gain, whatever financial gain, which was for her family, her family's survival. OK? That is absolutely the definition of prostitution." To then refuse to do this sacrifice is in flat contradiction with what primarily is a prostitute: "That's not a prostitute, that's just a crazy person. Just like the other person is just a mother, they are both mothers, it's irrelevant that they are prostitutes." So, if it is not relevant to analyze the mothers as prostitutes, we need only focus on the heroism of the true mother. Not the defiance of the bad mother, not the wisdom of Solomon, but the heroism and wisdom of the good mother is the whole point of the story. The traditional Jewish telling of the story emphasizes the mother, not Solomon. In the traditional telling the mothers are not presented as prostitutes because it isn't really important. Carol Stuart who grew up with this story as told in the synagogue was adamant about maintaining the traditional reading. "In the reform temple you rejoice over the mother not Solomon, Solomon was irrelevant." Similar emphasis on the heroism of the good mother can be found in feminist biblical scholarship as well.[42]

Carol could entertain sympathy for the other mother but maintained that this is not the point of the story: "I think there is a tragedy about a person who has lost her kid and I think that we should all feel something and we could all feel something but that is not what the story is about…this

42. Carole Fontaine, "The Bearing of Wisdom on the Shape of 2 Samuel 11–12 and 1 Kings 3," in Athalya Brenner (ed.), *A Feminist's Companion to Samuel and Kings* (Sheffield: Sheffield Academic Press, 1994), pp. 143–67 and Annelies van Heijst "Beyond Divided Thinking: Solomon's Judgment and the Wisdom-traditions of Women," *Louvain Studies* 19 (1994), pp. 99–117.

story is about what to do for your own child. This story is not about whether or not you're a whore or whether or not to give up your kid, or whose to blame." She agreed with Stuart Lasine on the absolute determinacy of this text and seeing the mothers as mothers: "Far from inviting us to explain the women's behavior in terms of their profession and low station, the fact that the women are harlots is designed to focus our attention precisely on the fact that their distinguishing characteristic is motherhood."[43] When we added to the discussion a real life parallel of Daisy Anarchy as an example of the rebellious sex worker activist mother, Carol still insisted that this was not a strategy that she would ever affirm. The main problem that Carol always came back to was "what is the strategy of killing the child? What is the strategy?"

Most of us could agree with Carol that a mother who would risk letting her child be harmed is quite a rarity: "let me tell you, the guy with the sword is way more violent, you have no idea how violent that motherfucker is and he will do it. He will do it…I ask you, if you were the mother, of you own child, what you would do, and I know what the answer is!" Due to Carol's argumentation, Robyn and I wavered over if we could really ever truthfully conceive of a mother who would call a killer's bluff, "OK, I am sorry Avaren you do too, any mother would know that truthfully. A woman who cares about her child is going to sacrifice herself no matter what, no matter what." Ultimately, despite the exercise in sympathy with the other mother, solidarity with her was difficult to maintain in a very strong way.

A Bad Economy for Women

It is clear that many of the elements of an exploitive economy exist in the texts of Solomon. What I will next examine is how women are depicted in the court narratives of David and Solomon and what this bodes for women under the emerging monarchy or during the Deuternomic reform. What is portrayed in these accounts it is the transition of Israel from the non-statist anarchy of Judges to the era of the monarchy. It is widely thought that there was a Deuternomic editor during the time period of King Josiah who was responsible for the particular ideology on kingship that blames bad kings for the misfortunes that befall Israel.[44] The Deuteronomic editors

43. Lasine, "The Riddle of Solomon's Judgment," p. 70.

44. For a detailed description of the characteristic traits of the Deuteronomistic Historian which are the bases for arguing an editorial unity, see the work of Martin Noth, *The Deuteronomistic History* (Sheffield: Sheffield Academic Press, 2001).

urge religious reforms and most particularly, a strict centralized place of worship in Jerusalem. Thus, due to editing of these narratives different voices can be heard, some old some new, such as those typologized by Polzin as the voices of "critical traditionalism" and the voices "authoritarian dogmatism."[45] In addition to this typology is that of the "Deuteronomic Template" as discussed by David Penchansky.[46] The "Deuteronomic Template" coerces readers to understand Israelite oppression as punishment for their sins, but the template frames other older stories that might perhaps have a different message. Wherever it comes from, there is definitely a voice critical of kingship that begins the narrative of monarchy in Israel. P. Kyle McCarter identifies an anti-monarchical voice when Israel demands a king in 1 Sam. 8:10–18.[47] God is against there being a king other than himself and tells Samuel to warn the people of the pitfalls of having a king:

> These will be the ways of the king who will reign over you: he will take your sons and appoint them to his chariots and to be his horsemen, and to run before his chariots; and he will appoint for himself commanders of thousands and commanders of fifties, and some to plow his ground and to reap his harvest, and to make his implements of war and the equipment of his chariots. *He will take your daughters to be his perfumers and cooks and bakers.* He will take the best of your fields and vineyards and olive orchards and give them to courtiers. He will take one tenth of your grain and of your vineyards and give it to his officers and his courtiers. He will take your male and *female slaves*, and the best of your cattle and donkeys, *and put them to work.* He shall take one tenth of your flock, and *you shall be his slaves.* And in that day you will cry out because of your king, who you have chosen for yourselves, but the Lord will not answer you on that day.

The crux of the warning is that having a monarch means extraction; having a king will cost the people dearly. In the list of what will be taken from the Israelites by kings are numbered daughters and female slaves, indicating that women will play a key role in this economy. Their labor as cooks, perfumers and bakers and slaves "put to work" will be taken from the people of Israel. In actuality, the narratives of the ensuing monarch show several

---

45. Polzin, Moses and the Deuteronomist: A Literary Study of the Deuteronomic History (New York: Seabury Press, 1980), p. 84.

46. David Penchansky, "Up for Grabs: A Tentative Proposal for Doing Ideological Criticism," *Semeia* 59 (1992), pp. 35–41.

47. P. Kyle McCarter, *1 Samuel* (Garden City, NY: Anchor Bible, Doubleday, 1980), p. 161.

women taken by King David and Solomon. How they fare in this new political economy might be instructive at least for demonstrating symbolic control of women in this text. While, the most narrative detail pertains to women at the top of the social hierarchy, what happens to these might be a good indication that things have occurred pretty much according to God's prediction in 1 Sam. 8:13 and 16. Bad economies often mean increases in the prostitution industry, which might then account for why the only two persons for whom Solomon's wisdom are displayed, are in fact, prostitutes.

Thus the treatment of Michal, Abigail, Bathsheba, the existence of multiple wives and extensive harems for both David and Solomon are perhaps indicative of a bad economy for women, where women are "taken" by monarchs and officers who are commanders of thousands (as was David for Saul before he became king himself). I assume that the reason they are taken is not only for their reproductive labor but also for their labor role in the new royal economy as outlined by God in 1 Samuel 8.

Many of the women who appear in the narratives are used as pawns for royal legitimation and then discarded, like when Saul gives his daughter Michal to David at 1 Sam. 18:20–28, then she is taken away and married to Palti/el at 25:44, then retaken by David when he is about the become king at 2 Sam. 3:14–16. Likewise at 2 Sam. 16:21–23, Absolom publicly takes David's concubines to bed as a way to assert his kingship, an act which was predicted by Nathan as a punishment for the crime of adultery with Bathsheba at 2 Sam. 12:11. The ten violated concubines of David were then discarded to live out their lives as widows according to 2 Sam. 20:3. When Adonijah requests as wife the beautiful Abishag, David's bed warmer, David takes it as treason against himself (1 Kgs 2:7,12, 23). Three different texts appear to indicate that David also took over the former wives of Saul. 1 Sam. 25:43 says that David married Ahinoam and 14:50 says that Ahinoam was Saul's wife. At 2 Sam. 12:8, when Nathan scorns King David for his adultery with Bathsheba, the word of God reproaches David with these words: "I gave you your master's house and, your master's wives into your bosom," which is a further indication that David's wife Ahinoam used to be married to Saul. These texts show that taking a wife or a daughter of a king gives one a claim to the throne.

Other wives of David are taken for the king's desire. While Michal loved David she never bore him a child and he is depicted as indifferent to her. David's wife Abigail was married to a rich fool, Nabal, who refused a possible shakedown by David's army of 600 men (1 Sam. 25:7,15–16). Nabal refused to feed the men of David in payment for not harming his flocks and shepherds (1 Sam. 25:11). David vowed to kill him and everyone belonging to him for this insult but Abigail, Nabal's wife, intervenes to stop the massacre by feeding his men: "two hundred loaves, two skins of wine, five sheep ready dressed, five measures of parched grain, one hundered clusters of raisens, and two hundred cakes of figs" (1 Sam. 25:18). Here David is depicted as demanding and taking the goods of a fellow Judahite and soon after, his wife as well. David marries Nabal's wife, Abigail after Nabal myseriously dies at the hand of God (1 Sam. 25:38).

With Solomon's mother, Bathsheba, David cannot wait but takes her even before her husband is killed through royal machinations on the battlefield. Bathsheba's husband, Uriah the Hittite, is loyally off fighting the Ammonites for David when David takes his wife. When she becomes pregnant by David, David tries to cover up his adultery by having Uriah sleep with Bathsheba so that her child will be thought her husband's. When this fails, David arranges with Joab to make sure Uriah dies in battle. When Uriah dies, David takes his wife as his own. God is displeased by such arrogant expropriation and cursed David with the same fate. The parable told by Nathan likened Bathsheba to a poor man's lamb who a rich man takes and eats despite the fact that he already has a large flock of his own. Thus again, woman, wealth and property are intertwined in a narrative that shows God's prediction in 1 Samuel 8 to be true.

Solomon is credited with having 700 wives and 300 concubines, on top of his marriage to Pharaoh's daughter (1 Kgs 11:3). These women are blamed for the downfall of the kingdom, for having led the king astray and for his tolerance of the foreign religious practices all these women brought with them. Given that Solomon is preeminently known as the richest king ever, perhaps all the women who belonged to him played a role in the production of his wealth. One thousand wives and concubines is a veritable factory worth of labor and not all of it need have been sexual or reproductive. Indeed it is during Solomon's reign where the God's prediction of royal expropriation comes full swing. Administrative officers are appointed with tithing and forced labor instituted in Kgs 4:6–7, 5:13–17 and 9:15–22. Jeroboam, whose rebellion split Israel in two, was the officer from the house of Joseph in charge of forced labor for Solomon (1 Kgs 11:28). Jeroboam's rebellion did not occur until the death of Solomon but it was instigated because the people were weary of their corveé work load: "your father made our yoke heavy, therefore now lighten the hard service of your father and his heavy yoke that he placed upon us, and we will serve you" (1 Kgs 12:4). The officer who was in charge of all the forced labor for Solomon, Adoniram, was stoned to death when the request was refused (1 Kgs 5:14 and 12:18).

This death would have been a good motivation for Jeroboam to lead a rebellion. While many see the extreme erotic behavior of Solomon (1000 wives and concubines) as separate from the overall economy, there is no good reason to assume that the women in Israel were not overworked as well. These were a lot of women in the king's court who we can assume *worked* for Solomon, since at 1 Sam. 8:13 and 16 it states that the daughters and slaves are taken in order to work.

Feminist and critical legal scholars of the Deuteronomic law have concluded that the Deuteronomy law code of chapters 12–26 indicate a constriction of women's rights. The legal ideology of the Deuteronomist can also be detected in the Deuteronomistic Historian level redaction of the Deuteronomistic History that extends from Joshua to the end of 2 Kings. Feminist Marxist scholar Gale Yee has done several analyses of the Deuteronomic ideology in conjunction with the role of the changing modes of production and its effect upon the lives of women during the monarchy as well as the periods of colonial rule that followed. She surmises that part of the negative ideology of "women as evil" serves as a mechanism for the state and religious institutions to control female sexuality and domestic labor in order to extract more labor.[48] This ideology she roots in the historical contexts of monarchy and the Josianic religious reform, which centralized worship in Jerusalem. The process of centralization first begins with the institution of monarchy itself which centralized power in the new state and away from independent extended families in which women might have exercised more informal power due to their important economic functions. According to Yee "Solomon's administration set into motion the breakdown of kinship authority through the redistricting of his kingdom."[49] For women, the laws that ensue in emerging states tend to focus on restricting sexuality. Female sexuality becomes regulated by the state in the public sphere where women have less power. The Josianic religious reform, according to Yee, instituted a more efficient method of appropriating peasant surpluses since the king could not raise taxes. Instead Josiah "reorganized the collection of taxes, tributes and fees that were already assessed so they flowed directly into Jerusalem's coffers. He thus bypassed

48. Gale Yee, *Poor Banished Children of Eve: Women as Evil in the Hebrew Bible* (Minneapolis, MN: Fortress Press, 2003).
49. Yee, *Poor Banished Children of Eve*, p. 66.

the local leaders, who had been collecting these revenues for him, but who had been taking their cut."[50]

Scholars focused on the effects of the Deuteronomic Law on poor women (widows, orphans, and aliens) indicate that it exacerbated their situation rather than ameliorated it. Harold Bennett and Cheryl Anderson both argue similar points with regard to how this code immiserates the powerless and constructs violence through assymetrical penalties and privileges and the centralized worship which gives more economic control to the religious hierarchy receiving/controlling the tithes. The economic shift detected by Bennett in Deut. 12–26 is that already overburdened peasants are given the responsibility of providing economic relief to widows, orphans and aliens.[51] Meanwhile, by centralizing worship the priests centralized the appropriation of tithes and "positioned themselves to oversee the allocation of commodities and to guarantee an influx of grain, wine, and meat into their personal coffers, while using charity toward a category of socially weak, vulnerable persons as a pretext."[52] An already burdened peasantry may or may not have had the ability to assist the indigent in their midst. Furthermore, given the relatively small amount of surpluses obtained in small-holding peasant production and given the limited periodic distribution to those needing assistance, such persons might be driven into debt slavery or prostitution in order to attain the necessary sustenance to live.[53] In the realm of sexual regulation, Cheryl Anderson argues that the Deuteronomic Law is addressed to a male audience and directs them to control the sexuality of their women who are controllable because economically dependent on men. However, "the laws also sexualize the bodies of women not under the control of free Israelite men, such as prostitutes and foreign women."[54] This is due to the different penalties

---

50. Gale Yee, "Ideological Criticism: Judges 17–21 and the Dismembered Body," in Gale Yee (ed.), *Judges and Method: New Approaches in Biblical Studies* (Minneapolis, MN: Fortress Press, 1995), p.155.

51. Harold Bennett, *Injustice Made Legal: Deuteronomic Law and the Plight of Widows, Strangers and Orphans in Ancient Israel* (Grand Rapids, MI: Eerdmans, 2002), p. 168.

52. Bennett, *Injustice Made Legal*, p. 171.

53. Bennett, *Injustice Made Legal*, p. 120, note 17 and discussed by Cheryl Anderson, *Women, Ideology, and Violence: Critical Theory and the Construction of Gender in the Book of the Covenant and the Deuteronomic Law* (New York and London: T &T Clark, 2004), p. 56.

54. Anderson, *Women, Ideology, and Violence*, p. 75.

that apply to different categories of women: "by clearly penalizing some sexual encounters (those with a woman in the household of another privileged Israelite man) but not others, the Book of the Covenant (BC) and Deuteronomic Law (DL) indirectly sexualize non-privileged women."[55] It is the conclusion of Anderson that asymmetrical laws such as those in Deuteronomic Law construct violence against women, but most especially against non-Israelite and economically marginalized women. The texts of the Deuteronomistic History certainly portray symbolic control of the women around David and Solomon and the Deuteronomic Laws undergird this control as well.

Analysis of Differences between Biblical Scholars and SWOP Activists

In contrast to the Rahab story, the prostitute identity of the mothers was an issue of contention and not unanimously emphasized. The major point of consensus in this reading was the corrupt and violent nature of Solomon's court. It was hard to sustain the idea that the heroism of the mother is somehow constitutive of her being a prostitute and not simply a "motherly thing" as Carol asserts. Prostitutes who become rights activists are rarely mothers of underage children and if they are, they are retired. Only former prostitute mothers or those with grown children will risk drawing the attention of the authorities upon themselves. Current courts arrest or seize the children of prostitutes who seek justice.

A sex worker standpoint exposes the corrupt and violent nature of Solomon's court. This violence is invisible even to many liberation oriented biblical scholars. Prostitutes' lack of equal access to a justice system is also not generally apparent to most people in our own culture. Thus SWOP members uncover this institutional injustice in both contexts. Acceptance of this state of affairs hinges on common assumptions that only sexually "decent" or "respectable" women are worthy of justice or have a right to resist violence, especially sexual violence. What I have come to see is that prostitutes' rights activists actually have an image problem similar to the unpopular "other mother" who won't give up her justice claim. The mother who gives in, who vacates her claim to custody for the sake of the child is much more palatable in a feminist politics that sees prostitutes as victims. Shamelessly demanding rights controverts that victim image and it is at that point that many withdraw support for the plight of prostitute mothers.

55. Anderson, *Women, Ideology, and Violence*, p. 71.

Damienne sums it up this way: "that whole thing of like, if you're a victim then we feel sorry for you, we need to get you out of this work, then you will be OK and you shouldn't be criminalized, but if you're somebody who likes it, and you're fine with it, and don't want to quit, and succumb to their idea of who they think you should be, then you're an evil, fallen, horrible person." A conventional religious morality of sexual "decency" feeds into this state of affairs.

Making visible the systemic economic circumstances that make prostitution a viable option for so many mothers, either in the time of Solomon or now is also a key issue for rights activists. SWOP activists object to the implicitly "decent" understanding of motherhood in Solomon's riddle offered by Stuart Lasine and many feminist readers. What prostitutes urge us to see is that if the exploitation is to end, sexual decency *and* the economic system it supports needs to be questioned. Viewing the riddle of Solomon as a parody of justice is a step in this direction.

SWOP Commentary of the Story of Solomon and the Two Prostitutes

In conclusion, I will now put together a commentary on the Solomon and Two Prostitutes text. We will exegete this story by threading quotes by these speakers: *Avaren*, Ms. Shiris, Robyn, Carol, Sweet, Gayle, Scarlot, Larry, Veronica, Kimberlee, Shemena and Rick.

> *This is a story of King Solomon in a context about where it is very ambivalent whether he is the good guy or the bad guy. Because some times it says that he is a bad guy, really bad guy, because he is violating all the norms of Israel, and what he does means the break up of the kingdom and Israel falls apart after him.* So the child is maybe a metaphor for Israel? Then why would they, in that metaphor, be prostitutes? That Israel is born of prostitutes, born of whores? That is a favorite metaphor for Israel whenever they are bad in the Bible, to describe it as a prostitute. To describe Israel as a prostitute! I was never told that these two women were prostitutes; I was always told that these two women were mothers. This is a very common story in my life. I'd also forgotten that they were prostitutes. I think that the reason that they are prostitutes is simply to explain why they were living together. *Well he just conquered Jerusalem, or his father just conquered Jerusalem and so…*so there were probably a lot of impregnated women from the raping and pillaging. So let's decontextualize the thing, why was it relevant at all that the women were whores? Like over the notion that, isn't this a motherly thing? We have to assume there was a specific reason that they were named as prostitutes. We have to, it is not just because there were a lot of prostitutes and there happened to be carpenters and

prostitutes, factory workers, no? Not just cuz there were so many that it didn't matter. So what are they even trying to say in the story, we have to figure that one out. So they are whores! They live together, maybe they are lesbians. Lesbians whores! I think what I am getting at is that it is significant that they are mentioned as prostitutes in this story, in a story that I have known since I was four years old, they are *only* mentioned because it is the only career outside of the family that we have. Because all women that are not invisible are whores. Tell that exact same story and only have it be just two women and not just prostitutes. I mean again why do they even bring the idea up? The reason, in my opinion, that they have to be prostitutes is really clear, because of the fact that you were either with your father or you were with your husband and if you were with your father or your husband you wouldn't even be allowed an audience with the king. You would be back at the home and your father or your husband would speak for you and put the moral quandary before the king. You'd be at home, you wouldn't get to talk anyway. Well because, she is a prostitute, because she did not have a husband, now the husband would have ultimate control over that child but because they are prostitutes there is no man speaking here for the children.

People, like really condescending men who interpret this story, say 'this shows that there was justice in the courts even for the lowly prostitute' that's how they take it and that the 'real true maternal nature will prevail over the fact that they are prostitutes,' that's what they say. What feminists say and this is even more interesting, feminists say 'clearly what the presupposition in this story is that all prostitutes are liars, because he doesn't even question them. Why question a liar?' You can't trust them. You can't trust them so you may as well be violent. Yeah, they had to be of ill moral character to be willing to go and steal another woman's baby and replace it with a dead one. Well, I've come to say there is an essence of heroism within our prostitutes in the Bible so far. And they also are especially good girls because they give up something or they martyr or they go along with the power blah blah. So yeah, even in the stories we can take that, like, essence that's in there, of heroism that is truly in both stories and we can then own it and magnify it, or, on the other hand... well, wait a minute, we can go with the feminists, what those people say or we might emphasize the something else, the bad parts, the hatred, the hatred... the fact that the Bible doesn't like the prostitutes. Now, so we could go the other way and say the heroism is good. But I still say that the overriding situation in this is that it is ridiculous that this king is going to cut the baby in half! Yeah, it was a bluff. It's still abusive and it's still sick. To even take then, to turn around and say you wanna push the heroism of a prostitute in a story that really should be focused on this violence...

More reasonable would have been a story of two women who weren't prostitutes, two women friends living together, had the two babies, one dies and the one whose child didn't die would be in empathy and would be 'oh my god, you poor thing you lost your child why don't we share mine?' but they wouldn't tell it that way they want to keep the women divided, that the women didn't care for each other. Maybe, maybe he benefited from the women being divided. Well because he could give that baby to someone, that's what they do now, they sell our children, they take our children from us they say we're incompetent and they sell them! They want mother's to be totally selfless. Martyrs; Martyrdom! Women are martyrs. We have Rahab who gives up her whole town to save her family. And now were talking about another woman who will give up her own fucking child. Martyrs! And if she is knowledgeable about how justice is being doled out up to that point, who's to say she is not being manipulative of what the likely outcome would be? I felt bad for the woman who, I felt bad for both women. Cuz of my mom and because of her issues, and because of her loosing me into the, and I went into the foster care system and all that, so for me, it had some pretty heavy duty significance and I was always, my sister and I were always being separated in that way, ya know, or because I was always being fought over because I was almost adopted by my foster mother. And my mother fought for me, so you get that I have a lot of that, I just felt incredible empathy for both women. I remember hearing that in church and thinking, there is not a lot of empathy going on for either women. Really. And I am like you, ya know, I am one of those people who is always for the underdog and I really felt that the women who is being seen as not the real mother, was maybe not getting very much empathy. And I thought, that kind of sucks! But that woman is suffering she is pain, her baby died, she is in pain and she is suffering and at this point she knows she has lost. OK she is in there and it's a loss, the guy is going to cut this baby in half, and give the two pieces to them, she has already, she has lost, she has lost, so she says yes, ya know she has already lost her baby and it is gone. So she figures that neither one will get the baby. It is like a no win situation. So it is trying to figure out the best way to work in the situation that is already bad. Why couldn't she be trumping his card? Maybe she is a mother who is fighting back. One of them said 'go ahead stupid shit cut him in half.' What about the Daisy Anarchy mothers? Daisy Anarchy is a resistance fighter! OK, come on, there is a fight, it is a fight for justice. He is allowed to even suggest murdering a baby with out being a bad guy but if she calls his bluff she is an evil mother. I was thinking, why aren't they going strait to jail for reporting themselves as prostitutes? I want to know why does he let a prostitute have a child? Because the culture I live in basically takes children away from prostitutes. The first thing that struck me when I was a little girl was, the prostitute gets to keep her baby? This culture, our government, operates as the husband and takes the children away if you're a prostitute. So I actually thought this is a bit of a more progressive culture, isn't it? Because the baby gets to stay with its mom. The prostitute was allowed to keep her child. Now, I don't know if maybe they felt that they had a social system where they could say 'well you're the child of a prostitute or you're a bastard child so therefore we're not worried about prostitutes having children because their children will never become part of accepted society.' And that seems to be, ya know, when you think about the Pharisees and the big bone that Christ had to pick with them it was about how they would wash their hands up to their elbows and they wouldn't touch unclean people and they tried to set themselves apart. They also had circumcision again as another way to set oneself apart through body and cleanliness. And it seems to me that we still live here in 2005 in a time where people want to have a separation between what they consider clean and dirty. And prostitutes are dirty so the most important thing really is not about eradicating us, because this culture, even the Catholic Church said 'you gotta have sewers,' um but rather to keep the sewer where it belongs. When I first read that story what I remember is feeling physical pain. That this powerful man that is supposed to be close to God would suggest such a thing. And I also felt overwhelmed because the patriarchs, I didn't have that term, but the older men, always get to do things that are bad and it is still good and that is what I always walked away with. How can he? Oh, OK, its not bad because wasn't really going to do it, is that it? But he made these women afraid and it was a horrible thing to even suggest. *Yeah, no, so but the same word for awe in Hebrew, is fear. And so you could interpret it as 'all of Israel was terrified by the king.' And if you interpret it that way then it's like 'OK I am not going to go to his court...I am going to just stay away from the authorities.'* That makes a lot more sense than being impressed! But they went before him with this argument. they took the argument to him. So there was that much trust. I mean, I don't know that I would take my argument to an invading conqueror that I didn't trust. So this one woman who needed justice, they went there somehow, they went before him with this argument ya know, it is pretty crazy you'd think that there was some other way. Don't go to fucking Solomon and those assholes to make our judgments; we need a fucking fairer court! I wouldn't take my shit to the courts to decide it either!

I don't think that Solomon is the hero. No, the mother is the hero. But historically, he is the one everybody rejoiced over, Solomon's decision.

Chapter 5

ANOINTING WOMAN: 'IN MEMORY OF HER': THE PREQUEL

Jn 12:1–8 (NRSV)

12 Six days before the Passover Jesus came to Bethany, the home of Lazarus, whom he had raised from the dead. ² There they gave a dinner for him. Martha served, and Lazarus was one of those at the table with him. ³ Mary took a pound of costly perfume made of pure nard, anointed Jesus' feet, and wiped them with her hair. The house was filled with the fragrance of the perfume. ⁴ But Judas Iscariot, one of his disciples (the one who was about to betray him), said, ⁵ 'Why was this perfume not sold for three hundred denarii and the money given to the poor?' ⁶ (He said this not because he cared about the poor, but because he was a thief; he kept the common purse and used to steal what was put into it.) ⁷ Jesus said, 'Leave her alone. She bought it so that she might keep it for the day of my burial. ⁸ You always have the poor with you, but you do not always have me.'

Lk. 7:36–50 (NRSV)

³⁶ One of the Pharisees asked Jesus to eat with him, and he went into the Pharisee's house and took his place at the table. ³⁷ And a woman in the city, who was a sinner, having learned that he was eating in the Pharisee's house, brought an alabaster jar of ointment. ³⁸ She stood behind him at his feet, weeping, and began to bathe his feet with her tears and to dry them with her hair. Then she continued kissing his feet and anointing them with the ointment. ³⁹ Now when the Pharisee who had invited him saw it, he said to himself, 'If this man were a prophet, he would have known who and what kind of woman this is who is touching him—that she is a sinner.' ⁴⁰ Jesus spoke up and said to him, 'Simon, I have something to say to you.' 'Teacher,' he replied, 'speak.' ⁴¹ 'A certain creditor had two debtors; one owed five hundred denarii, and the other fifty. ⁴² When they could not pay, he canceled the debts for both of them. Now which of them will love him more?' ⁴³ Simon answered, 'I suppose the one for whom he canceled the greater debt.' And Jesus said to him, 'You have judged rightly.' ⁴⁴ Then turning toward the woman, he said to Simon, 'Do you see this woman? I entered your house; you gave me no water for my feet, but she has bathed my feet with her tears and dried them with her hair. ⁴⁵ You gave me no kiss, but from the time I

came in she has not stopped kissing my feet. [46] You did not anoint my head with oil, but she has anointed my feet with ointment. [47] Therefore, I tell you, her sins, which were many, have been forgiven; hence she has shown great love. But the one to whom little is forgiven, loves little.' [48] Then he said to her, 'Your sins are forgiven.' [49] But those who were at the table with him began to say among themselves, 'Who is this who even forgives sins?' [50] And he said to the woman, 'Your faith has saved you; go in peace.'

Mk 14:3–9 (NRSV)

[3] While he was at Bethany in the house of Simon the leper, as he sat at the table, a woman came with an alabaster jar of very costly ointment of nard, and she broke open the jar and poured the ointment on his head. [4] But some were there who said to one another in anger, 'Why was the ointment wasted in this way? [5] For this ointment could have been sold for more than three hundred denarii, and the money given to the poor.' And they scolded her. [6] But Jesus said, 'Let her alone; why do you trouble her? She has performed a good service for me. [7] For you always have the poor with you, and you can show kindness to them whenever you wish; but you will not always have me. [8] She has done what she could; she has anointed my body beforehand for its burial. [9] Truly I tell you, wherever the good news is proclaimed in the whole world, what she has done will be told in remembrance of her.'

Mt. 26:6–13 (NRSV)

[6] Now while Jesus was at Bethany in the house of Simon the leper, [7] a woman came to him with an alabaster jar of very costly ointment, and she poured it on his head as he sat at the table. [8] But when the disciples saw it, they were angry and said, 'Why this waste? [9] For this ointment could have been sold for a large sum, and the money given to the poor.' [10] But Jesus, aware of this, said to them, 'Why do you trouble the woman? She has performed a good service for me. [11] For you always have the poor with you, but you will not always have me. [12] By pouring this ointment on my body she has prepared me for burial. [13] Truly I tell you, wherever this good news is proclaimed in the whole world, what she has done will be told in remembrance of her.'[1]

> Fill up the cup and say again, again, again, 'Heliodora's.' Speak the sweet name, temper the wine with but that alone. And give me, although it be yester night's, the garland dripping with scent to wear, *in memory of her*. Look how the rose that favours love is weeping, because it sees her elsewhere and not in my bosom.[2]

1. *The Holy Bible: New Revised Standard Version* (Nashville, TN: Thomas Nelson, 1996 [1989]).
2. An amatory epigram by Meleager, from the *Greek Anthology*, Vol. I (trans. W.R. Paton; Loeb Classical Library, Cambridge, MA: Harvard University Press, 1960). Book V.136, p. 192, emphasis mine.

Scholar Standpoints

The Biblical prostitution text(s) that is most frequently and affirmatively referenced by sex workers themselves is that of the woman who anointed Jesus (Lk. 7:36–50, Mk 14:1–9, Mt. 26:6–13, and Jn 12:1–8). She is still most commonly but erroneously, identified as Mary Magdalene.[3] As stated previously, sacred prostitution or Goddess religion is also a popular topic for prostitutes, but it is generally described in the Hebrew Bible in a negative way, if mentioned at all. Oddly enough, it was in these traditions of the anointing woman where SWOP readers were able find the Goddess affirmed and with this, their selves as well.

Every prostitute activist I have ever met has asked some form of question about the anointing traditions such as, "Didn't Jesus hang out with prostitutes and other social outcasts?" or "Mary Magdalene herself was a prostitute, wasn't she?" or "a prostitute anointed Jesus' feet, right?" These questions accord well with what both Gabriela Leite and Margaret Guider assert about the religiosity of Brazilian activist prostitutes who derive esteem from this association between Jesus and prostitutes.[4] That a popular Tijuana prostitutes' union call themselves the "Mary Magdalenes" also bears witness to this strong notion among rights activists.[5] Chung Hyun Kyung writes about how Korean prostitutes identify with Mary Magdalene, even though the "teaching may be wrong," for this case it is a good thing.[6] Thus, the story of anointing woman was the most important text for our group to interpret. This importance stands despite the results of much feminist scholarship that has definitively argued against the tradition that Mary Magdalene was a prostitute or that she anointed Jesus. Kudos from SWOP

3. See Jane Schaberg for an account of how the tradition developed in her article "How Mary Magdalene Became a Whore," *Bible Review* (October 1992), pp. 31–52 and *The Resurrection of Mary Magdalene: Legends, Apocrypha and the Christian Testament* (New York: Continuum, 2003), chapter 3 in particular. See also Ingrid Maisch, *Mary Magdalene: The Image of a Woman through the Centuries* (trans. Linda Maloney; Collegeville, MN: Liturgical Press, 1998).

4. Leite, "The Prostitute Movement in Brazil," pp. 425–26 and Guider, *The Daughters of Rahab*, pp. 96, 200–201.

5. Sally Hughes, "Women's Work," *Freedom Review* (1 September), 1995; http://www.jornada.unam.mx/2002/07/04/ls-norte.html; Richard Marosi, "Making Nice on Vice," *Los Angeles Times*, 4 January 2005.

6. Chung Hyun Kyung, "Your Comfort Vs. My Death," in Mary John Mananzan, Mercy Amba Oduyoye, Elsa Tamez, J. Shannon Clarkson, Mary C. Grey, Letty Russell (eds.), *Women Resisting Violence: Spirituality for Life* (Maryknoll, NY: Orbis Books, 1996), pp. 129–40, p. 138.

readers goes to Jane Schaberg for recognizing the complex issue of prostitutes' identification with Mary Magdalene, when she grapples with the ramifications of removing the prostitute label from Mary Magdalene. Instead of simply insisting on the non-prostitute identity of Mary Magdalene, she instead leaves space for prostitute interpreters: "Only a prostitute's commentary on the legends seen 'from the vantage point of branded women' and from the vantage point of solidarity, would lay bare the mechanisms of injustice in the context of women's struggle for autonomy."[7] This book is trying to provide exactly such a "prostitute commentary" for which she called.

This feminist re-visioning of the Jesus/Mary Magdalene/prostitute association has also extended to whether the woman who anointed Jesus was an actual prostitute and to the whole idea of whether "the women around Jesus were really prostitutes."[8] It is for this reason that Margaret Guider chose Rahab of Joshua 2 and 6 as the most liberating biblical model for prostitutes, since she seemed the only suitable prostitute left for a feminist "hermeneutic of retrieval."[9] Guider states that "although Mary Magdalene is an important character, her longstanding reputation in the Christian tradition as repentant prostitute has been undone, at least in the minds of biblical scholars."[10] The same can be said of anointing woman who is not necessarily labelled a prostitute anymore by biblical scholars, except perhaps in reference to Luke's redaction of the story.

Due to this anointing story, the issue of Jesus' solidarity with sex workers is a primary issue of contention in liberation and feminist readings of the Bible for sex workers. Exactly *who* is being remembered for her action "wherever the Gospel is preached in the whole world" as written in Mk 14:9? The answer given most recently by Kathleen Corley is: "she was not sinful or a prostitute, as in Luke, but respectable."[11] Sex workers feel that feminist biblical scholarship might be pulling the rug out from under their political strategy of claiming the endorsement of Jesus in their struggles for justice and liberation. Even worse is their erasure from involvement in

7. Schaberg, *The Resurrection of Mary Magdalene*, p. 106.

8. Kathleen Corley, "Were the Women around Jesus Really Prostitutes? Women in the Context of Greco-Roman Meals," in Davis J. Lull (ed.), *Society of Biblical Literature 1989 Seminar Papers* (Society of Biblical Literature, 1989), pp. 487–521.

9. Guider, *The Daughters of Rahab*, p. 27.

10. Guider, *The Daughters of Rahab*, p. 27.

11. Kathleen Corley, "The Anointing of Jesus in the Synoptic Tradition: An Argument for Authenticity," *JSHJ* 1.1 (2003), p. 72.

such past struggles as in the biblical story, a recurring theme in history according to rights activists. Since the women's movement in general is split on the issue of prostitution, prostitutes' rights activists do not expect that feminist intellectuals in any discipline are going to be automatic allies. There is also a strong class component to the whore stigma and the desire to be "good girls" that may prevent many women from fully identifying with sex workers. SWOP readers speculate on the agenda of feminist biblical scholars with regard to Mary Magdalene and anointing woman. These characters seemed to be undergoing a sexual purification at the expense of prostitutes. "If the objective is to say 'oh, we want get her as far away from sex as possible,' I have a problem with that," says sex worker activist Veronica Monet. SWOP readers assume that it is an issue of claiming the respectability of the women in the Jesus Movement so that they too, as Christian women scholars, can better identify with these women as their own role models and historical forerunners. Veronica feels split, but sympathetic with this need:

> I also like the idea of her being a role model for women who want to see *themselves* in a more powerful roles, vies a vie, I guess, what the culture considers powerful, so that is where my spilt takes place. I can see where changing the paradigm might be useful to young women growing up, to think that there was a female apostle.

Most biblical scholars are generally not sex workers and it was often assumed by SWOP readers that such women do not usually know many prostitutes intimately as family members, neighbours or friends. Thus, the feminist identification of Mary Magdalene as the "first resurrection witness" or "female apostle" is seen as perhaps more empowering than as the "repentant whore," especially for women who are ignominiously labelled "whores" if they take on leadership roles in contemporary churches. The feminist scholarly critique of the patriarchal silencing of the witness of early Christian women by labelling them whores unfortunately comes with an implicit acceptance that such women are unworthy of being heard. As more and more women become theologians and ministers, the notion of women's (chaste) leadership in the early Christian movement seems to have increased in popularity. Veronica and Dammine Sin critique this move toward respectability as "half measures." As is voiced by Sweet, in the end, the most liberating role model would be, "to have a woman who was powerful AND sex positive in terms of her view on the world."

From another angle, there is also a trend in New Testament studies lately to question whether the first Christians were really of the lowest sectors of society but perhaps instead more of a middle stratum of working people. Scholars speculate that early Christians were a group mixed perhaps of the decent, deserving working class and respectable middle strata with status inconstancy.[12] This status increase of early Christianity would be another way prostitutes could be excised from among the early Jesus Movement, at least for the prostitutes from among the slave classes. To their credit, feminist scholars Schüssler Fiorenza and Schottroff argue for the definite inclusion of prostitutes among the early followers of Jesus.[13] Kathleen Corley and Theresa Hornsby, however, argue against this view and while liberation scholars would emphasize the "gospel to the poor" and "God's preferential option to the poor and oppressed" not all liberation oriented scholars deal with Jesus as a friend to prostitutes or prostitutes as a likely type of poor and marginalized person in New Testament times.[14] The point here is that prostitutes' presence in the Jesus Movement cannot be simply asserted as a norm for biblical scholars who are either feminist or liberation oriented.

12. See Luise Schottroff, *Lydia's Impatient Sisters* (Louisville, KY: Westminster John Knox Press, 1995), pp. 145–51 for a helpful discussion of this trend. Wayne Meeks' study of *The First Urban Christians: The Social World of the Apostle Paul* (New Haven, CT: Yale University Press, 1983), is an influential argument for the middle stratum constituency of early Christianity.

13. Schüssler Fiorenza argues that prostitutes were part of the early Jesus Movement but argues that Mary Magdalene and the historical anointing woman were not prostitutes, see *In Memory of Her: A Feminist Theological Reconstruction of Christian Origins* (New York: Crossroad, 1985), pp. 122–41. Luise Schottroff argues that prostitutes were a category of the poor and that anointing woman, at least in Luke, is definitely a prostitute, see Luise Schottroff and Wolfgang Stegemann, *Jesus and the Hope of the Poor* (Maryknoll, NY: Orbis Books, 1986), p. 15. See also Regene Lamb and Claudia Jansen, "Zoellnerinnen und Prostituierte gelangen eher in das Reich Gottes als ihr (Mt. 21, 31)," in Kuno Fuessel and Franz Segbers Hgs, *So lernen die Voelker des erdkreises Gerechtigkeit: ein Arbeitsbuch zu Bibel und Oekonomie* (Salzburg: Verlag Anton Pustet, 1995), pp. 275–84.

14. Corley, "The Anointing of Jesus in the Synoptic Tradition," pp. 520–21 and Teresa Hornsby, "Why is She Crying? A Feminist Interpretation of Luke 7.36–50," in Harold Washington, Susan Lochrie Graham and Pamela Thimmes (eds.), *Escaping Eden: New Feminist Perspectives on the Bible* (New York: New York University Press, 1999), pp. 91–104. Richard Horsley, who otherwise supports the idea of a revolutionary Jesus Movement, doesn't think it likely that prostitutes would be included in the Jesus Movement, see *Jesus and the Spiral of Violence: Popular Jewish Resistance in Roman Palestine* (Minneapolis, MN: Fortress Press, 1993), p. 223.

While prostitutes in antiquity, as now, were not always poor and oppressed, there exists a very strong association in antiquity between being a slave and being a prostitute. In fact, "the words *porne* and *doule* occur together so commonly that a study by Italian scholar Citti has concluded that mention of the term *porne* in ancient Greek necessarily evokes the mental image of a *doule*.'[15] Edward Cohen argues that being a slave was associated with earning money. Slave prostitutes would be among those most likely to buy their freedom through their earning given that their wages were higher than any other type of labour female slaves were likely to do.[16] Rebecca Flemming uses the literal meaning of the Latin word *meretrix* in her definition of prostitution, "she who earns," in order to examine economic patterns of prostitution in ancient Rome.[17] This parallels the Greek word *porne*, which derives from the verb *pernemi* meaning "to sell as a slave."

Thomas McGinn argues that "discourse on prostitution reads as a kind of shorthand for a prescriptive ordering of society on the basis of sexual behaviour, or at least reputation. It is inexorably linked to a larger discourse on sex, gender, and reproduction, both biological and social. In an ideal sense, social status was tied directly to sexual honour, more acutely and directly for women."[18] Prostitution was often an institutionalized means of providing sex for the poor masses of male workers and slaves. According to Plutarch, Cato the Elder preferred that slave prostitutes sexually service his male slaves, instead of forming family ties.[19] Prostitution is a means for capital accumulation by women and their dependants, or more commonly, their owners. Rebecca Flemming asserts that "female bodies clearly counted amongst the economic resources not only of slave dealers and owners, but also of any family network, available for short- or long-term for the avoidance of penury and probably in some cases also for the pursuance of more

15. Edward Cohen, "Free and Unfree Sexual Work," in Christopher Faraone and Laura McClure (eds.), *Prostitutes and Courtesans in the Ancient World* (Madison, WI: University of Wisconsin press, 2006), p. 103.

16. Cohen, "Free and Unfree Sexual Work," p. 106.

17. Rebecca Flemming, "*Quae Corpore Quaestum Facit:* The Sexual Economy of Female Prostitution in the Roman Empire," *Journal of Roman Studies*: 89 (1999), pp. 38–61, p. 42.

18. See Thomas McGinn's *Prostitution, Sexuality, and the Law in Ancient Rome* (Oxford: Oxford University Press, 1998), p. 9.

19. Plutarch, Cato Elder, 21.2, see Carolyn Osiek and David Balch's *Families in the New Testament World* (Louisville, KY: Westminster/John Knox Press, 1997), p. 78.

particular and ambitious economic strategies."[20] The association between female slavery and prostitution was so strong that restrictive clauses were written into slave sale contracts to the effect that women *not* be prostituted, known as the "Ne Serva Prostituatur" clause.[21] Many ancient moralists, most notably Dio Chrysostom, denounce the procurers and profiteers of prostitution showing clearly the war spoil route to slavery and prostitution:

> They must not take hapless women or children (*aichmalota somata*) captured in war or else purchased with money, and expose them for shameful ends in dirty booths which are flaunted before the eyes in every part of the city, at the doors of houses of magistrates and in market-places, near governmental buildings and temples, in the midst of all that is holiest.[22]

Women in antiquity by and large became prostitutes by a few specific routes. The infamous prostitute Neaera, prosecuted by pseudo-Demosthenes, is the quintessential ancient Greek prostitute. She was bought by the Madame Nikarete and reared from childhood to be a prostitute.[23] Indeed, most prostitutes were slaves in ancient Greece and Rome and thus did not choose their vocation.[24] Women generally became enslaved in three different ways: First, many women became slaves as war spoil via conquest of their homeland.[25] Death tolls of the male population were much higher than the female, and the majority of enslaved survivors were women and

20. Flemming, *"Quae Corpore Quaestum Facit,"* p. 42.

21. Thomas McGinn, Prostitution, Sexuality and the Law in Ancient Rome (Oxford: Oxford University Press, 1998), pp. 288–319.

22. Dio Chrysostom, *Euboean Discourse*, vol. 1 (trans. J.W. Cohoon; Loeb Classical Library, Cambridge, MA: Harvard University Press, 1971), 7:133–34, pp. 362–63. Please note the use of the word *soma* in reference to prostitute women, just as in Rev. 18:13.

23. Demosthenes, *In Neaeram*, vol. iv (trans. A.T. Murray; Loeb Classical Library; Cambridge, MA: Harvard University Press, 1988), pp. 18, 365. See also the discussion by Regene Lamb and Claudia Jansen, "Zoellnerinnen und Prostituierte gelangen eher in das Reich Gottes als ihr," p. 279.

24. See Rebecca Flemming, *"Quae Corpore Quaestum Facit,"* p. 41 and also Keuls, *The Reign of the Phallus* (New York: Harper and Row, 1985), p. 154.

25. See Sarah Pomeroy, *Goddesses, Whores, Wives and Slaves: Women in Classical Antiquity* (New York: Schocken Books, 1975), pp. 191–92 and Richard Bauckham, "Economic Critique of Rome in Revelation 18," in Alexander Loveday (ed.), *Images of Empire* (Sheffield, JSOT Press, 1991), pp. 74–75. He relies on recent work by W.V. Harris, who argues that foundling children are a significant source of slaves, see his article: "Demography, Geography and the Source of Roman Slaves," *Journal of Roman Studies*: 89 (1999), pp. 62–75.

children. This would have been the case for the women who survived the destruction of Jerusalem. Another major method by which women became slaves was via debt. Debt bondage was more likely to happen to women than men because daughters were more expendable than male heirs. In the event that there was no land, people only have their own bodies or the bodies of their families to pledge for debt. Finally, female child exposure was the most favoured form of infanticide in the Greco-Roman world and provided a steady source of foundling girls to be reared to work in brothels.[26] According to some estimates, half of all newborns were exposed in Hellenistic cities during certain eras.[27] For these reasons, there are indications that the number of female slaves was over-determined, while citizenship tended to be more of a male prerogative. Demographic studies of gender ratios in Roman Egypt bear this out.[28] Thus, being female would have had a major class component since the majority of slaves and non-citizens were female. And being a female slave would have also connoted being a prostitute. This inference is true too for Jewish women during second temple period and under rabbinic law. Tal Illan points out that women slaves did not go free in the seventh year, by biblical law since the maidservant "is also a sexual object for the males of the house" and for this reason is different from the male slave.[29] The maidservant is in the same category as a prostitute, her children are considered fatherless, and even if she is freed she cannot marry legitimately.

Free women who became prostitutes or prostituted their young usually did so because of poverty. Prostitution was often the only means of obtaining adequate sustenance for the masses of unattached, unskilled, non-owning women and their dependents, displaced in the harsh colonial economy. It was the only way to make ends meet in many professions, which were too low paying to sustain a single woman, much less a single woman with children or elderly dependents. Textile work is most often mentioned as the other profession of prostitutes; and vase paintings of prostitutes often

---

26. Justin Martyr, *Apol* 1:27, denounced the practice of child exposure for just this very reason, cf. McGinn, *Prostitution, Sexuality*, p. 269.

27. Harris, "Demography, Geography," p. 74, n. 93.

28. Roger Bagnall who has seen this skewed sex ratio repeatedly in demographic data makes this argument. He sees foundling girls as a main source of the slave population in "Missing Females in Roman Egypt," *Scripta Classica Israelica*: 16 (1997), pp. 121–38.

29. Tal Ilan, *Jewish Women in Greco-Roman Palestine* (Peabody, MA: Hendrickson Publishers, 1996), pp. 205–21.

depict props of textile work, such as looms or spindles.[30] Widows with children seemed to be in this predicament often. This passage by Lucian tells a common story of a mother who is forced to prostitute her girl:

> Let me give you the rest of my instructions about what to do and how to behave with men; for we have no other means of livelihood, daughter, and you must realize what a miserable life we've had these two years since your father died...After his death, first of all I sold his tongs, his anvil and his hammer for 2 minae, and that kept us for 7 months; since then I've barely provided a starvation diet, now by weaving, now by spinning thread for woof or warp. I've fed you and waited for my hopes to be realized.[31]

Lucian's text here recounts the intentional rearing of a courtesan, or *hetaira*, by her own mother. The *hetaira* is often distinguished from the lower class slave prostitute by being a freeborn citizen with education, refinement, and power via the powerful men they were attached to such as Aspasia who was the lover of Pericles, the Athenian leader. Nevertheless, many see the *porne* and *hetarae* as being more on a fluid status continuum and not necessarily as distinct as previously thought.[32] I do not distinguish a great deal between the social status or titles of *pornae* and *hetairae* but consider them synonymous, as confirmed by the interchangeability of usage in the ancient prostitution literature (Demosthenes, Lucian, Alciphron and Athenaeus). *Hetaira* (companion) is what Athenaeus explains is a euphemism for a prostitute and perhaps was a way to make the practice feel more genteel for higher paying customers or high class "johns."[33] A frequent job description for a prostitute/*hetaira* in Lucian, and Demosthenes' *In Naearam*, is "to drink with men and sleep with them for pay."[34] Naeara was a good example of a *hetaira* who was also a slave, a slave who nevertheless earned enough from high paying clients to buy her freedom.

30. See Keuls, *The Reign of the Phallus*, pp. 155, 190, also see image of the loom on p. 183 and Cohen, "Free and Unfree Sexual Work," p. 104. Natalie Kampen reports the same theme for Roman women in *Image and Status: Roman Working Women in Ostia* (Berlin: Gebr. Mann Verlag, 1981), p. 121.

31. Lucian, *Dialogues of the Courtesans*, 6.1, p. 387.

32. See Keuls, *The Reign of the Phallus*, pp. 194–99 and Cohen, "Free and Unfree Sexual Work," pp. 98–99.

33. See *Deipnosophistae* 13.571d, p. 87.

34. Lucian, *Dialogues of the Courtesans*, 6.2, p. 389 and Demosthenes, *In Neaeram*, 48, p. 387.

Martin Hugo Córdova Quero, in a recent queer reading of Mary Magdalene asks the same thing SWOP readers ask: "the question that still remains is: What if Mary of Magdala was in fact a former prostitute? Can she still be the first and main witness of the resurrection?"[35] His task is to analyze scholarship in terms of the binary of "in/decency" coined by Marcella Althaus-Reid. He argues that while feminist scholars rightly critique the repentant, weeping sinner-whore image of androcentric scholarly tradition, they also commit a similar error and stay within the confines of a heterosexist patriarchal understanding of power by not addressing the sexuality of Mary Magdalene: "what feminist theologians clearly avoid is the sexual aspect of Mary." Furthermore "this has indeed non-innocent consequences: in gaining a status of equality for Mary in the midst of a male world implies to disembody and desexualize the female Mary. Paradoxically she is saved as a servant of God by being *assumed* (co-opted) by maleness." Thus the binary of in/decency remains a constant in these readings because Mary is made into a decent woman.

Córdova Quero, as do SWOP readers, wants to know "what would happen if Mary were a lesbian, or Jesus bisexual, or transgender or intersex…what if, in fact, Mary of Magdala was a prostitute? Is she less witness of the risen Christ then?" This is the main point that SWOP readers also make in their reading: that such gestures towards respectability and decency work against the liberation of all women because they are also stuck in the whore/saint or in/decent binary and cannot entertain the blurred boundaries of both/and. Says SWOP reader Damienne Sin:

> She can be a very powerful woman *and* a sex worker and my hope is that these women who are very powerful in Bible scholarship and they are trying to rewrite Mary Magdalene as a powerful woman and not necessarily a sex worker, that eventually they will discover the power of their own sexuality, they will eventually be able to rewrite Mary Magdalene as I really believe she really was.

To proceed, SWOP prostitutes tabled the issue of Mary Magdalene as anointing woman. However, SWOP prostitutes still read the anointing woman as a prostitute and a woman in the Jesus Movement. This reading functions as an illustration of Jesus' solidarity with prostitutes and other marginalized groups. It is furthermore presupposed that prostitutes and

---

35. Martín Hugo Córdova Quero, "The Prostitutes Also Go Into The Kingdom of God. A Queer Reading of Mary of Magdala," in Marcella Althaus-Reid (ed.), *Liberation Theology and Sexuality: The New Radicalism from Latin America* (Aldershot, Hampshire, UK: Ashgate Publishing).

other types of poor people were important components of the Jesus Movement. Exegetes have given many reasons why the anointing woman is inferred to be a prostitute. Luke's version provides the most evidence for the prostitute argument. That she is labelled a "sinner" by the narrator, the Pharisee and Jesus, supposedly underscores the moral evaluation. The text of Lk 7:37 says "And a woman in the city, who was a sinner, having learned that he was eating in the Pharisee's house, brought an alabaster jar of ointment." That she is from the city and present at a dinner party (that is to say a symposium setting) are other reasons given. At Lk 7:38 the text continues: "She stood behind him at his feet, weeping, and began to bathe his feet with her tears, and to dry them with her hair. Then she continued to kiss his feet and anoint them with the ointment." That she touches Jesus, that she anoints Jesus, that she owns costly perfumed ointment, that her hair is unbound are other signs of her "loose" character. SWOP prostitutes identify the act of anointing, either head or feet and the possession of anointing oil as the chief reason for her identification as a sex worker. Finally, the mental disapproval by Simon the Pharisee to the actions of anointing woman indicates that there is something untoward about her behaviour: "If this man were a prophet, he would have known who and what kind of woman this is who is touching him—that she is a sinner." (Lk 7:39). This scandalized reaction of Simon and the variant onlookers in the other versions is also mentioned as another reason for seeing her behaviour as risqué and which resists excision from the tradition.[36] These reasons cut across all four Gospels. In Mk 14:4b–5 it says: "But some were there who said to one another in anger, 'Why was the ointment wasted in this way? For this ointment could have been sold for more than three hundred denarii, and the money given to the poor.' And they scolded her." Matthew's version (26:8–9) is close to Mark's: "But when the disciples saw it, they were angry and said, 'Why this waste?' For this ointment could have been sold for a large sum, and the money given to the poor." Finally in John's version (12:4–6) it is Judas who objects to her act: "But Judas Iscariot, one of his disciples (the one who was about to betray him), said, 'Why was this perfume not sold for three hundred denarii and the money given to the poor?' (He said this not because he cared about the poor, but because he was a thief; he kept the common purse and used to steal what was put into

36. Burton Mack, *A Myth of Innocence* (Philadelphia, PA: Fortress Press, 1988), p. 200 and J.D. Derrett, "The Anointing at Bethany and the Story of Zacchaeus," in *Law and the New Testament* (London: Darton, Longmann & Todd, 1970), pp. 266–78, p. 268.

it)." For this reason Burton Mack detects a shorter *chreia* (a saying by a famous person, like Jesus) behind all versions that has been elaborated variously but all originally including an element of sexual innuendo.

Other scholars are not persuaded by this evidence and point to the fact that nowhere does any anointing woman passage actually name this woman as a prostitute.[37] It is often an historical or form-critical argument that is trying to recover the historical woman behind the story. The most famous statement of this argument is made in Elisabeth Schüssler Fiorenza's *In Memory of Her*. Herein it is argued that the original historical event is the anointing of Jesus' head by a woman performing the prophetic sign action that makes Jesus the "Christ" or literally, "anointed one."[38] This prophetic anointing is a dangerous memory that shows the importance of women as prophets and in leadership roles in the early Jesus Movement. In this line of interpretation, the sexualization of the act occurs later, probably invented by Luke, as a way to undermine the leadership roles of women in the emerging church. That the anointing woman is identified as a prostitute, and Mary Magdalene as well, is a form of slander designed to oppress women in the critical view of such scholars. Overturning or removing this whore slander is thus a task of feminist scholarship because it is a creation of a sexist misogynistic interpretive history beginning with Luke, not the real story of women in the historical Jesus Movement.

A major issue at stake is Luke's characterization of the anointing woman as a "sinner." This "sinner" label is a major stumbling block to her glorification as the prophetic woman who anoints Jesus and must be remembered forever for it. Many assume that this story depicts sex as sinful and women as particularly guilty of this kind of sin. Ingrid Rosa Kitzberger gives a very good description of a typical feminist reader response to the Lukan rendition of the episode:

> Therefore, my first reaction to Luke 7:36–50, or rather, the effect that the text has on me, is quite negative, because whereas in the other texts a very positive view and the role of a woman is presented, the woman in our story is conceived of as a sinner. This implies a negative connotation

37. Theresa Hornsby argues this for even the Lukan version. Corley argues a non-prostitute identity for only the non-Lukan versions where the woman may not "deserve" the slur. See Corley, "Were the Women around Jesus Really Prostitutes?" pp. 520–21.

38. Schüssler Fiorenza, *In Memory of Her*, pp. xiv and 128–29. Schüssler Fiorenza argues that Jesus' anointing was as a prophet not king. For a Jesus-as-king version of this argument see J.K. Elliott, "The Anointing of Jesus," *Expository Times* (1974) 85:4. pp. 105–107.

for me because too often women have been considered by men as being prone to sin, especially sexual sin, to be potential or actual harlots. Because of this 'text written on my soul' I resist this definition of the woman as a sinner, the characterization of the woman in Mark/Matthew and John appeals to me more. Her subsequent acts of weeping upon Jesus' feet and wetting them with her tears, drying them with her hair, kissing his feet and anointing them is embarrassing, humiliating.[39]

SWOP readers object to the sinner label also but for different reasons. They are offended that the woman is labelled a sinner for being a prostitute and the patronizing forgiveness of Jesus in light of her repentance. If Jesus sees prostitution as a sin needing his forgiveness, then he is just arrogant not an empowering agent of liberation to the poor and oppressed. Indeed one of our SWOP interpreters, Carol Leigh aka Scarlot Harlot, has recently written a book entitled *The Unrepentant Whore*[40] so it was clear early on that this kind of "repentant sinner" interpretation would not be very popular for our readers.

From a feminist-liberation angle, Luise Schottroff has written on the story of the anointing woman in Luke that offers resources for an unrepentant whore.[41] She consciously uses the word "whore" in solidarity with sex workers who have reclaimed this word as a strategy of empowerment. She is one of the few scholars that maintain the prostitute identity in a somewhat positive manner. Her reading argues against the repentance of Luke's anointing woman as meaning she is quitting her work or that her sex work is an issue of her personal morality: "I understand the woman as a whore, but not a repentant whore" and what she knows about the modern day prostitutes' struggle is the reason "to fight against the Christian tradition of prostitution as a moral problem, and the Christian idea that prostitution can be overcome by the repentance of whores."[42] She argues that the typical Christian interpretation assumes that anointing woman is acting out her feelings of repentance, however "conversion—a

39. Ingrid Rosa Kitzberger, "Love and Footwashing: John 13:1–20 and Luke 7:36–50 Read Intertextually," *Biblical Interpretation* 2 (1994), pp. 198–99.

40. Carol Leigh, *Unrepentant Whore.*

41. Luise Schottroff, "Through German and Feminist Eyes: a Liberationist Reading of Luke 7:36–50," in Athalya Brenner (ed.), *The Feminist Companion to the Hebrew Bible in the New Testament* (Sheffield: Sheffield Academic Press, 1996), pp. 332–41. An earlier statement of this argument is in her book *Let the Oppressed Go Free: Feminist Perspectives on the New Testament* (trans. Ann Marie Kidder; Louisville, KY: Westminster/John Knox Press, 1993), pp. 138–55.

42. Schottroff, "Through German and Feminist Eyes," p. 334.

turning away from sinning—is a matter of both practicality and economy, which certainly was not possible for this woman. The text, however, leaves all these questions open and does not tell of the prostitute's repentance but of a prostitute's love for Jesus."[43] Schottroff asserts that the story is showing us the proper way of relating to prostitutes, with love and solidarity, in distinction to the way many super pious people were accustomed to treating prostitutes. Nor is this an anti-Judaistic story about Christian gospel versus Jewish law: "the text is not about the difference between the Pharisee's concept of God and that of Jesus but about the difference between the way they relate to prostitutes."[44] Unfortunately most people do not follow the example of Jesus.

The issue is complicated by the erotophobic interpretive traditions of Christian dualism that sees sex and the erotic as part of the carnal fleshy realm incompatible with spirituality. This is dealt with or incorporated into the interpretation as either anointing woman as a "repentant" sinner who has renounced her former evil lifestyle or that her anointing was somehow a chaste love act or a clean eroticism not associated in any way with meretricious behaviour. Two extremes of the in/decency binary function in these interpretations. Anointing woman is either an abject sinner begging mercy or is engaging in a kind of non-erotic Christian divine love that has nothing to do with lust. This tendency may be influenced by the old rubric of Christian theology that would like to distinguish between Christian *agape* and pagan *eros*.[45] A prominent theorist of this thesis was Anders Nygren in the 1930s. His task of distinguishing these kinds of love was complicated by the Platonic version of a sublimated *eros*, or "heavenly *eros*" which is somewhat similar to Christian *agape*.[46] Both of these kinds of love are distinguished from "vulgar Eros" which is the child of πάνδημος Αφροδίτη, or "vulgar Aphrodite" as first articulated in Plato's *Symposium*.[47] Atheneaus' *Deipnosophistae* has several instances where Aphrodite is

43. Schottroff, *Let the Oppressed Go Free*, p. 153.

44. Schottroff, *Let the Oppressed Go Free*, p. 145.

45. The classic statement of this view is made by Anders Nygren in trans. Philip Watson; *Agape and Eros* (London: SPCK, 1953). For a sex positive critique of such traditions, see James B. Nelson, and Sandra P. Longfellow, *Sexuality and the Sacred: Sources for Theological Reflection* (Louisville, KY: Westminster/John Knox Press, 1994).

46. Nygren, *Agape and Eros*, p. 51, and Plato, *Symposium*, 180D–81.

47. An epigram of the *Greek Anthology* V.177, has Eros as Aphrodite's bastard child.

labeled a courtesan or prostitute.[48] This is also the kind of *eros* that prostitutes are associated with and a similar adjective, πάγκοινος, "vulgar" or "common" is used to describe their activities.[49] This bad *eros* is equated with sexual love and a desire for material, sensible and transient things, which in this view, is non-spiritual, female and low class.[50]

Another element in this discourse is the more recent strain of thought among feminists about prostitution wherein sexual commerce is closely identified with male domination and exploitation. Such feminist readers are rightly concerned about the biblical text's lack of critique of such issues. For this reason Judith Applegate worries that while the Lukan portrait of anointing woman has liberative elements, it can also be used in oppressive ways, such as encouraging women to exchange sexual favours for love, forgiveness, or security.[51] Theresa Hornsby sees the ascription of prostitute identity as a way of slandering "physicality as deviant" and seems to be searching for a purer kind of eroticism "without debasement." She is looking for a sex-positive way of reading the text which is the very same agenda of SWOP readers. However, the prostitute labelling is disqualified by Hornsby because it is seen as a tainted version of sexuality that edifies degradation.[52] SWOP activists do not see prostitution per se as inherently exploitive or a debased kind of eroticism (any more than, say, marriage). Thus the objections raised in the readings of these feminists are more of a hindrance to a liberating reading to prostitutes because they assume too much negativity within the prostitute identity.

Luise Schottroff, Jane Schaberg and Elisabeth Schüssler Fiorenza, in their interpretations of Luke's anointing, are also critiqued by Hornsby as perhaps representing a more conservative anti-sex strain of biblical feminism.[53] This is due to their ongoing ascription of the prostitute label to Luke's version of anointing woman which is the focus of Hornsby. What she does

48. Athenaeus, *Deipnosophists,* Vol. VI (Loeb Classical Library; Cambridge, MA: Harvard University Press, 1959), XIII.559a, p. 22; XIII.571c, p. 86; XIII.572e, p. 92.

49. *Greek Anthology,* Vol. 5 (trans. W.R. Paton; Loeb Classical Library; Cambridge, MA: Harvard University Press, 1960), epigram 175, p. 212.

50. Nygren, *Agape and Eros,* pp. 310, 390.

51. Judith Applegate, "'And she wet his feet with her tears': A Feminist Interpretation of Luke 7:36–50," in Harold Washington, Susan Lochrie Graham and Pamela Thimmes (eds.), *Escaping Eden: New Feminist Perspectives on the Bible* (New York: New York University Press, 1999) pp. 84–85.

52. Hornsby, "Why is She Crying?" pp. 100–101.

53. Hornsby, "Why is She Crying?" p. 99.

not consider in her critique is the importance of maintaining the label in terms of a liberation hermeneutic, given that prostitution is an extremely common occurrence among the poor. I believe this is a motivation of these feminist scholars even though they might also see Luke's redaction as a dangerous slandering of women's involvement in the Jesus Movement. In this liberation vein the celebration of the loving act of a sex worker still has the ability to affirm the erotic, especially among the poor in the complicated circumstances of poverty. In a 1996 article not addressed by Hornsby, Schottroff actually looks at the Luke passage with the help of Audre Lorde's definition of the erotic as being closely connected to the search for justice.[54] Herein, the anointing woman crying in Luke is crying for justice. Her anointing is a form of erotic, uncensored love which Jesus does not eschew: "He does not distinguish between what she shares with him and what she may have even shared with some of her 'johns'—or what she shares with God." Her love is not tainted to Schottroff, nor to SWOP readers.

There is a very big stream of social theory that investigates the function of institutional control of sex in authoritarian societies. Beginning with Freud's theory that sex needed to be repressed in order for there to be civilization, in his work *Civilization and its Discontents*,[55] this kind of theorizing became the special task of Frankfurt school intellectuals who lived through the horrors of Nazism and WWII. Wilhelm Reich was one of the first to link sexual repression to fascist social control.[56] Max Horkheimer also was interested in how socialization in the family prepared individuals to function in a totalitarian society.[57] Herbert Marcuse theorized that for a more democratic society to occur, *eros* also needed liberation.[58] Subsequent theorists of sex, such as Michel Foucault and Judith Butler, have focused attention on sex as not simply repressed and having some sort of pure existence prior to repression but as always created, shaped and controlled

54. Schottroff, "Through German and Feminist Eyes," p. 340. The reference for Audre Lorde is "Uses of the Erotic: The Erotic as Power*," from *Sister Outsider* (Freedom, CA: Crossing Press, 2000), pp. 53–58.

55. Peter Gay (ed.), *The Freud Reader* (NY and London: Norton and Norton, 1989), pp. 722–72.

56. Wilhelm Reich, *The Mass Psychology of Fascism* (New York: Noonday Press, 1970 [1946]).

57. Max Horkheimer, "Authority and the Family," from *Critical Theory: Selected Essays* (New York: Continuum, 1999 [1968]).

58. Herbert Marcuse, *Eros and Civilization: A Philosophical Inquiry into Freud* (Boston, MA: Beacon Press, 1966 [1955]).

in certain ways by technologies of power.[59] Whatever their particular stance on sex and social control, these theorists all point to the relevance of linking the erotic to the struggle for justice which Schottroff asserts via Audre Lorde in the anointing woman text of Luke. Similar assertions about sex and justice are made frequently by sex worker activists. The taboo on sexual commerce can rouse contradictory feelings for many that contribute to the stigmatization of prostitutes and other sex outlaws. That sex is such a subconscious source of shame is perhaps why people can get so emotionally agitated over the justice claims of sex workers.

In line with of such insights on sex and the body, Vernon Robbins used the traditions of anointing woman to work through his new integrative method of socio-rhetorical poetics. In an article that was a precursor to full length book advocating for a more integrated mode of exegesis, Robbins makes a call for further investigation into the social meaning of anointing woman's action.[60] He believes that New Testament scholars overvalue a "culture of the mind" in their interpretations and that "there may be deep reasons why New Testament scholars do not search for intertextual data that exhibit various possibilities for the social meaning of the woman's action...intertextual data then may push us into social and cultural issues that we are not accustomed to talk about."[61] What is needed is a frank engagement with the "culture of the body." Kathleen Corley's subsequent work on the social meaning of women at Greco-Roman meals is very helpful toward this end but comes to equivocal conclusions in terms of identifying prostitute women as prominent among the followers of Jesus.[62] Corley does not eliminate prostitutes from among the followers of Jesus per se, but argues that Christian women who engaged in table fellowship in mixed

59. Michel Foucault, *The History of Sexuality: An Introduction,* Vol. I, (New York: Vintage, 1990 [1978]) and Judith Butler, *The Psychic Life of Power: Theories in Subjection* (Stanford, CA: Stanford University Press, 1997).

60. Vernon Robbins, "Using a Socio-Rhetorical Poetics to Develop a Unified Method: The Woman who Anointed Jesus as a Test Case," in *Society of Biblical Literature 1992 Seminar Papers* (Society of Biblical Literature: 1992), pp. 302–19. The book I refer to is *Exploring the Texture of Texts: A Guide to Socio-Rhetorical Interpretations* (Valley Forge, VA: Trinity Press International, 1996).

61. Robbins, "Using a Socio-Rhetorical Poetics to Develop a Unified Method," pp. 312–13.

62. Kathleen Corley, *Private Women, Public Meals: Social Conflict in the Synoptic Tradition* (Peabody, MA: Hendrickson Publishers, 1993). See also other articles by Corley: "Were the Women around Jesus Really Prostitutes?" and "The Anointing of Jesus in the Synoptic Tradition."

Alabastra featuring conjugal situations. Reprinted with permission of University of California Press, from Eva Keul's *Reign of the Phallus: Sexual Politics in Ancient Athens*, Berkeley, CA: University of California Press, 1993

Prostitutes with anointing flasks are a feature of ancient Greek vase painting. Reprinted with permission of University of California Press, from Eva Keul's *Reign of the Phallus: Sexual Politics in Ancient Athens*, Berkeley, CA: University of California Press, 1993

company would get the label whether they "deserved it" or not and that the label may not have any correlation to the actual professions of many women in the Jesus Movement.[63] While her larger focus is on the social meaning of dining in Greco-Roman antiquity, part of her investigation addressed the passage of anointing women and the specific social significance of the woman's actions. The focus of SWOP readers is on the anointing act as a form of sex work in conjunction with the customary presence of prostitutes at symposia (which means literally, a "drinking party"). To this end, Corley's work is still a good pathway to this SWOP focus.

Corley carefully reconstructs the social presuppositions that might get triggered by the presence of a woman at a dinner. There is a great deal of evidence from antiquity that respectable women present at a symposium ran the risk of being associated with prostitution. However, it was exactly during the time of the early Christian movement that such non-prostitute women began to start attending symposia. The symposium type scene in an abundance of Greco-Roman literature features prostitutes, hetaerae or flute girls, as the stereotypical female attendees at such functions, thus the moralists of the time spilled a lot of ink over the reputations of non-prostitutes who dared come to dinner parties. Courtesans attended to symposia as guests of men, the musical entertainers were generally prostitutes and servant slaves were considered sexually available: "central to Greco-Roman meal ideology was the continued association of sexuality, slavery, and prostitution with banquet settings."[64] It was customary for guests to be anointed on their head or feet by servants of the host as reflected in the text of Lk 7:44–46. This anointing was a common form of hospitality *and* festive banquet behaviour.

It is a common topic of articles on anointing woman to argue about what is original, head anointing or foot anointing, generally due to the Christological significance of head anointing. A question important to feminist scholars regards the historical reality behind the various versions of the anointing found in the Gospels. Schüssler Fiorenza sees a prophetic, Christologically significant sign action in the anointing. Thus, the head anointing in Mark 14 is for her the earliest layer of the tradition. If foot anointing is seen as an anomaly then perhaps it is cloaking a more original head anointing of the Messiah, so the argument goes. In counterargument, a list of contemporaneous parallels to foot anointing is given in an article

63. Corley, "Were the Women around Jesus Really Prostitutes?" p. 520, and *Private Women*, p. 79.
64. Corley, *Private Women*, p. 78.

by J.F. Coakley in order to make the argument for the priority of the Johannine tradition.[65] Kathleen Corley recently argued that the attribution of a Christological intention to the anointing woman, especially anointing for burial, could only be post-Easter redaction.[66] Corley contends that what is portrayed is banquet anointing, either of the foot or head, it doesn't matter for the action to be scandalous.[67] In Attic comedy, both head and feet were euphemisms for the phallus.[68] A Christological emphasis would have certainly been obscured in the redactional process since none of the existing anointing texts actually use the messianic verb χρίω to describe her action. Instead, the verb to pour (χέω) or μυρίζω and αλείφω, other anointing verbs, are used for the act of anointing. If the messianic overtones came later in the redactional process it certainly didn't emphasize it lexically. In terms of a prostitute interpretation, it is a moot issue. The verb χρίω is used for erotic banquet head anointing, even in the Jewish author Josephus.[69] Since the anointing of head and feet both have strongly erotic associations whatever the verb, it does not necessarily matter which one is original for the behaviour to be labelled sexual. The SWOP reading mostly focuses on head anointing or anointing in general as the main reason for identifying the woman as a sex worker (or someone totally unafraid of the whore stigma) that cuts across all accounts. A witty text attributed to a prostitute by Athenaeus shows an easy switch from foot to head loaded with sexual innuendo: "As Diphilus bade her wash his feet, Gnatheana asked 'Why need I, indeed have you not come to me on your head?'"[70] Corley's claims are an important basis upon which SWOP readers reassert a prostitute presence back into the story of early Christianity. It is time to turn to the interpretive work of these sex worker activists.

Sex Worker Standpoint on the Anointing Woman Traditions

The themes that emerged for the SWOP readers were fairly unified with a few minor places of debate. The most important and strongest point of

65. J.F. Coakley, "The Anointing at Bethany and the Priority of John," *JBL* 107 (1988), p. 247.

66. Corley, "The Anointing of Jesus in the Synoptic Tradition," p. 63.

67. Corley, "The Anointing of Jesus in the Synoptic Tradition," p. 71.

68. Jeffery Henderson, *The Maculate Muse: Obscene Language in Attic Comedy* (Oxford: Oxford University Press, 1991 [1975]), pp. 113, 129.

69. Josephus, *Jewish Antiquities*, Vol. IX (trans. Louis Feldman; Loeb Classical Library; Cambridge, MA: Harvard University Press, 1965), XIX.239, p. 324.

70. Athenaeus, XIII.583f, p. 147.

consensus was that anointing is sex work for the SWOP readers and this was the most important reason for interpreting the woman in all versions as a sex worker. There was substantial discussion around the ideological reasons, class based and related to respectability, that recent feminist scholarship would minimize the participation of sex workers in the Jesus Movement. The main reason that was identified was the strict dichotomy of sex and spirituality in Christian tradition. The stigmatizing view of anointing woman as a sinner because of her sexual status was a place of disputation. The readers recognized that it was only in Luke where this is an issue so the discussion mainly revolved around whether the woman was really viewed in a negative way by Jesus in this account. Some of the readers assumed that Jesus saw the woman as a sinner and was dispensing his forgiveness with patronizing arrogance and covert domination. This kind of Jesus was not viewed as liberating. If Jesus could be seen as arguing against conventional notions of sin and status, then perhaps even Lk 7: 36–50 could be viewed in a positive way. Finally, the most exciting aspect of the SWOP reading was examining the view of anointing woman as personating a goddess in a sacred ritual. One overarching goal of all the readers was to try to integrate the sexual and sacred in the story. However, Ms Shiris, who herself identifies as a modern day sacred prostitute, played a very central role in actually discerning the Goddess in this story. The other readers have simply desired evidence of the feminine as divine, having been influenced by the matriarchy theories of radical feminism. I have done subsequent research to facilitate this reading and was shocked at the plethora of evidence that links erotic prostitute anointing with the worship of Aphrodite and Adonis.

Is Anointing Woman a Prostitute? Anointing as Sex Work

The issue of the anointing woman's identity was clarified forthwith in the SWOP symposium dedicated to the four gospel parallels. The act of anointing was immediately and unanimously recognized as sex work. That the story setting was a banquet made it unlikely that her behaviour was respectably chaste. Gayle gives her reasons for reading the anointing as sex work:

> I would have made the assumption even if it didn't come out and say: 'this was a prostitute.' It's because the righteous women were very rarely mentioned, the women who stayed at home with their husbands and cared for their children and the house, they are rarely mentioned. So this is sort of an assumption, but this wouldn't be something a respectable woman, single or married, would do to a stranger. Coming into

somebody's house and anoint? Only a prostitute would feel good about doing it. It was traditional to have prostitutes at such a gathering.

There was also a great range of behaviours connected to anointing: perfumes and perfumed oils, incense, aromatherapy of scented candles, lubricants, bathing, massage, exfoliation, caresses and kisses. Gayle also explains this range very well:

> It is not unusual in my practice, with my clients, to pamper them. In fact, that is part of what I do, it is, sorry, that is MAINLY what I do. I pamper them and I stroke them from head to toe, and I also give them a really good massage which includes the feet and the head. So it just depends on what kind of service you provide. I don't differentiate that much between the sensual and the sexual. It is for the receiver to determine what belongs in what category. It is a total experience and in addition to any of the more overt sexual practice, there is the touching and the holding and the caressing the cuddling and sometimes bathing together, which could be interpreted as a form of anointing.

A commonplace among sex workers is that the strictly sexual labour of intercourse and penile stimulation is a very small fraction of the services that they provide which is actually a fuller emotional package deal. Kimberlee below compared what she does with clients with what happens in the foot anointing versions of the Gospels:

> I have seen clients who climax within minutes, you know, you get close to them and they are just done. Now you have got this guy still who wants the other 58 minutes of his appointment and you're done! And every single time I have lifted out the exfoliant and a bowl of hot water and a cloth and I wash their feet. That is what I do. It is like this client right now needs something, he needs you to connect with him and there is a level, like I can lay with them and cuddle with them or whatever for five or ten minutes but I can't do it for fifty minutes, it just like, it starts to interfere with my personal boundaries. And so, it's like I have this sense that this person really needs to connect with me and I wash their feet. But I exfoliate, I do a whole thing with the ones I need to take time with. And they love it! And they don't ever receive that...It is definitely a form of worship and sexual.

Other readers discussed foot fetishism in their trade and their experiences with "foot work." Everyone agreed that foot work is sex work and the foot is an extremely erogenous zone. Kimberlee knows from experience: "I have had an orgasm from just having my foot rubbed. You know, only on my feet." The head also was an erogenous zone, and head rubs were common enough but head anointing was not a customary act for contemporary sex workers. Damienne Sin, who has done a lot of reading on theories of early matriarchal civilizations, wondered if perhaps the whole "anointing for burial" explanation was also a sexual thing:

> I think it is important to keep in mind that in antiquity during the whole matriarchal cultures, graves were shaped like vaginas so when you died you were put back into a vagina. Exactly, that was the whole thing, so the whole idea of lubing up before you enter a woman's vagina...I am wondering...anointing for burial, anointing before...?

So, the act of anointing itself is the main reason for identifying anointing woman as a prostitute for these modern sex workers. This connection is not something anachronistically imported from the modern sex industry. Nor is it a misogynistic assumption of male interpretation. The associations that pertain to anointing in Classical and Hellenistic Greek literature and art have a very strong erotic valence. Anointing is a typical sex prefatory behaviour between conjugal couples (see photos on p. 138). Some examples of this marital anointing are from Aristophanes.[71] In *Lysistrata*, Myrrhine tries to delay intercourse with her sex-starved husband Cinesius via elaborate preparations which include anointing with oil in an *alabastron*.[72] In another comedy, the *Acharnians*, Dicaiopolis advises a bride about how to anoint her groom using the phallic shaped *alabastron* like a penis. However, scented oil or μύρον and anointing is also strongly associated with prostitutes at symposia.[73] A good example of this linkage comes also from the comedy the *Acharnians* by Aristophanes. In an invitation to dinner by the priest of Bacchus, Dicaiopolis is told to hurry and that "all things else are ready and prepared, the couches, table, sofa-cushions, rugs, wreathes, sweetmeats, myrrh (μύρον), the harlotry are there (αι πόρναι)."[74] Reclining

71. *Aristophanes* Vol. III (trans. B.B. Rodgers; Loeb Classical Library; Cambridge, MA: Harvard University Press, 1996), 939–49, p. 90–92. *Acharnians* in *Aristophanes*, Vol. 1 (trans. B.B. Rodgers; Loeb Classical Library; Cambridge, MA: Harvard University Press, 1992), 1051–1066, p. 102. Henderson, *The Maculate Muse*, p. 120.

72. Christopher Faraone has recently argued that the play gets its humour from depicting Myrrhine and Lysistrata simultaneously as brothel workers and devotees of Athena, so the scene is perhaps not so respectably conjugal as it might seem. His article is "Priestess and Courtesan: The Ambivalence of Leadership in Arisophanes' *Lysistrata*," in Christopher Faraone and Laura McClure (eds.), *Prostitutes and Courtesans in the Ancient World* (Madison, WI: University of Wisconsin Press, 2006).

73. See Eva Keuls, *The Reign of the Phallus*, pp. 117–20, 170–73. Also the same point is made by Kathleen Corley (following Keuls) about anointing in the synoptics in *Private Women, Public Meals*, p. 104.

74. *Acharnians*, 1089–1091, pp. 104–106

couches, μύρον, and hetaerae are also grouped together in Plato's *Republic* as constituent elements of a symposium.[75] In the poetry of Catullus there is a symposium that features a slave girl or prostitute wielding an unguent given her by Venuses and Cupids.[76] Even at the eschatological banquet described in the Septuagint's version of Isa. 25:6, everyone will be anointed (χρίσονται μύρον) and drink wine.[77]

In the works on prostitutes by Lucian, Alciphron and Athenaeus, anointing oil is frequently listed as a form of harlot's hire or gift and as an attribute of prostitutes.[78] Athenaeus describes a drinking cup of the prostitute Callisto which she dedicated to Aphrodite full of anointing oil.[79] The Jewish writer, Philo, associates prostitutes and anointing oil.[80] Prostitutes depicted with anointing flasks are a feature of ancient Greek vase painting (see photos on p. 139).[81] Prostitutes and their lovers with anointed heads are found repeatedly in the amatory epigrams of Greek Anthology.[82] It is very safe to say that anointing has strong erotic associations in Greek literature and art. This erotic behavior ranges in type from the respectably conjugal to the extreme of the orgiastic group sex of the symposia.[83] A plethora of intertexts to explain the meaning of anointing as erotic exists but is not usually brought to bear on the New Testament

75. Plato, *Republic*, Vol. 1 (trans. Paul Shorey; Loeb Classical Library; London: Wm. Heinemann, 1924), II.373a, p. 160.

76. Catullus, *Catullus, Tibillus, and Pervigilium Veneris* (Loeb Classical Library; Cambridge: Harvard University Press, 1956), 13.11, p. 19.

77. This text was pointed out to me by M. Sabbe's "The Anointing of Jesus in John 12.1–8 and its Synoptic Parallels," in F. Van Segbroeck, C.M. Tuckett, G. Van Belle and J. Verheyden (eds.), *The Four Gospels 1992: Festschrift Frans Neirynck* (Leuven: University Press, 1992), pp. 2051–2082. p. 2058.

78. Lucian, *The Dialogues of the Courtesans*, Vol. VII (Loeb Classical Library; Harvard University Press: Cambridge, 1961), Alciphron, *The Letters of the Courtesans* (Loeb Classical Library; Harvard University Press, Cambridge, 1959. Myrrh/μύρον in Lucian: Dialogue 7, p. 395 and Dialogue 14, p. 457. In Alciphron: Letter 9, p. 271. In Athenaeus: XIII.577e, p. 119; XIII.580e, p. 129; XIII. XII.596c, p. 215.

79. Athenaeus, Vol. V, XI.486b, p. 158.

80. See Corley, *Private Women*, pp. 72–74 where she discussed Philo's *Sacrifices of Abel and Cain*, pp. 21–24.

81. Keuls, *The Reign of the Phallus*, pp. 170–73.

82. *Greek Anthology*, Vol. I, V.136, p. 193; V.175, p. 213, V.198–200, p. 227.

83. Eva Keuls documents this with vase painting. The kylix or drinking cup used in symposia were quite often pornographic in painted depictions of symposium sex with prostitutes, see *The Reign of the Phallus*, p. 165.

texts under study. There is no evidence that the woman who anointed Jesus was his wife so the erotic action remains outside the bounds of sexual propriety for being non-conjugal and public. This is exactly the kind of behaviour associated with the symposium or banquet type scene. This intertextual material can explicitly elucidate why the action of anointing is so often seen to be scandalous, even in the non-Lukan versions. In/decency may be a reason for not applying this material to Jesus' anointing.

A very strong case can be made for viewing biblical anointing in erotic terms as well. For example, Ruth, Judith, Esther, the Shulamite in Song of Songs, the foundling bride of YHVH, Israel, in Ezekiel 16 all anoint or use myrrh/perfumed oil/μύρον for sexually imbued reasons. Naomi advised Ruth to bathe and anoint herself and put on her best clothes in order to seduce Boaz in Ruth 3:3. Strange Woman in Prov. 7:17 says: "I have perfumed my bed with myrrh, aloes, and cinnamon. Come let us take our fill of love until morning; let us delight ourselves with love." YHVH himself anoints his foundling bride in Ezekiel 16 only to lose her to harlotry. Judith and Esther anoint themselves to seduce colonial powers (Judith 10:3 and Est. 2:9, 2:12). Song of Songs is a very oily, scented pastoral scene: "Your anointing oils are fragrant, your name is perfume poured out" (1:3), "While the king was on his couch, my nard gave forth its fragrance." (1:12) "Perfumed with myrrh and frankincense" (3:6) "I arose to open to my beloved, and my hands dripped with myrrh, my fingers with liquid myrrh" (5:5). Ann Winsor reads these very passages from the Song of Songs to interpret intertextually John's version of the anointing woman in Jn 12:1–8.[84]

In Hos. 2:5, 8, and 12 basic "oil" is listed as a form of harlot's hire.[85] However, anointing oil can also be a sign of decadent wealth, which YHVH will take away from wayward Israel in punishment for her religious harlotry in prophetic texts using the prostitution metaphor, as well as the negative use of myrrh in the case of Sophia's foil, the strange woman in Prov. 7:17. Decadent rich exploiters who anoint are in Wisdom of Solomon 2:7: "Let us take our fill of costly wines and perfumes," or in Isa. 3:20, Mic. 6:15,

---

84. Ann Roberts Winsor, *A King is Bound in the Tresses: Allusions to the Song of Songs in the Fourth Gospel* (New York: Peter Lang, 1999).

85. For a detailed explanation on the ancient production of perfumed oil (generally with the base being olive oil), or μύρον, see Theophrastus' treatise *On Odours*, in *Enquiry into Plants and Minor Works on Odours and Weather Signs*, Vol. II (trans. Sir Arthur Hort; Loeb Classical Library; Cambridge: Harvard University Press, 1949), especially section IV, p. 340.

Amos 6:6. Clearly, there is an erotic valence to anointing here in all these stories, but also, a latent critique at times associated with erotic anointing and its connection to decadent wealth. This linkage could also be at work in the Mark/Matthew/John passage when objectors critique the woman's act of anointing as an extravagance at odds with their mission to the poor. J.D. Derrett operates with the premise that the anointing oil was a form of harlots hire and thus a tainted gift or offering.[86] He explains the scene in legal terms; if the tainted oil were sold then the offering would be acceptable, thus explaining the objection of onlookers. This reading however is part of the anointing-woman-as-sinner type of reading which is problematic to both feminists and SWOP readers.

Anointing Woman as Sinner. Prostitution as Sin?

It was Scarlot Harlot, the famous "Unrepentant Whore"[87] who really took the lead in critiquing the prostitute-as-sinner way of viewing Luke's anointing woman. Almost everyone had something to say about this issue, almost everyone has had their morality questioned and has been told that Jesus will love them if they repent. Not only is this interpretation of anointing woman problematic for prostitutes but also for what it means for the characterization of Jesus:

> He meters out his forgiveness to the poor person that is all like, at his feet, you know, like the big sinner, and then really, Jesus is playing a domination game and he like totally wins. But he is just like, I think he is being really a jerk and teaching people that, you know, well that you have to go around and both buy into these subtleties that I am putting out about who is dominant and part of his trip for domination is to be, like, generous. I think it is really nasty.

No one likes this Jesus. Says Kimberlee: "it sounds like Jesus considers prostitution a sin. So, OK I do not think this passage is liberating to prostitutes." Related to this Jesus characterization is the opposition of her action with the care of the poor. If Jesus is the exceptional case where such anointing is acceptable, then this is another reason for reading his behaviour as arrogant. Kimberlee quickly chimed in to agree with Scarlot:

> Of course she has this expensive perfume for *my* feet, and you will always have the poor people but you won't always have me. So it is OK for us to indulge when it's about *me* but, you know, we have this vow of

86. Derrett, "The Anointing at Bethany and the Story of Zacchaeus," p. 270.
87. Carol Leigh, *Unrepentant Whore*.

poverty otherwise. I think ew, Jesus must have been hot, and that is just totally bad because there is this totally self deprecating thing about being attracted to guys that are dominating pricks! I just broke up with a dominating prick. So, that behaviour, the way you describe the domination by doling out his compassion and generosity but then saying 'I am so much better than you, I dominate you because of this generosity', is right on.

Since there were other versions of the story, there was a way out of the sinner scenario. Both Veronica and Sweet pointed out how the other versions that did not name her a sinner seemed more focused upon her action as something wonderful to remember. It also solves the problem of an arrogant Jesus to focus on her action:

> That version (Mk 14) is very different. It doesn't sound so self-serving. This sounds more generous and giving and kind to me. In the previous version it is like the poor are going to be around forever, but I am not, so let her do what she want disrespecting herself cuz *I'm Jesus*. One of the most obvious differences, I just want to show in terms of the last two that we just read, is that there is much more reference to the woman in the Mark version.

Veronica, however, argued that it is not necessary to understand Jesus as agreeing with the sinner label. Instead, she saw a contrast between how Simon the Pharisee, as a model of piety, viewed the prostitute, and how Jesus viewed the prostitute. This reading is very close to Luise Schotroff's described earlier. Veronica's way of doing this was to compare Jesus' parable argumentation with how he talks about Samaritans in order to push people's paradigms a bit further:

> And so he comes and says 'actually if you come and take a look at this, these people are more gracious, more humble, more helpful', that's why there is the parable about the good Samaritan, the reason he picked a Samaritan is because these were a people that were reviled. So it was like, 'I want to show you what a good person does.' I don't think he was necessarily saying 'I believe that Samaritans were bad people', but he was saying 'I understand that *you* think you are better than them. Let me tell you a parable about a Samaritan doing a good thing cuz I want to get you to start thinking about what really matters.'

This reading accords well with Luise Schotroff's assertion that Luke's story is trying to contrast Jesus' attitude towards prostitutes with that of a conventional religious leader. The early Q tradition of Jesus's frequent table fellowship with tax collectors and prostitutes, as reflected in Mt. 21:31, is the basis for seeing the historical Jesus as being unconcerned about the propriety of associating with social outcasts.[88] This association is part of the basis for claiming that Jesus has a preferential option for the poor and the oppressed thus his behaviour does not need to be seen as patronizing arrogance but perhaps instead, solidarity, and is something prostitutes wish to maintain for their present day struggles for human rights.

In this struggle, the rights of the poor are not at odds with the behaviour of anointing woman. This is a false dichotomy set up by self righteous and greedy people to divide the poor into deserving and non-deserving. It is much easier to blame the poor and to scapegoat sex workers when sexual pleasure is seen as sinful and the reason for the existence of poverty. In a 1990 article on the phrase "for the poor are always with you," R.S. Sugirathrajah argued something similar, even though he does not mention prostitutes. "Jesus knew selling perfume wasn't going to end poverty" but only a "radical social redesign" could accomplish this.[89] Says Damienne Sin: "I think it goes beyond expunging sexuality; it is expunging any kind of pleasure, fun, enjoyment, period, because you should just be miserable and help the poor all your life." Ms. Shiris agrees: "something I learned very early on in life is that those who claim to believe in happiness but attack luxuries, are forgetting that happiness is essentially about leisure and time off for aesthetic embodiment."

Sex worker activists in general see themselves as an integral part of this struggle out of poverty because being poor is not a spiritual good. Sex workers are generally sex workers because they are poor. As Gayle states: "then as now, women in this profession are almost always in it because they can make very good money for the amount of time they spend, and they *need* that time to work on their masters degrees or to take care of their children or to pursue their other career in painting or writing, or whatever…to join the revolutionary Jesus Movement!" Sex workers have often been leaders in or funded progressive social movements. Gayle says of the people who object to anointing woman's behaviour:

88. For discussion of the earlyness of this tradition in Q see Schüssler Fiorenza, *In Memory of Her*, p. 122; Schottroff and Stegemann, *Jesus and the Hope of the Poor* (Maryknoll, NY: Orbis Books, 1986), pp. 15, 33; Corley, *Private Women*, pp. 156–57, 178–79.

89. R.S. Sugirtharajah, "'For you always have the poor with you,' An Example of a Hermeneutics of Suspicion," *Asia Journal of Theology* 4 (April 1990), pp. 102–107, p. 105.

> Now she doesn't defend herself and say 'I did sell some yesterday and gave 12 million denarii, whatever it is, to the poor.' But she doesn't have a comeback. But it is a very false assumption. Personally I give so much to charity. I give more than 10 percent of my income to a variety of important charities...I think it is a false assumption that we're greedy. I don't see a conflict between her action and the needs of the poor. I could see Mary doing the same thing out in the market place for somebody, who is obviously really poor, that wasn't Jesus. This is someone, like 'Oh, look at this person, they need some kindness' or something like 'Look at their poor feet, or *HER* poor feet' and just do it.

So, it is not prostitutes and poor people who are really in opposition to one another. For SWOP readers, the separation of the sexual from the divine is really about society's control of women and the poor via sexuality. And it is prostitutes who are the special vortex for all of the emotional baggage society has about sex: "you are absolutely a vector for all the love and the hatred that people hold around on sexuality," asserts Damienne Sin. Veronica agrees: "the Bible says 'if your right hand offends thee chop it off!' But they never think to kill the guy with the hard on!"

When SWOP readers reject the opposition between eroticism and social justice, what they are also doing is attempting to reintegrate the sexual and the sacred. There is an enormous amount of social resistance to this. Veronica and others discussed how upsetting it was to their family members that they were doing Bible study: "If I am studying her, it's *her* Bible evidently, then I am going to get my own spin on it now, which means she can't just tell me what the word of God is, right? And apparently, I come up with some cockamamie idea that spirituality and prostitution can coexist." All the SWOP readers agreed that God is not opposed to sex per se but rather it is domination, coercion, and exploitation that offend whatever divinity they pray to. SWOP readers yearn for spiritual affirmation of what they do as sex professionals and they saw it in this story. Gayle sees that "there is no separation for Mary between the sacred and the profane, as they would say, or the sexual and the erotic. I think it is a wonderful example of her humanity. Her behaviour demonstrated her integration of the spiritual and the sexual." Ms. Shiris took this one step further to discern anointing woman as a personification of a goddess:

> It is not typical of me to defend Christianity or Jesus but this story has a very different meaning to me, anointing yes, is a symposium gesture, you have to understand 'context symposium.' Socrates' teacher Diotima, who was an hetaera, she is also a sacred prostitute priestess, it is very unclear historically how closely those roles were linked, but there is a heavy religious component even in Greek culture. It is even more obvious

when you look at Mesopotamian, or if you look at the cultures that all become Phoenicia. You anoint in a sacred prostitution ceremony and anointing is typically a prefatory phase in the ceremony. The same this is true I believe though my research is incomplete here, of the Eleusinian Mysteries. But this is very much a part of a religious ritual. And specifically what it does, in either a male or female, the Canaanite priest the pagan would take on the guise of the Baal or Ashtorah as in either male or female, in an Adonis or Aphrodite figure. And the point is that I think what it is saying, what Jesus is saying, 'use that oil on me' the point is that it is a stage, if you think of this strictly in terms of the mystery of the Trinity which actually makes a bit of sense to me, oddly enough, I see this as a nexus point of Jesus qua immortal and Jesus qua Baal as a ceremony of realization. Mary of Bethany or Mary of Magdala taken as an equivalent, is, takes on a goddess figure, that is a classic pose of sacred prostitution from Gilgamesh all the way to the 21st century. That is what it seems to me is the reason it is worth putting this 300 denarii in, well 'around here, how many people have been paid 300 denarii for a night?' I mean that may seem odd but I think that is very much the point, in that the amount of preciousness worthwhile to have the excellence of achieving this kind of ex-temporal aesthesis or aesthetics, or incarnation, to use the Christian sense, this is an example of it and a crucial one.

I initially had a concept of Jesus and anointing woman as enacting something relating to Sophia as a divine erotic figure. I also knew well from Lucian, Alciphron and Athenaeus that ancient prostitutes are repeatedly portrayed as worshipping Aphrodite. However, Ms. Shiris pushed me to go even further in this line of investigation subsequent to our symposia.

I have a special fondness for Aphrodite because this is what they call me in Greece. In fact, this is my Christian name. When I was 18 years old I was anointed from head to toe in an adult baptism to the Greek Orthodox Church in order to marry my Greek lover. After three days of marinating in this oil, I was made to bathe in the ocean, like the rebirth of Aphrodite from the sea. My baptism occurred in the chapel of St. Panteleimon above the archeological site of Kommos in southern Crete. This was an ancient site of worship of Phoenician Aphrodite, according to Stephanie Budin who has written the new definitive book on *The Origin of Aphrodite*.[90] When I was young and romantic, I liked being identified with the goddess of love, and I do even more so in middle age. However, the real reason that

90. Stephanie Budin, *The Origin of Aphrodite* (Bethesda, MD: CDL Press, 2002), p. 196.

I got that nickname was probably because the villagers thought me a "whore" for being 18, American, blond, and travelling alone around the Mediterranean like a heroine from an ancient Greek romance. I never did marry that guy. I have become a religion scholar instead. Eventually I married a man named Thomas, who I occasionally like to call Tammuz, the Babylonian name for Adonis. I know from personal experience that modern Christian ritual can reverberate with very ancient pagan elements. The next section gives a summary of what I found that would substantiate to biblical scholars Ms. Shiris' assertions about sacred erotic anointing.

Is There a Goddess Hidden in the Account of Jesus' Anointing?

Given the current disfavour in biblical scholarship of the theory of sacred prostitution (see the discussion in chapter 3, Rahab's Deal), what I am attempting here is simply to show the connections in ancient literature between prostitutes, Aphrodite and anointing. I am not arguing for the existence of an institution of sacred prostitution where prostitutes work at a temple that is really a kind of brothel where their earnings are dedicated the goddess of love.[91] What I feel I can show in a very strong way, however, is that prostitutes are depicted in ancient literature as the special devotees of Aphrodite. Here is an ancient Greek prayer to Aphrodite from a prostitute:

> Goddess who hauntest Cyprus, and Cythera and Miletus to the fair plain of Syria that echoes to the tread of thy horses, come in gracious mood to Calliston who never repulsed a lover from her door.[92]

I can also show that prostitutes' clients are often represented as "Adonises" and what occurs between the two, including anointing, is thought of as divine. I can show that unlike current Christian attitudes, there once was a time when sex was divine and prostitutes were thought to be sexual experts. This sense of the female divine is what the SWOP readers yearn for in a reading of the Bible that they deem liberating to prostitutes. Such an affirmation goes beyond pity or mere tolerance of prostitutes but is something that wants to go to the heart of all sexual shame to reorient it completely towards the sacred. This sense of sacred sex is not a glorification of exploitation where Aphrodite, or any other god, becomes some kind of

---

91. I follow Stephanie Budin's definition in "Sacred Prostitution in the First Person," in Faraone and McClure (eds.), *Prostitutes and Courtesans*, pp. 78–79.
   92. *Greek Anthology,* Vol. IV, XII.131, p. 348.

divine pimp.[93] A modern day Indian sacred prostitute summed up her professional identity in this way: "I am a *Devadasi*; I believe sex with men is divine and draws me closer to my Gods."[94]

A very strong association attached to anointing relates to the cult of Aphrodite. In many literary texts Aphrodite anoints herself and her lovers in a manner homologized by prostitutes. Μύρον is a feature the festival of Adonis. In the Fifteenth Idyll of Theocritus the dirge sung over dead Adonis honours him "with Syrian perfume in golden *alabastra*."[95] In a votive plaque found in Locri, Aphrodite and Hermes elope with cupids pulling their chariot and holding an *alabastron* of μύρον.[96] The initiation celebrated in their cult was not conjugal; they are lovers, not the prototype of a married couple. Aphrodite as the goddess of sexuality is the patron deity of prostitutes and a common epithet of desirable young lovers is "Adonis" or sometimes Phaon and Anchises, all young mortal lovers of Aphrodite.[97] Hermes is perhaps a youthful god version of these young lovers. The Greek Anthology features many amatory epigrams with prostitute head anointing

93. Sheila Jeffreys, a staunch opponent of the prostitutes' rights movement had devoted a whole section in her book to imputing such motives to scholars as wishing to legitimate the exploitation of women in prostitution. This is not my goal. See Sheila Jeffreys, *The Idea of Prostitution*, pp. 48–54. This Australian feminist contacted our Alameda County Supervisor to try to get him to rescind his endorsement of decriminalizing prostitution in Berkeley during the 2004 campaign for Measure Q. I and a group of four sex workers spent a good hour trying to keep his endorsement. We did keep the endorsement, but another supervisor backed down due to such pressure from anti-prostitution feminists.

94. http://www.healthdev.org/eforums/cms/inv-archives.asp. This is from a letter from Kama, posted on 1 August 2005 on the SEX WORK eforum.

95. *The Greek Bucolic Poets* (trans. J.M. Edmonds; Loeb Classical Library: London: Wm. Heinemann, 1923), Theocritus Idyll XV.114, p. 191 and Bion I.77, p. 392.

96. Nanno Marinatos, "Striding across Boundaries: Hermes and Aphrodite as Gods of Initiation," in David Dodd and Christopher Faraone (eds.), *Initiation in Ancient Greek Rituals and Narratives: New Critical Perspectives* (London and NY: Routledge, 2003), pp. 130–51, p. 145 for discussion and 148 for image.

97. "Adonis": Alciphron Letter 14, pp. 297, 301 and 17, pp. 309–15; Luican, Dialogue 7, p. 399: Athenaeus XIII.580e; *Greek Anthology*, Vol. I, V.113, p. 183. "Phaon": Lucian, Dialogue 12, p. 435. "Anchises" *Greek Anthology* Vol. V, XVI.278, p. 327 here Anchises is equated with Adonis, both compared to a lover of the musican Maria who personates Aphrodite.

98. Nossis in the *Greek Anthology*, Vol. I (trans. W.R. Paton; Loeb Classical Library; Cambridge: Harvard University Press, 1960), VI.275, p. 447.

that is given religious valence through comparison with the famous love affair between Aphrodite and her young lover:

> With joy, methinks, Aphrodite will receive this offering from Samytha, the caul that bound her hair; for it is delicately wrought and hath a certain sweet smell of nectar, that nectar which with she, too, anoints lovely Adonis.[98]

The classical scholar Marilyn Skinner has analyzed this homology between prostitutes and clients and Aphrodite and Adonis in the poetry of Nossis, a Hellenistic poetess.[99] According to Skinner, "use of rich balms and incenses was intrinsic to the cult of the dying god, Aphrodite's consort.....perfumed oils, too, have an erotic as well as ritual significance. Nossis thus sets up a sly correlation between Aphrodite and Samytha: both derive sensual enjoyment from unguents – and from the company of a young male friend."[100] It was common for prostitutes to dedicate to Aphrodite locks of anointed hair, garlands dripping with myrrh,[101] mirrors,[102] and anointing vessels.[103] It was also prostitutes that were the typical models for statues of the goddess Aphrodite which makes a strong argument for seeing prostitutes as the special "avatars of a goddess honored as the demiurgic principle of sexuality operating outside the sphere of marriage."[104]

In the realm of biblical studies, personified Sophia has been interpreted as having absorbed many characteristic attributes of various Ancient Near Eastern goddesses. Schüssler Fiorenza writes that "divine Sophia is Israel's God in the language and *Gestalt* of the goddesss."[105] This is likely the result of the Hebrew religion going monotheistic: the Godhead takes within itself

---

99. Marilyn Skinner, "Nossis *Thelyglossos*: The Private Text and the Public Book," from Sarah Pomeroy (ed.), *Women's History and Ancient History* (Chapel Hill, NC: University of North Carolina Press: 1991), p. 25.

100. Skinner, "Nossis *Thelyglossos*," p. 25.

101. *Greek Anthology*, Vol. I, V.198–200. p. 226.

102. Andrew Stewart, "Reflections," in Natalie Kampen (ed.), *Sexuality in Ancient Art: Near East, Egypt, Greece and Italy* (Cambridge: Cambridge University Press, 1996), pp. 136–54, p. 143.

103. Athenaeus, Vol. V, XI.486b, p. 158.

104. Skinner, "Nossis *Thelyglossos*," pp. 25–27 and note 22, p. 42. The quote is from p. 27. The famous courtesan Phryne was the model for the famous statue of Aphrodite by Praxtiles and a painting by Apelles, see Athenaeus, Vol VI, XIII.591a, p. 186. For a recent article on this phenomenon see Catherine Keesling, "Heavenly Bodies: Monuments to Prostitutes in Greek Sanctuary," in Christopher Faraone and Laura McClure (eds.), *Prostitutes and Courtesans*.

105. Schüssler Fiorenza, *In Memory of Her*, p. 133.

both the male and female divinities that it is usurping. However, Tikva Frymer Kinsky writes "there is only one goddess who escaped this eclipse: Ishtar (Inanna) not only did not disappear but continued to grow in importance. Ishtar (Inanna) was not easily eradicated."[106] One characteristic of this goddess of love (Aphrodite is her Greek parallel) shared by Sophia is eroticism. Thus, scholars of Sophia have linked her to these love goddesses. Martin Scott does this specifically with reference to Sophia in the Gospel of John.[107] Silvia Schroer likewise links the dove, a symbol of Near Eastern love goddesses, to Sophia.[108] Lester Grabbe writes that there are two models of Sophia in the tradition: "One of these is that of a goddess-like figure; and the other is that of seducer or lover or erotic figure."[109] The erotic aspect of Sophia also has a relationship to prostitutes since Proverbs likes to carefully distinguish the two, even though or perhaps because, they tend to behave in similar ways. Claudia Camp has noted the slippage between Sophia and Strange Woman of Proverbs who is portrayed as a harlot: "the contrast begins to blur, however, when the protection offered by Wisdom's truth is itself purveyed in terms familiar from the Song of Songs and Egyptian love poetry."[110] Camp also sees a bit of Strange Woman in the behavior of Tamar, Judith and Ruth which defies the whore/virgin binary.[111] There also is a strong connection between the prostitute and the Ancient Near Eastern love goddess, Innana/Ishtar.[112] This may account for the erotic aspect of personified Sophia as seen in wisdom literature. If Song of Songs is classified as wisdom literature, then anointing gains an even stronger erotic aspect that links it to divine Sophia. The Canticles are often interpreted as a sublimated allegory of the soul's love for God (and vise versa) which is quite on par with the personified Sophia, ardently loved and pursued by the true seeker of wisdom. This line of interpretation is germane to the study of anointing woman since so many scholars see traces of Sophia in

106. Tikva Frymer-Kensky, *In the Wake of the Goddess: Women, Culture and the Transformation of Pagan Myth* (New York: Fawcett Columbine, 1992), p. 77.

107. Martin Scott, *Sophia and the Johannine Jesus* (Sheffield: Sheffield Academic Press, 1992), p. 42.

108. Silvia Schroer, *Wisdom has Built her House: Studies on the Figure of Sophia in the Bible* (Collegeville, MN: Liturgical Press, 2000 [1996]) p. 134.

109. Lester Grabbe, *Wisdom of Solomon* (Sheffield: Sheffield Academic Press, 1997), p. 68.

110. Claudia Camp, *Wise, Strange, and Holy: Strange Woman and the Making of the Bible* (Sheffield: Sheffield Academic Press, 2000), pp. 26, 76–77.

111. Camp, *Wise, Strange, and Holy*, pp. 76–77.

112. Frymer-Kensky, *In the Wake of the Goddess*, pp. 28–29.

the gospel characterizations of Jesus, especially in the Gospel of John where there are abundant allusions to the Canticles, particularly in the story of anointing woman in John 12:1–8. [113] While the allegory makes the eroticism "respectable," there is always something suspicious about it and that evades complete domestication.

In *The Gardens of Adonis,* a book length structuralist study on the meaning of Adonis and spices, Marcel Detienne argues that in ancient Greek culture, μύρον symbolizes both eroticism and its opposite, religious sacrifice. According to Detienne, the function of spices "were threefold: culinary, religious, and erotic" however, the spices "of the frankincense and myrrh type were used almost exclusively for making ointments and perfumes or else in sacrifices that were part of the worship of divine powers."[114] Μύρον is used as a label for Adonis in two poems.[115] One, from the Greek Anthology features a prostitute who nicknamed her Adonis "μύρον." Another, by the bucolic poet Bion depicts the ritual mourning of Adonis: "Pour out upon him unguents of Syria, perfumes of Syria. For he that was thy perfume (μύρον) is perished and gone." In another epigram in the Greek anthology by Asclepiades is depicted a slave on a shopping spree for a dinner party. She is sent to a myrrh shop owned by Αίαχρα or "Shameful" who has already been paid with kisses and her bed was a witness.[116] In an article that discusses this poem, Alan Cameron shows that perfumers had a bad reputation and were thought of as loose women.[117] Being a perfumer should be strictly a woman's profession according to Athenaeus.[118] The relationship of myrrh/perfume to the unregulated sexuality of women with "Adonises" is a recurring constant.

Non-conjugal eroticism, such as that practiced by prostitutes and that was most especially associated with the luxuriance of perfumes, was also commonly disdained as fruitless and a distraction from the worship of the gods. The festival of Adonis was a marginal rite looked upon with suspicion

---

113. Ann Winsor, *A King is Bound in the Tresses: Allusions to the Song of Songs in the Fourth Gospel* (New York: Peter Lang, 1999).

114. Marcel Detienne, *The Gardens of Adonis: Spices in Greek Mythology* (Princeton: Princeton University Press, 1994), p. 37.

115. *Greek Anthology,* V.113, p. 182. *Greek Bucolic Poets,* Bion I.77, p. 392. See Detienne, *The Gardens of Adonis,* p. 63.

116. V.181, p. 216.

117. Alan Cameron, "Asclepiades' Girlfriends," in Helene Foley (ed.), *Reflections of Women in Antiquity* (New York: Gordon and Breach Science Publishers, 1981), pp. 275–302, pp. 286–87.

118. Athenaeus, Vol VI. XIII.612a, p. 297.

by many. Prostitutes are depicted in literature as the most notable of Adonis' devotees.[119] Detienne writes that "the festivals of Adonis were characterized by the abandoned enjoyment of lovers, the drunkenness of courtesans, *recherché* meals and *risqué* talk."[120] With Aphrodite, eroticism and worship could be operative simultaneously as shown by Athenaeus who writes that in the Golden Age, before the advent of male war gods, Aphrodite or "Cypris only was their queen. Her that folk appeased with painted offerings and richly scented salves, with sacrifices of pure myrrh and fragrant frankincense."[121] Furthermore, this kind of worship symbolized pleasure over virtue in the discussion of Athenaeus.

In many mythical accounts of Aphrodite anointing is a motif. Before she went off to seduce Anchises (the father of Aeneus who founded Rome), in the *Homeric Hymn to Aphrodite*, the Graces anointed the goddess with heavenly perfumed oils.[122] In Aelian, a story is told of the ferryman Phaon, another young lover of the goddess. Phaon was a ferryman who Aphrodite rewarded with an *alabastron* of μύρον, which gave him special charm to seduce. Many scholars equate Phaon and Adonis.[123] As previously mentioned, anointing oil was a feature of the Adonia. In the Adonia, the death of Adonis is ritually enacted with weeping and loose hair, as well as anointing oil. Adonis is resurrected yearly and it is perhaps the oil that bestows the immortality.

From the direction of ancient Greco-Roman love magic, Christopher Faraone lists oils and ointments as conventional types of love potions. Moreover, in literary representations, prostitutes were stereotypical practitioners of aggressive love magic, which is more typically considered a male behaviour.[124] Many magic spells that were for charm, love, health and favour were enacted with anointing oils or unguents and addressed the love goddess in prayer. A good example is a spell summoning Aphrodite

119. Detienne, *The Gardens of Adonis*, pp. 65–66.

120. Detienne, *The Gardens of Adonis*, p. 66.

121. Athenaeus, Vol V, XII510d, p. 294d.

122. Hesiod, *Hesiod, the Homeric Hymns and Homerica* (trans. Hugh G. Evelyn-White; Loeb Classical Library; Cambridge, MA: Harvard University Press, 1970), V.61, p. 410.

123. Aelian, *Historical Miscellany* (trans. N.G. Wilson; Loeb Classical Library; Cambridge, MA: Harvard University Press, 1997), 12.18, p. 367, note c. See also Detienne, *The Gardens of Adonis*, pp. 68–70.

124. Christopher Faraone, *Ancient Greek Love Magic* (Cambridge, MA: Harvard University Press, 1999), pp. 146–60.

to gain the grace or χάριν she had given Adonis.[125] This grace was poured over the head of Pandora by Aphrodite in the mythical account of Hesiod in *Works and Days*.[126] An Egyptian love spell asking for grace equates the goddess Isis with Aphrodite (as Cypris) in address and describes her as anointing her face before going to revive her dead husband Osiris.[127] It was not only pagans who practiced such love magic but, also, Christians, following the same rituals. A Christian Coptic spell reads:

> Oil! Oil! Oil! Holy Oil! Oil that flows from under the throne of Yao Sabaoth! Oil with which Isis anointed Osiris's bone(s)! I call you oil. The sun and the moon call you. The stars of heaven call you. The servants of the sun call you. I want to send you. You must come so that I may bring you and you may bring N. daughter of N. to me—N. son of N.[128]

The *Greek Magical Papyri* (in Latin, *Papyrae Graecae Magicae* or PGM) features a very long ritual, known as the Mithras Liturgy that includes an ointment recipe that will bestow immortality: "Say the successive things as an initiate, over his head, in a soft voice, so that he may not hear, as you are anointing his face with the mystery."[129] Another spell for charm in the PGM, or "*charitesion*," features head and face anointing together as one and the same action.[130] Clearly, the act of anointing was imbued with magical properties that can attract lovers and bestow favour and ward off death. For this reason dead bodies were anointed. According to Detienne, vultures were thought to be magically repelled by μύρον.

125. Robert Daniel and Franco Maltomini (eds.), *Supplementum Magicum*, Vol. II (Opladen:Westdeutscher Verlag GmbH, 1992), spell 63, p. 61; cf Faraone, *Ancient Greek Love Magic*, pp. 28, 96, 134–35. See also Faraone's article "Aphrodite's KESTOS and Apples for Atalanta: Aphrodisiacs in Early Greek Myth and Ritual," *Phoenix* 44 (1990), pp. 224–43.

126. Hesiod, *Hesiod, the Homeric Hymns and Homerica* (trans. Hugh G. Evelyn-White; Loeb Classical Library; Cambridge, MA: Harvard University Press, 1970), *Works and Days*, line 65, p. 7. See Faraone's (*Ancient Greek Love Magic*) discussion on pp. 98–99.

127. Daniel and Maltomini, *Supplementum Magicum*, spell 72, p. 106.

128. Marvin Meyer and Richard Smith (eds.), *Ancient Christian Magic: Coptic Texts of Ritual Power* (Princeton, NJ: Princeton University Press, 1999 [1994]), spell 82, p 175.

129. Betz, Hans Dieter (ed.), *The Greek Magical Papyri in Translation: Including the Demotic Spells* (Chicago, IL: University of Chicago Press, 1992), PGM IV.747, p. 52.

130. Betz, *The Greek Magical Papyri in Translation*, PGM.XXXVI.214, p. 274.

According to James Frazer, the anointing of Israelite kings derived from the Goddess of love anointing Adonis. Thus writes Frazer: "the history of the Hebrew kings presents some features which may perhaps, without straining them too far, be interpreted as relics or traces of a time when they or their predecessors played the part of a divinity, and particularly Adonis the divine lord of the land." [131] The work of Fraser is over a century old and has been disputed on many levels, particularly his penchant for paralleling all religious rituals into one universal fertility myth. However, Detienne also more recently makes such a linkage back to Syria for the whole cult of Adonis. [132] Says Detienne in his 1994 afterword: "Etymolgy calls. Adonis-*Adon* means lord just as Baal means master. The Phoenicians are there, the Syro-Palestinian world too and the Caananite traditions as well. Then there is Sumer, Dumuzi before Tammuz. The sleuths go back in time." Here anointing as worship and the sexual meaning of myrrh comes full circle as both Christological and erotic. This brings to mind the important fact that the cult of Adonis in Byblos was a very short distance from Galilee. Lucian's *Syrian Goddess* describes the cult centre in Byblos where the yearly ritual of lamentation for Adonis occurs. James Frazer even went so far as to place Adonis worship in Bethlehem. [133] The ritual lament for Tammuz, the Babylonian version of Adonis, is mentioned in Ezek. 8:14. Therefore, there is sufficient reason to assert the possible influence of the Adonis cult ritual upon the story of Jesus' anointing. Anointing can be both erotic and sacred. There is no necessary dichotomy between the spiritual and sexual.

Analysis of Differences between Biblical Scholars and SWOP Activists

Feminists are ambivalent at best about identifying anointing woman as a prostitute. Not so with sex workers. They feel that their very history may be under threat of erasure. This is one of the very few Christian traditions that is still currently meaningful to prostitutes; that at least Jesus is on their side in their justice struggle. Feminists with a consciousness of issues of class do best with prostitutes as protagonists of liberation but most others seem to see "prostitute" and "apostle or woman leader" as mutually exclusive terms. This may be a sign that they are invested in decency or protecting

131. James Frazer, *Adonis, Attis, Osiris: Studies in the History of Oriental Religion* (Hyde Park, New York: University Books, 1961), pp. 20–21.
132. Detienne, *The Gardens of Adonis,* Afterword, pp. 133–39.
133. Frazer, *Adonis, Attis, Osiris*, p. 257.

their class prerogatives as decent feminist biblical scholars. Many feminists, Christian or otherwise, have a long way to go in terms of sex positivity.

Feminists object to the characterization of anointing woman as a sexual sinner because it has been used to marginalize her as a leader in the Jesus Movement. Sex workers object to the whole repentant sinner scenario in a manner similar to Luise Schottroff as discussed earlier. Prostitutes reject being the scapegoat for society's unease with sex and sexual commerce. Individual repentance will not change the economic and cultural structures that create a market for sex. The repentant whore theory is bad social analysis that does nothing to liberate sex workers. In fact, this interpretation does a lot of damage. Many social reformers and do-gooders who try to work on the issue of prostitution work with similar assumptions and instead of reducing harm, they create it.

Finally, sex workers have the boldness to ask for the sacralization of sex, even commercial sex. I don't know that many liberation or feminist scholars are willing to go this far, but I am certainly trying to facilitate this consideration of the idea with this book. Sex as an element of the divine and a key to libratory resistance are affirmations we feminist biblical scholars, in the company of Carter Heyward and Audre Lorde, need to carefully consider.[134]

Exegetical SWOP Quotes on Anointing Woman

In conclusion to the section on anointing woman, we explain the story by threading quotes by speakers: *Avaren,* Sweet, Gayle, Scarlot, Veronica, Damienne Sin, Kimberlee and Ms. Shiris:

> *The woman who anointed Jesus was a sex worker.* I would have made the assumption even if it didn't come out and say: 'this was a prostitute.' It's because the righteous women were very rarely mentioned, the women who stayed at home with their husbands and cared for their children and the house, they are rarely mentioned. So this is sort of an assumption, but this wouldn't be something a respectable woman, single or married, would do to a stranger. Coming into somebody's house and anoint? Only a prostitute would feel good about doing it. It was traditional to have prostitutes at such a gathering. Then as now women in this profession are almost always in it because they can make very good money for the amount of time they spend, and they need that time to

134. See Carter Heyward, *Touching Our Strength: The Erotic as Power and the Love of God* (San Francisco, CA: Harper and Row, 1989), and Audre Lorde, "Uses of the Erotic."

work on their masters degrees and to take care of their children or to pursue their other career in painting or writing, or what ever, to join the revolutionary Jesus Movement! So the fact that she definitely has enough money to buy this expensive ointment means that she is respected in that way anyway, because she would be able to pay her taxes and who is to say that she doesn't give money to the poor? Wasn't that an assumption!

It is not unusual in my practice, with my clients, to pamper them. In fact, that is part of what I do, it is, sorry, that is MAINLY what I do. I pamper them and I stroke them from head to toe, and I also give them a really good massage which includes the feet and the head. So it just depends on what kind of service you provide. I don't differentiate that much between the sensual and the sexual. It is for the receiver to determine what belongs in what category. It is a total experience and in addition to any of the more overt sexual practice, there is the touching and the holding and the caressing the cuddling and sometimes bathing together, which could be interpreted as a form of anointing.

I have seen clients who climax within minutes, you know, you get close to them and they are just done. Now you have got this guy still who wants the other 58 minutes of his appointment and you're done! And every single time I have lifted out the exfoliant and a bowl of hot water and a cloth and I wash their feet. That is what I do. It is like this client right now needs something, he needs you to connect with him and there is a level, like I can lay with them and cuddle with them or whatever for five or ten minutes but I can't do it for fifty minutes, it just like, it starts to interfere with my personal boundaries. And so, it's like I have this sense that this person really needs to connect with me and I wash their feet. But I exfoliate, I do a whole thing...with the ones I need to take time with. And they love it, and they don't ever receive that, and so that is the only way it overlaps for me. It is definitely a form of worship and sexual.

I seem to end up a lot of the time kissing somebody's feet all over the place and it seems to be very well received as well. I have to say, the rubbing of the hair, that's very erotic. What about the just kissing of the feet? How can you possibly kiss somebody's feet without being erotic? I was going to say, that whole time she was just kissing his feet? Right, uh huh! Lots of foot fetishist clients I see are totally into feet, and that is all I do. It is a very erotic part of the body. I have had an orgasm from just having my foot rubbed. You know, only on my feet.

So it sounds like Jesus considers prostitution a sin (in Luke's version). So, OK, I do not think this passage is liberating to prostitutes. I just think this is obnoxious because here is Jesus and then he is so cool, that he just can come in, like he is the dominant guy, its like he is the A male. So the other guy is not cool enough and doesn't forgive this, thinks he is better than this sinner whatever, who doesn't think that, but Jesus is so cool that he meters out his forgiveness to the poor person that is all like, at his feet, ya know, like the big sinner, and then really, Jesus is playing a domination game and he like totally wins. But he is just like, I think he is being a really jerk and teaching people that, ya know, well that you have to go around and both buy into these subtleties that I am putting out about who is dominant and part of his trip for domination is to be like, generous. I think it is really nasty.

I kind of felt that crux of it too maybe is that he justifies her that, they are supposed to have this vow of poverty or whatever, but of course she has this expensive perfume for *my* feet, and you will always have the poor people but you won't always have me. So it is ok for us to indulge when it's about me but, you know, we have this vow of poverty otherwise. I think ew, Jesus must have been hot, and that is just totally bad because there is this totally self deprecating thing about being attracted to guys that are dominating pricks! I just broke up with a dominating prick. So, that behaviour, the way you describe the domination by doling out his compassion and generosity but then saying I am so much better than you, I dominate you because of this generosity. That was so right on.

On the other hand, I think a lot of times when Jesus talks in parables, he, I mean, it, is coming from his cultural reference, but usually he is trying to push people's paradigm a little further. And so he comes and says 'actually if you come and take a look at this, these people are more gracious, more humble, more helpful. That's why there is the parable about the Good Samaritan, the reason he picked a Samaritan is because these were a people that were reviled. So it was like, 'I want to show you what a good person does.' I don't think he was necessarily saying 'I believe that Samaritans were bad people,' but he was saying 'I understand that *you* think you are better than them. Let me tell you a parable about a Samaritan doing a good thing' cuz I want to get you to start thinking about what really matters.

Notice too that in Matthew and Mark she is not a sinner. Or at least she is not pointed out specifically as a sinner, though. If you read the whole Bible it is doesn't mention women without them being of sin. Eve's origin is sin and all the women that intersect with Jesus, except for his mother, are sinners. Everybody is a sinner. I never read a good woman except maybe Ruth. But Ruth is giving Boaz a blow job.

That version (Mk 14) is very different. It doesn't sound so self-serving. This sounds more generous and giving and kind to me. In the previous version it is like the poor are going to be around forever, but I am not, so let her do what she want disrespecting herself cuz *I'm Jesus*. One of the most obvious differences, I just want to show in terms of the last two that we just read, is that there is much more reference to the woman in the Mark version.

She was trying to seduce him, that is what I saw, and that the other guys are jealous that she tried to seduce him and not them and that is why they got mad. Exactly! Which is where all this righteous comes to the fore. Which is so much worse! Now she is a whore because 'we are trying to care for the poor and we're all righteous'. I think it goes beyond expunging sexuality; it is expunging any kind of pleasure, period, fun, enjoyment, because you should just be miserable and help the poor all your life. Something I learned very early on in life, is that those who claim to believe in happiness but attack luxuries, are forgetting that happiness is essentially about leisure and time off for aesthetic embodiment.

The other characters, like the master of the house is the traditional macho uninformed man who really has no idea of what goes on in real life. And he also has money. And he doesn't have any concept of those who are of lower station than him can actually be very wonderful people. The fact that he gets Jesus into this, it is almost like he is criticizing Jesus too. And Jesus was poor too so he is just critical of anybody that is not of his class.

Whoever these were saying 'how dare you! Why didn't you sell this and give it to the poor?' Now she doesn't defend herself and say 'I did sell some yesterday and gave 12 million denarii, whatever it is, to the poor.' But she doesn't have a comeback. But it is a very false assumption. Personally I give so much to charity. I give more than 10 percent of my income to a variety of important charities. I think it is the least I can do. Organizations like the Women's Building in San Francisco that helps mostly poor Hispanic women get education and helps with childcare and how to educate your children. I think it is a false assumption that we're greedy. I think it is a wonderful example of her humanity. I could see Mary doing the same thing out in the market place for somebody, who is obviously really poor, that wasn't Jesus. This is someone, like 'Oh, look at this person, they need some kindness' or something like 'Look at their poor feet, or HER poor feet' and just do it.

Then as now women in this profession are almost always in it because they can make very good money for the amount of time they spend, and they need that time to work on their masters degrees of to take care of their children or to pursue their other career in painting or writing, or what ever, to join the revolutionary Jesus Movement! So the fact that she definitely has enough money to buy this expensive ointment means that she is respected in that way anyway, because she would be able to pay her taxes and who is to say that she doesn't give money to the poor? Wasn't that an assumption!

Apparently, I came up with some cockamamie idea that spirituality and prostitution can coexist. There is no separation for Mary between the sacred and the profane as they would say, or the sexual and the erotic.

Her behaviour demonstrated her integration of the spiritual and the sexual.

The truth is that whores were goddesses and were worshiped. Because you *are* a goddess, you are absolutely a vector for all the love and the hatred that people hold around on sexuality, and that is god, god is that force, that creation, that creative force, that birth force and that is what a vagina is, and that is what women symbolize as prostitute, specifically as prostitutes.

Is not typical of me to defend Christianity or Jesus but this story has a very different meaning to me, anointing, yes, is a symposium gesture; you have to understand 'context symposium.' Socrates' teacher Diotima, who is an hetaera, she is also a sacred prostitute priestess, it is very unclear historically how closely those roles were linked, but there is a heavy religious component even in Greek culture. It is even more obvious when you look at Mesopotamian, or if you look at the cultures that all become Phoenicia. You anoint in a sacred prostitution ceremony and anointing is typically a prepatory phase in the ceremony. The same thing is true I believe, though my research is incomplete here, of the Eleusinian mysteries. But this is very much a part of a religious ritual. And specifically what it does, in either a male or female, the Canaanite priest, the pagan, would take on the guise of the Baal or Ashtorah, as in either male or female, in an Adonis or Aphrodite figure. And the point is that I think what it is saying, what Jesus is saying, 'use that oil on me' the point is that it is a stage, if you think of this strictly in terms of the mystery of the Trinity which actually makes a bit of sense to me, oddly enough, I see this as a nexus point of Jesus qua immortal and Jesus qua Baal as a ceremony of realization. Mary of Bethany, or Mary of Magdala taken as an equivalent, is, takes on a goddess figure, that is a classic pose of sacred prostitution from Gilgamesh all the way to the 21st century. That is what it seems to me is the reason it is worth putting this 300 denarii in. Well around here, how many people have been paid 300 denarii for a night? I mean that may seem odd but I think that is very much the point, in that the amount of preciousness worthwhile to have the excellence of achieving this kind of ex-temporal aesthesis or aesthetics, or incarnation, to use the Christian sense, this is an example of it and a crucial one.

Can I point out something what I think is interesting in what you said, because whether it is a 'sacred' act of prostitution or regular act of prostitution but bottom line is that it is sexual, erotic, whether she was the holiest priestess in the joint, or was a woman off the street. It does not matter, it was still sexual, it was still an act of gratification taking place.

But it is only prostitution if she is getting compensated for it. I don't see her getting any compensation any where at all this story.

That is not true. Legal codes in many states still define prostitute as someone who gives herself generally and in the ancient concept. Prostitutes have been equated with actresses in many cultures. Wives? Only if she gives herself sexually to all comers, to many people. No, actually that is very much not true. Prostitution, both as a positive spiritual experience and as something with negative connotation in patriarchy, especially in societies which have no distinctions of money and non money as we have, in the middle ages and in Ancient India and Japan prostitute and actress were sometimes the same word.

I think it is important to keep in mind that in antiquity during the whole matriarchal cultures, graves were shaped like vaginas so when you died you were put back into a vagina. Exactly, that was the whole thing, so the whole idea of lubing up before you enter a woman's vagina...I am wondering...Anointing for burial, anointing before....?

Whether or not she was a rich lady apostle or if she is a hooker, and which one is more empowering? I am personally kind of split down the middle. If the objective is to say 'oh, we want get her as far away from sex as possible,' I have a problem with that.

But on the other hand, I also like the idea of her being a role model for women who want to see *themselves* in a more powerful roles, vies a vie I guess what the culture considers powerful, so that is where my spilt takes place. I can see where changing the paradigm might be useful to young women growing up, to think that there was a female apostle. I am split. I can see where it could have a positive impact on women. Just because people right now have a hard time with the sex thing, and as a feminist sometimes I feel like certain sacrifices have to be made in order to go forward. I am real glad that I get to wear my lipstick and high heals but I am glad for all the women with their asexual hats on who bust into corporate America. That is what I am saying...half measures. I am not always going to fight my sisters even if they don't care about my rights to live; sometimes I just see the worth of their work. Even when they are out to get me, I can still see the worth in their work. I am more inclined to say, to have a woman who was powerful and sex positive in terms of her view on the world is better. I agree that she can be a very powerful woman **and** a sex worker and my hope is that these women who are very powerful in Bible scholarship and they are trying to rewrite Mary Magdalene as a powerful woman and not necessarily a sex worker, that eventually they will discover the power of their own sexuality they will eventually be able to rewrite Mary Magdalene as I really believe she really was. Just because it doesn't come out and say, 'Mary Magdalene is a prostitute' doesn't mean that she wasn't, because of her behaviour. I mean again, why can't you be rich and smart and beautiful and make money and still be drawn to Jesus because of his purity of heart and the great message he brought?

Chapter 6

THE WHORE BABYLON: VIOLENCE AGAINST PROSTITUTES

Rev. 17:1–19:10 (NRSV)

17 Then one of the seven angels who had the seven bowls came and said to me, 'Come, I will show you the judgment of the great whore who is seated on many waters, ² with whom the kings of the earth have committed fornication, and with the wine of whose fornication the inhabitants of the earth have become drunk.' ³So he carried me away in the spirit into a wilderness, and I saw a woman sitting on a scarlet beast that was full of blasphemous names, and it had seven heads and ten horns. ⁴ The woman was clothed in purple and scarlet, and adorned with gold and jewels and pearls, holding in her hand a golden cup full of abominations and the impurities of her fornication; ⁵ and on her forehead was written a name, a mystery: 'Babylon the great, mother of whores and of earth's abominations.' ⁶ And I saw that the woman was drunk with the blood of the saints and the blood of the witnesses to Jesus.

When I saw her, I was greatly amazed. ⁷ But the angel said to me, 'Why are you so amazed? I will tell you the mystery of the woman, and of the beast with seven heads and ten horns that carries her. ⁸ The beast that you saw was, and is not, and is about to ascend from the bottomless pit and go to destruction. And the inhabitants of the earth, whose names have not been written in the book of life from the foundation of the world, will be amazed when they see the beast, because it was and is not and is to come.

⁹ 'This calls for a mind that has wisdom: the seven heads are seven mountains on which the woman is seated; also, they are seven kings, ¹⁰ of whom five have fallen, one is living, and the other has not yet come; and when he comes, he must remain only a little while. ¹¹ As for the beast that was and is not, it is an eighth but it belongs to the seven, and it goes to destruction. ¹² And the ten horns that you saw are ten kings who have not yet received a kingdom, but they are to receive authority as kings for one hour, together with the beast. ¹³ These are united in yielding their power and authority to the beast; ¹⁴ they will make war on the Lamb, and the Lamb will conquer them, for he is Lord of lords and King of kings, and those with him are called and chosen and faithful.'

¹⁵ And he said to me, 'The waters that you saw, where the whore is seated, are peoples and multitudes and nations and languages. ¹⁶ And the ten horns that you saw, they and the beast will hate the whore; they will make her desolate and naked; they will devour her flesh and burn her up with fire. ¹⁷ For God has put it into their hearts to carry out his purpose by agreeing to give their kingdom to the beast, until the words of God will be fulfilled. ¹⁸ The woman you saw is the great city that rules over the kings of the earth.'

18 After this I saw another angel coming down from heaven, having great authority; and the earth was made bright with his splendor. ² He called out with a mighty voice,

'Fallen, fallen is Babylon the great!

It has become a dwelling place of demons,
a haunt of every foul spirit,
    a haunt of every foul bird,
    a haunt of every foul and hateful beast.
³ For all the nations have drunk
    of the wine of the wrath of her fornication,
and the kings of the earth have committed fornication with her,
    and the merchants of the earth have grown rich from the power of
        her luxury.'
⁴ Then I heard another voice from heaven saying,

'Come out of her, my people,
    so that you do not take part in her sins,
and so that you do not share in her plagues;
⁵ for her sins are heaped high as heaven,
    and God has remembered her iniquities.
⁶ Render to her as she herself has rendered,
    and repay her double for her deeds;
    mix a double draught for her in the cup she mixed.
⁷ As she glorified herself and lived luxuriously,
    so give her a like measure of torment and grief.
Since in her heart she says,
    'I rule as a queen;
I am no widow,
    and I will never see grief,'
⁸ therefore her plagues will come in a single day—
    pestilence and mourning and famine—
and she will be burned with fire;
    for mighty is the Lord God who judges her.'

⁹ And the kings of the earth, who committed fornication and lived in luxury with her, will weep and wail over her when they see the smoke of her burning; ¹⁰ they will stand far off, in fear of her torment, and say,

    'Alas, alas, the great city,
        Babylon, the mighty city!
For in one hour your judgment has come.'

[11] And the merchants of the earth weep and mourn for her, since no one buys their cargo anymore, [12] cargo of gold, silver, jewels and pearls, fine linen, purple, silk and scarlet, all kinds of scented wood, all articles of ivory, all articles of costly wood, bronze, iron, and marble, [13] cinnamon, spice, incense, myrrh, frankincense, wine, olive oil, choice flour and wheat, cattle and sheep, horses and chariots, slaves—and human lives. [14] 'The fruit for which your soul longed

has gone from you,
and all your dainties and your splendor
    are lost to you,
    never to be found again!'
[15] The merchants of these wares, who gained wealth from her, will stand far off, in fear of her torment, weeping and mourning aloud,
[16] 'Alas, alas, the great city,
    clothed in fine linen,
        in purple and scarlet,
    adorned with gold,
        with jewels, and with pearls!
[17] For in one hour all this wealth has been laid waste!'

And all shipmasters and seafarers, sailors and all whose trade is on the sea, stood far off [18] and cried out as they saw the smoke of her burning,
'What city was like the great city?'
[19] And they threw dust on their heads, as they wept and mourned, crying out,
    'Alas, alas, the great city,
        where all who had ships at sea
        grew rich by her wealth!
    For in one hour she has been laid waste.
[20] Rejoice over her, O heaven,
    you saints and apostles and prophets!
For God has given judgment for you against her.'
[21] Then a mighty angel took up a stone like a great millstone and threw it into the sea, saying,
    'With such violence Babylon the great city
        will be thrown down,
        and will be found no more;
[22] and the sound of harpists and minstrels and of flutists and trumpeters
    will be heard in you no more;
and an artisan of any trade
    will be found in you no more;
and the sound of the millstone
    will be heard in you no more;
[23] and the light of a lamp
    will shine in you no more;
and the voice of bridegroom and bride

will be heard in you no more;
for your merchants were the magnates of the earth,
    and all nations were deceived by your sorcery.
[24] And in you was found the blood of prophets and of saints,
    and of all who have been slaughtered on earth.'
19 After this I heard what seemed to be the loud voice of a great multitude
in heaven, saying,
    'Hallelujah!
Salvation and glory and power to our God,
[2]   for his judgments are true and just;
he has judged the great whore
    who corrupted the earth with her fornication,
and he has avenged on her the blood of his servants.'
[3] Once more they said,
'Hallelujah!
The smoke goes up from her forever and ever.'[1]

> You know something, it doesn't matter if you're on a jet airplane or
> if you're working the street, bottom line is everyone of us is a
> legitimate target to be raped or murdered. That is what brings us
> all together. [2]

Scholar Standpoints

The text with the most negative reputation among sex workers is the vision
of the Great Whore, Babylon, in Revelation 17–18. While some SWOP
readers felt somewhat empowered by how mighty and feared this prostitute
is portrayed, strongly sensing a sublimated and repressed goddess figure in
the whore, a unanimous majority understand this text as an extremely
dangerous divine sanction to "kill the whore" as Veronica Monet so bluntly
puts it. That this is what is enacted by so many men, from wife beaters to
rapists and serial killers of prostitutes, makes the experienced ideology of
this text incredibly potent and lethal. It is precisely because the SWOP
readers really are whores and the text imagines licit violence against such
women that this story is so literally painful. Thus, sex workers provide a
new reason for critiquing the whore metaphor: their own beaten and dead
bodies. Not because it is offensive to call a woman a whore but because it is
offensive to use the identity of whores as an insult. Nor is the imagined
violence mitigated because it was really aimed at the leaders or oppressors
of prostitutes, not prostitutes themselves. Being a metaphor is no excuse

1. *The Holy Bible: New Revised Standard Version* (Nashville, TN: Thomas
Nelson, [1996]).
2. Veronica Monet, SWOP Symposium, Berkeley CA, 12 January 2005.

for SWOP readers. Being oppressed oneself is also no excuse for using the whore metaphor. The whore metaphor is just all around bad news to prostitutes.

Many feminist scholars object to the whore metaphor for its violence and misogyny. A key issue for these critics is whether Revelation's depiction of women legitimates violence and whether the celebration of the fall of Babylon is vindictive. Tina Pippin and Adele Yarbro Collins are prominent representatives for these points.[3] Yarbro Collins operates with the concept of catharsis and that the violent imagery of Revelation was an outlet for the rage and anger of those in "perceived crisis." Even though she argues that it was written to avoid violence, there is the danger that "what is cathartic for one person can be inflammatory for another."[4] Tina Pippin reads the ideology of gender in her study of Revelation and concludes that "Women in the Apocalypse are victims—victims of war and patriarchy. The Apocalypse is not a safe space for women. In effect what I am saying is that the Apocalypse is not liberating for women readers."[5] She acknowledges that read as resistance literature, Revelation has had an important message for some but "can any misogynistic text be truly liberating?" What happens instead is that "this world turned upside down dumps all the women out; the mothers of the revolution are excluded."[6] The readers of SWOP pretty much agree with and substantiate these critiques.

3. Tina Pippin in *Death and Desire: The Rhetoric of Gender in the Apocalypse of John* (Louisville, KY: Westminster John Knox Press, 1992). A similar critique of the misogyny of John's gender ideology can be found in Marla Selvidge's article "Reflections on Violence and Pornography: Misogyny in the Apocalypse and Ancient Hebrew Prophesy," in Athalya Brenner (ed.), *A Feminist Companion to the Hebrew Bible in the New Testament* (Sheffield: Sheffield Academic Press, 1996), pp. 274–85 and also in Gail Corrington Streete's *The Strange Woman: Power and Sex in the Bible* (Louisville, KY: Westminster John Knox Press, 1997), pp. 150–58. See also David Barr's response in "Towards an Ethical Reading of the Apocalypse: Reflections on John's Use of Power, Violence and Misogyny," in *SBL Seminar Papers* (1997), pp. 358–73. The issue of Revelation's vindictiveness has been treated by Adele Yarbro Collins in many of her writings but most notably "Persecution and Vengeance in the Book of Revelation," in David Hellholm (ed.), *Apocalypticism in the Mediterranean World and the Near East. Proceedings of the International Colloquium on Apocalpticism, Uppsala, 1979* (Tubingen: Mohr, 1989). See also Yarbro Collins, *Crisis and Catharsis: The Power of the Apocalypse* (Philadelphia, PA: Westminster, 1984).
4. Yarbro Collins, *Crisis and Catharsis*, p. 171.
5. Pippin, *Death and Desire*, p. 80.
6. Pippin, *Death and Desire*, pp. 91–92.

Other feminists argue for a more positive reading of Revelation along with liberation scholars who identify with the oppressed who were imagined to have written Revelation. These scholars emphasized that the whore metaphor is simply that, a metaphor. Elisabeth Schüssler Fiorenza has the most famous of such interpretations. Says Schüssler Fiorenza: "the female imagery of Revelation, therefore, would be completely misconstrued if it were understood as referring to the actual behaviour of individual women."[7] Such scholars emphatically argue that the "whore Babylon" is a literary figure and has nothing to do with real prostitutes; it is strictly a political metaphor or conventional literary topos. Schüssler Fiorenza argues the necessity of reading the symbolic world of Revelation as a "'fitting' response to its historical-rhetorical situation."[8] Barbara Rossing has made the definitive literary argument for the city-as-a-woman topos interpretation of the whore Babylon. Barbara Rossing emphatically argues that the imagery of the destruction of Babylon is of a city, not "the torture and rape of a woman's body."[9] Male liberation scholars sensitive to feminist concerns are careful to navigate through all these feminist readings. Wes Howard Brook and Anthony Gwyther write:

> For Elisabeth Schüssler Fiorenza to choose to treat Revelation's sexual imagery as 'conventional literary language' is one thing; she is after all one of the world's leading feminist critics of ecclesial and social patriarchy and sexism. For two first world men of privilege to jump on the bandwagon is another. We hear Tina Pippin's experience of the text as degrading, violent and hateful of women. We offer no excuses for John's language…In case there is doubt, let us be clear at the outset. *The images of women used by Revelation were not intended to, nor should they ever, legitimate violence against women of any kind…*any effort to associate them with actual people represents a gross misuse of the text.[10]

7. Elisabeth Schüssler Fiorenza, *Revelation: Vision of a Just World*, (Minneapolis, MN: Fortress Press, 1991), p. 96; see also her discussion in *The Book of Revelation: Justice and Judgment* (Minneapolis, MN: Fortress Press, 1998), pp. 219–22.

8. Schüssler Fiorenza, *The Book of Revelation*, p. 183.

9. Barbara Rossing, *The Choice Between Two Cities: Whore, Bride, and Empire in the Apocalypse*, Harvard Theological Studies 48 (Harrisburg, PA: Trinity Press, 1999), pp. 87–90.

10. Wes Howard-Brook's and Anthony Gwyther's, *Unveiling Empire: Reading Revelation Then and Now* (Maryknoll, NY: Orbis Books, 1999), p. 162, original emphasis.

Such interpreters advocate for better, more ethical readings of the text that do not literalize the whore metaphor. The long history of readers who read otherwise are still a problem in that they persist in their misreading.

Political readings of Revelation are numerous, especially among liberation scholars.[11] These types of readings are often interested in Revelation as resistance literature describing and denouncing the political economy of Imperial Rome. Often these scholars are writing in contexts of political oppression that makes their interpretations especially poignant. Such readings of Revelation find it a hopeful and liberating text. However, none acknowledge or analyze prostitution as a possibly integral component of the unjust political economy being denounced in Revelation's use of the whore metaphor. This omission is partly due to an understanding of the whore metaphor that sees no correspondence with reality and real prostitutes in the language of Revelation, which is the argument of Schüssler Fiorenza and Rossing. Therein is a dualism on the level of language that argues for the complete separation of metaphors from the material contexts that might have played a role in producing them. Another reason for the omission of sex work from the political economy is possibly related to in/decency. Whatever the reason, there is a trend in exegesis of biblical prostitution to utterly separate whore metaphors from real prostitutes.

11. Richard Bauckham, "Economic Critique of Rome in Revelation 18," in Alexander Loveday (ed.), *Images of Empire* (Sheffield, JSOT Press, 1991), pp. 47–90, pp. 55, 78; Dagoberto Ramirez Fernandez, "The Judgment of God on the Multinationals: Revelation 18," in Leif Vaage (ed. and trans.), *Subversive Scriptures: Revolutionary Readings of the Christian Bible in Latin America* (Valley Forge, PA: Trinity Press International, 1997), p. 92; Wes Howard-Brook and Anthony Gwyther, *Unveiling Empire: Reading Revelation Then and Now* (Maryknoll, NY: Orbis Books, 1999); J.N. Kraybill, *Imperial Cults and Commerce in John's Apocalypse* (JSNTSup 132; Sheffield: Sheffield Academic Press, 1996); Nestor Miguez, "Apocalyptic and the Economy: A Reading of Revelation 18 from the Experience of Economic Exclusion," in Fernando Segovia and Mary Ann Tolbert (eds.), *Reading From This Place: Social Location and Biblical Interpretation in a Global Perspective* Vol. 2 (Minneapolis, MN: Fortress Press, 1995), pp. 250–62; Pablo Richard, *Apocalypse: A People's Commentary* (Maryknoll, NY: Orbis Books, 1995), p. 137; Elizabeth Schüssler Fiorenza, *Revelation: Vision of a Just World,* Proclamation Commentaries (Minneapolis, MN: Fortress Press, 1991); Klaus Wengst, "Babylon the Great and New Jerusalem: The Visionary View of Political Reality in the Revelation of John," in Henning Graf Reventlow, Yair Hoffman and Benjamin Uffenheimer (eds.), *Politics and Theopolitics in the Bible and Postbiblical Literature*, JSOT Supplemental Series 171 (Sheffield: JSOT Press, 1994), pp. 189–202.

Following in the lead of these kinds of political and feminist readings of Revelation, I attempted a feminist materialist reading of Rev. 17–19:10 in a recent publication.[12] In this paper, I tried to insert prostitutes into the text's political economy as well as among the community of the oppressed whose language usage might also have turned up in the text. Thus, I was interested in a possible connection to reality for the whore metaphor among the speech community of readers. My inquiry benefited from years of study of the phenomenon of prostitution in which exploitive extraction economies tend to be correlated with a very high level of prostitution activity. By exploitive "extraction" economies I refer to economies where the most labor is extracted in exchange for the least wages. When wages fall below sustenance level, prostitution increases.[13] Liberation scholars also make frequent comparisons between the exploitive international trade in Revelation 18 and what is happening currently with Third World debt, structural adjustment policies of the of treaties and institutions like the General Agreement on Treaties and Tariffs (GATT), North American Free Trade Agreement (NAFTA), International Monetary Fund (IMF), World Bank (WB), and the World Trade Organization (WTO), but all seem generally ignorant to the fact that these institutions and agreements have also been equally implicated in the explosion of prostitution under globalization.[14] This steep rise in global prostitution makes it a feminist post-colonial issue par excellence and suitable for similar comparisons between ancient and modern exploitive economies.

Jean Kim critiques Revelation scholarship in exactly this manner because it "has not engaged in considering the possibility that the metaphorical

12. Avaren Ipsen, "Political Economy, Prostitution, and the *Eschaton* of the Whore Babylon: A Feminist Integration of Sex into an Economic Analysis of Revelation 17–19," in Frank Crusemann, Marlene Crusemann, Claudia Janssen, Rainer Kessler and Beate When (eds.), *Dem Tod Nicht Glauben: Sozialgeschichte der Bibel* (Gutersloher: Gutersloher Verlagshaus GmbH, 2004), pp. 504–27.

13. Such exploitive "extraction" is happening now with the global downsizing, deskilling, and outsourcing of labour. Another way to extract more labour for less wages is to restructure work so that most new job creation is temporary, part-time, or contract (also called flex-labour) which puts it outside of the legal structure that exists to protect labour rights.

14. Recall Maria Mies' "International of Pimps," 1998, p. 137. Chung Hyun Kyung makes similar points in her 1996 article "Your Comfort Vs. My Death" in Mary John Mananzan, Mercy Amba Oduyoye, Elsa Tamez, J. Shannon Clarkson, Mary C. Grey, Letty Russell (eds.), *Women Resisting Violence: Spirituality for Life* (Maryknoll, NY: Orbis Books, 1996).

figure, 'the whore', in Revelation 17 might have had something to do with a colonized woman's life in a (de)colonizing context."[15] Also, a common correlate in twentieth century militarism is that rape of women and ensuing prostitution of the women of an occupied territory are the second and third phases of warfare.[16] This was even truer in biblical times when the whore metaphor was created writes Kim: "Hebrew prophets were prophesying when Israel was under the control of foreign powers such as Syria, Assyria, Babylon, and Egypt, whose military intrusions were not simple invasions of native land, but were quasi-automatically accompanied by the invasion of native women's bodies. We therefore cannot overlook the possibility that the feminized city can also refer to sexually invaded women in a colonizing context."[17] What Rossing does not address is the recurring topos of the violated or enslaved woman, which also accompanies biblical accounts of siege warfare. Consider the Song of Deborah in Judg. 5:30: "Are they not finding and dividing the spoil? A girl or two for every man." Isa. 13:16 declares against Babylon: "Whoever is found will be thrust through. And whoever is caught will fall by the sword. Their infants will be dashed to pieces before their eyes; their houses will be plundered and their wives ravished." Zech. 14:2 predicts for Jerusalem that "the city shall be taken and the houses looted and the women raped." Lam. 5:11 mourns that the "women are raped in Zion and the virgins in the towns of Judah." Even more specific for my argument is the fate that Amos' oracle predicts for Amaziah's wife in 7:17: "your wife shall become a prostitute in the city, and your sons and your daughters shall fall by the sword, and your land shall be parcelled out by line." In such a context stripping the city and making it naked like a "raped woman" can operate on multiple levels and should not be narrowed down to only metaphorically apply to siege warfare, that is to

15. Jean Kim, "'Uncovering her Wickedness': An Inter(con)textual Reading of Revelation 17 from a Postcolonial Feminist Perspective," *JSNT* 73:61–81 (1999), p. 62. See also Caroline Vander Stichele, "Just a Whore: The Annihilation of Babylon According to Revelation 17:16," *Lectio Difficilor* 1 (2000) http://www.lectio.unibe.ch/00_1/1-2000-j.pdf. Stichele also argues against the separation of metaphors from material reality. Another scholar who argues for connecting the book of Revelation to the material reality of women is Luzia Rehmann Sutter, in *Vom Mut, genau hinzusehen: Feministisch-befreiungstheologische Interpretationen zur Apokalyptik* (Luzern: Edition Exodus, 1998).

16. Brock and Thistlethwaite, *Casting Stones*, pp. 6 and n.10, 55–56, 71, 109.

17. Kim, "Uncovering her Wickedness", p. 74.

say, breaking the walls of a city and plunder of wealth, as Rossing argues.[18] Athenaeus, too, relates this typical feature of militarism—that women are taken as spoil, raped and prostituted—in his book on prostitutes. In fact, the editor of the volume wonders if the word *strateuein* might mean "to go whoring" in slang usage, in addition to the conventional definition, "to go to war."[19] These stark realties of warfare make untenable the strict separation in the whore metaphor between destroyed cities and real prostitutes and raped women. Newer emerging studies of the political economy of prostitution in Greece and Rome evaluate the economic institution of prostitution in concert with militarism and slavery is paving the way for biblical scholars to do likewise.[20]

The main reason I attempted a reading that inserted prostitutes among the oppressed community of Revelation is because of my own upbringing in the underclass within the revolutionary left. The men of my ghetto childhood were often in a very unstable solidarity with the women. The men and women of my upbringing were sometimes part of the same struggle, sometimes not. Thus, it is a conflicted, ambivalent insertion at best. But with a lifetime of hearing the reverse slander of calling oppressive leaders and institutions "whores," Arundhati Roy, Dead Prez and Tupac Shakur[21] gave me the idea of analyzing the whore metaphor in this same way as reverse, parodic slander. Arundhati Roy has called "freedom" the "free world whore" of neo-liberal imperialism.[22] The Hip-hop group, Dead

18. Rossing, *The Choice Between Two Cities*, pp. 90–97.

19. Athenaeus, *Deipnosophistae,* 565b p. 53 also 556f, p. 11 uses the verb in a similar way.

20. Rebecca Flemming, *"Quae Corpore Quaestum Facit:* The Sexual Economy of Female Prostitution in the Roman Empire," *Journal of Roman Studies*: 89 (1999), pp. 38–61; Thomas McGinn, *The Economy of Prostitution in the Roman World: A Study of Social History and the Brothel* (Ann Arbor, MI: University of Michigan Press, 2004); Thomas McGinn, "Zoning Shame in the Roman City," in Christopher Faraone and Laura McClure (eds.), *Prostitutes and Courtesans*, pp. 161–76; and Edward Cohen, "Free and Unfree Sexual Work: An Economic Analysis of Athenian Prostitution," in Christopher Faraone and Laura McClure (eds.), *Prostitutes and Courtesans,* pp. 95–124.

21. Tupac Shakur, *2pacalypse Now,* "Words of Wisdom," 1991: "But if you ask me it's all about hypocracy, The constitution, Yo, it don't apply to me, Lady Liberty still the bitch lied to me." I found the lyrics at http://www.tupacnet.org/lyrics/0106.htm

22. Arundhati Roy, "Instant-Mix Imperial Democracy (Buy One, Get One Free)" A speech given at Riverside Church in New York City on 13 May 2003 and published in *Common Dreams,* 18 May 2003. "Democracy, the modern

Prez, call the police the "ho-lice," which they define as an "expression of revolutionary culture."[23] Finally, the late rapper Tupac Shakur, in his album called *2pacalpse Now* has a song called "Words of Wisdom" wherein he insults the statue of liberty: "Lady Liberty, still the bitch lied to me." This one lyric made me imagine the author of Revelation denouncing a statue of Roma as a "whore" in a similar manner: as deconstruction of imperial propaganda such as giant statues that promise the good life but do not deliver. I know Tupac was raised by a mother, Afeni Shakur, who herself was a left radical leader in the Black Panther Movement and that her son was not necessarily a misogynist, despite the "bitch" language.[24] Hip-hop and Rap music were my hermeneutical point of access to Revelation's whore metaphor because this music also is frequently denounced and dismissed for its language of violence, negative reciprocity, misogyny and homophobia. What Pablo Richard says of Revelation might be analogous to the use of whore and bitch language in Hip-hop:

> The function of these texts is not to generate violence or hatred, but rather to express the situation of extreme oppression and suffering that the people of God are experiencing...we cannot expect the poor to speak the refined diplomatic language of the powerful...if Revelation uses such language it is partly to bring about a catharsis in its hearers but it is also so that they may feel that they have attained their identity and through the message of Revelation may transform their hatred into awareness.[25]

Thus, I was interested in how Revelation has an imperfect liberation message, because oppressed people often don't have perfect liberation

---

world's holy cow, is in crisis. And the crisis is a profound one. Every kind of outrage is being committed in the name of democracy. It has become little more than a hollow word, a pretty shell, emptied of all content or meaning. It can be whatever you want it to be. *Democracy is the Free World's Whore*, willing to dress up, dress down, willing to satisfy a whole range of taste, available to be used and abused at will," (italics mine). http://www.commondreams.org/views03/0518-01.htm

23. Dead Prez, *Turn Off the Radio: the Mix Tape, Volume 1*, 2002, from the song "Get Up": "When I hear the woop-woop, I be duckin them hoes, I can smell a pig comin, so I stay on my toes, on the low from po-po, so fuck the Ho-lice," http://www.hhdb.com/lyrics/705/Get-Up-Lyrics; as an "expression revolutionary culture" see the song "Hood News" on the same album.

24. However, in 1994 Tupac Shakur was convicted and imprisoned on three counts of sexual abuse, a reduced rape charge, as shown in the film *Tupac Resurrected*.

25. Pablo Richard, *Apocalypse: A People's Commentary*, p. 31.

messages, but they have flaws and gaps in their social theories of change, just like academic social theorists. Still this flawed message can only be accepted with ambivalence because, as I know from my youth, some Black Power movement men were brothers in struggle and there were others who also beat their women and failed to support their children.[26] Places of poverty and oppression are spaces with complex ties and affinities.

All of these scholarly views are the pertinent ideas that SWOP readers engaged during our third symposium. There were many points of overlap between SWOP readers and feminist scholars on the issue of violence, the use of metaphors and the ethics of language.

Sex Worker Standpoint on the Whore Babylon

Revelation's whore metaphor was the major overarching topic of discussion for SWOP readers. We had many of the same types of concerns and questions as feminist and liberation scholars: Does the language of Revelation support violence against women? If we read Revelation as countercultural resistance literature, does that change things? If it used as a political metaphor, does this make the whore language acceptable? Are actual prostitutes referenced in the text and how does that change anything in the way it is interpreted? When, if ever, it is acceptable to use the word "whore" in a violent or negative context?

Reality of Violence against Prostitutes

The message of "kill the whore" is the first and loudest thing that SWOP readers hear when reading the vision of Rev. 17–19:10. This is predominantly because all of the SWOP activists became activists because of experiences of violence. One of the first actions of SWOP in 2003 was to institute 17 December as the International Day to End Violence against Sex Workers.[27] This violence is perceived by sex workers as heavily institutionalized via police, courts, prisons, the mental health establishment, and rehabilitation programs for prostitutes. The violence occurs on multiple levels in that these institutions often treat sex workers as moral imbeciles who need to be disciplined by the state and also do not extend equal

26. See Traci West for a black feminist critique of the black male violence among some Black Panther party members, in Rap music and the writings of Amiri Baraka, in *Wounds of the Spirit: Black Women, Ethics and Resistance Ethics* (New York: New York University Press, 1999), pp. 126–31.

27. http://www.swop-usa.org/greenriver.html

protection to sex workers as citizens or full human beings. Both Repressive and Ideological State Apparatuses (RSA and ISA) are involved in this institutional violence.[28] The RSAs would include the police, courts, jails, military, mental hospitals, and mandatory court diversion programs. The ISAs would be the cultural institutions that provide legitimating texts and discourses for the institutions that operate with force: Family values, academic disciplines like sociology and psychology, legislation, religion, etc. According to the conceptualization of Louis Althusser, "what distinguishes the ISA's from the (Repressive) State Apparatus is the following basic difference: the Repressive State Apparatus functions by violence, whereas the Ideological State Apparatus *function 'by ideology.'*"[29] Sex workers experience coercion, rape and abuse by cops, lawyers, judges, prison guards and of course, clients. Prostitutes are also heavily pathologized in mental and public health care arenas as incest victims, drug addicts, and STD carriers. Social workers often enact a kind of soft domination upon prostitutes as benevolent rescuers but who nevertheless often get their funding by the state and work in concert with the criminal justice system.[30] In past times, it was the church, an ideological apparatus, who was most interested in the reformation of prostitutes. Now, there are a multitude of ISAs and RSAs that are involved with policing the bodies and minds of prostitutes.

In/decency and the whore stigma provide ideological legitimation for the repression. Christianity has played a big role in this ideology. That biblical texts narrate even metaphorical violence contributes to this state of affairs. The general public often feels entitled to insult, revile, rape, beat and abuse prostitutes knowing that the state authorities generally don't exist to protect sex workers. This lack of equal protection is especially true

28. See Louis Althusser, "Ideology and Ideological State Apparatus (Notes Towards an Investigation)," *Lenin and Philosophy and Other Essays* (New York: Monthly Review Press, 2001), pp. 85–126, p. 97.

29. Oddly enough, the theorist who coined the concepts "Repressive State Apparatus" (RSA) and "Ideological State Apparatus" (ISA), Louis Althusser, murdered his own wife. He also distinguishes between RSA's as public, that is to say the police, and ISA's as private, like the family. But if you murder your wife and no one punishes you and battered women's shelters don't exist, is the violence public or private? Or perhaps it is a matter of police power devolving upon individual husbands, thus both. SWOP readers wonder if Althusser called his wife a "whore" when he killed her.

30. Laura María Agustín, "Helping Women Who Sell Sex: The Construction of Benevolent Identities," *Rhizomes* 10 (2005), http://www.rhizomes.net/issue10/agustin.htm.

for African American women. In a study of violence against African American women, Traci West found that it is particularly difficult for black women to get social recognition as victims of violence.[31] Prostitutes who report crimes often go to jail for outing themselves as sex criminals while the crimes they came to report go unsolved. It is no surprise that the majority of women jailed for prostitution are black. It is for this reason that SWOP readers think that rapists and serial killers like to prey on sex workers in particular. Think of Jack the Ripper, or more recently the Yorkshire Ripper, the Southside Murderer,[32] and the Green River Killer, Gary Leon Ridgeway, who killed as many as 70 women, most of them prostitutes, during the 1980s and 1990s.[33] According to Ridgeway's confession he said, "I want to be put down in history as killin' prostitutes,"[34] and told detectives "I am good in one thing, and that is killing prostitutes."[35] The Green River Killer, Gary Leon Ridgeway, as a prime example of heinous violence against prostitutes in general, was a motivation for SWOP to organize politically and for the first International Day to End Violence against Prostitutes a few days after he was sentenced in 2003. This event was a memorial to his victims. Due to the efforts of SWOP, by 17 December 2005, the third annual International Day to End Violence against Prostitutes was institutionally recognized by the California State Assembly and Senate as well as by the cities of San Francisco and Berkeley.

Gary Ridgeway thought he was "helping the police to rid the world of prostitutes, whom they couldn't control but he could"[36] and claimed to be operating according to a code of ethics.[37] He was known to have been an avid Bible reader and fundamentalist Christian before he began killing prostitutes and again after going to prison.[38] He saw the prostitutes he killed as sub-human: "Its just garbage, something to screw and kill her and

31. Traci West, *Wounds of the Spirit*, p. 145.

32. For an account of US PROStitutes Collective (US PROS) response to the South Side Slayer, see International Prostitute's Collective, *Some Mother's Daughter: The Hidden Movement of Prostitute Women against Violence* (London: Crossroads Books, 1999), p. 169.

33. David Reichert, *Chasing the Devil: My Twenty Year Quest to Capture the Green River Killer* (New York: Little, Brown and Co, 2004), p. 241.

34. Reichert, *Chasing the Devil*, p. 288.

35. King County Journal Staff, *Gary Ridgeway: The Green River Killer* (Seattle: King County Journal, 2003), p. 177.

36. King County Journal Staff, *Gary Ridgeway*, p. 176.

37. Reichert, *Chasing the Devil*, p. 288.

38. Reichert, *Chasing the Devil*, p. 277 and p. 306; King County Journal Staff, *Gary Ridgeway*, p. 24.

dump her"[39] and "screw 'em, kill 'em, bury 'em and maybe have sex with them a few times afterwards."[40] He even confessed his fantasies about cannibalizing them, just as happens in Rev. 17:16.[41] In addition to these kinds of rationalizations Ridgeway claimed he chose prostitutes to be his victims because they were "the easiest" and that "he picked prostitutes and runaways because he knew that no one would miss them quickly, if at all. His assessment was correct, prosecutors wrote in their summary."[42] Furthermore, Ridgeway "also knew police and prostitutes were not on friendly terms."[43] In terms of media attention, the story of the Green River Killer was voted the most under reported story of 1986, probably due to the status and race of the victims.[44] A very high number of the victims were African American: "'I'd much rather have white,' he told detectives. 'But black was fine.'" This testimony bears out what prostitutes say about no one caring about violence committed against them. The prostitutes' rights movement is at its core an anti-violence campaign. This protest against violence has been true repeatedly throughout history when prostitutes politically organize.

So when we read Revelation, Gary Ridgeway quickly came up in our discussion. Kimberlee said: "it says in here they strip and beat her, or something?" "Yes", I chimed in "and they eat her flesh." Immediately Veronica noted: "If you were Gary Leon Ridgeway and you were reading this, you'd feel like you were on a holy mission of God wouldn't you?" Shemena added: "And then she is burned like a sacrifice, that's what it always reminds me of, she is the sacrificial lamb who is burnt forever and ever and ever." In addition to this sacrifice imagery was a discussion of how prostitutes were scapegoats. Said Veronica:

> This chapter reminds me of being blamed for everything, for whatever is going on: serial killers, drugs, crime, bad neighbourhoods, drug problems, moral decay of the family, husbands cheating on their wives; that's all laid at the feet of the whore, spread of STDs, we're blamed for everything.

Gayle continued the interpretation by analyzing why: "It's a scapegoating. They need a scapegoat that they don't know personally. They have to take

---

39. King County Journal Staff, *Gary Ridgeway*, p. 32.
40. Reichert, *Chasing the Devil*, p. 282.
41. Reichert, *Chasing the Devil*, p. 283.
42. King County Journal Staff, *Gary Ridgeway*, pp. 31, 172.
43. King County Journal Staff, *Gary Ridgeway*, p. 33.
44. King County Journal Staff, *Gary Ridgeway*, pp. 79, 32.

it away from their lives. It's too close, so you attack people that are *out there*." This is precisely what a religious sacrifice does: it transfers guilt upon another. This scapegoating is something Gary Ridgeway does too.

Robyn and Kimberlee looked at the God angle of the violence. That it happened because "God judges her. Because it starts out 'come to see God's judgment on the whore of Babylon.' And it is so violent because we justify all violence with God, right? That is because, if God says it, let it be so, get out the ax and chop somebody's head off!" Due to God, said Robyn "her demise is within, what, one hour? She is done, this powerfully huge, powerful woman is undone within a matter of moments." When the question is posed, "Does this text legitimate violence against prostitutes?" the immediate answer from Robyn is, "Yes it does. Just ask Gary Leon Ridgeway. How did he vindicate himself every day when he went to bed? He read it in the Bible that it was OK to kill some whores." It was a serial killer of prostitutes who provided the most important hermeneutical key for reading Revelation.

However, it is not just exceptional psychopathic killers who read Revelation in this way. Many of the SWOP readers talked about the abusive treatment they have received from conservative Christians. Veronica and other sex worker activists with a public profile receive a steady stream of hate mail: "Well, there are right wing religious fanatics who send me and other sex workers hate mail every month. And they have the nerve to say prostitutes and whoremongers are all going to burn. And then at the bottom they ask me for money!" I found a Christian website, called Bible Doctrine News, which explicitly connected Gary Ridgeway to Revelation. The author of this site, Larry Wood, claimed that, "Ridgeway murdered prostitutes to represent the Satanic attack on the Prostitute of Babylon, the evil female who is often empowered by Satan as the goddess of love throughout history."[45] Furthermore it is predicted that "The destruction of Satan and his demon armies at the Second Advent will bring to an end the reign of the symbolic Prostitute of Babylon over the kings of the earth. Ever since the Garden of Eden, she has usurped authority in Marriage and led the nations astray." This line of interpretation interprets the symbolic whore as "the female attack on authority through the power of Satan as the goddess of love." A specific example given of this kind of female attack on authority is Gary Ridgeway's mother "Ridgeway's mother was a dominant usurper of authority, who fit the description of a person under the power of the Prostitute of Babylon." The web page concludes that "The Prostitute of

45. http://www.biblenews1.com/history3/20031105.htm

Babylon symbolizes the female attempt to usurp authority through false love. This is Bible Doctrine." Gary Ridgeway also echoed this point about false love as a reason for killing prostitutes: "Ridgeway said that in the beginning his hatred of prostitutes who service him for a fee boiled over into murder when he felt that they regarded him with disgust and disdain."[46] For this reason Ridgeway asserted that: "I wanna be put down in history as killin' prostitutes," he added, because they were people society rejected. "Money was the thing they wanted," he added. "Money was their downfall."[47]

However, it was not just prostitutes that Ridgeway blamed for his behaviour; it was also his first and second wives. He claimed his first wife had "become a 'whore'" while he was in the military (although he himself was a frequent customer of Filipino prostitutes while on tour with the Navy in the Western Pacific).[48] In terms of his second wife, "Ridgeway opined that some of the blame for the murders should be placed on Winslow. If he had killed her like he wanted to when they divorced, it might have 'changed my life. I'd only have one murder instead of 50 plus.'"[49] The media and Sheriff Reichert's descriptions of Ridgeway's mother fit with the Bible Doctrine News, reporting that she was domineering and "dressed like a prostitute." The King County Journal reported that "Ridgeway's mother dominated...stranger was the way Ridgeway's mother dressed. She wore tight clothes and excessive makeup, Winslow said. She looked like a prostitute."[50] Says Sheriff Reichert: "In contrast with his portrait of a snivelling father, Ridgeway's mother comes across as an aggressive, sexually provocative woman who dressed like a prostitute and applied her makeup with a trowel."[51] In terms of the whore identity of Babylon, SWOP readers spent time analyzing what it means to "dress like a whore" which I will get to in the next section.

Thus, when Veronica Monet asserts that Revelation advocates the killing of whores she knows what she is talking about. When going on Fox News a few years ago a congressman asked: "'Veronica have you read the Bible?' And I said 'Yes, I have read it cover to cover, have you?' And he said, 'Well what does your Bible tell you?' and I said, 'It says, kill the whore.' And he

---

46. Reichert, *Chasing the Devil*, p. 277.
47. Reichert, *Chasing the Devil*, pp. 288–89.
48. King County Journal Staff, *Gary Ridgeway*, p. 23.
49. King County Journal Staff, *Gary Ridgeway*, p. 23.
50. King County Journal Staff, *Gary Ridgeway*, p. 18.
51. Reichert, *Chasing the Devil*, p. 274.

and the other woman who was representing this right wing organization said 'Oh no, Jesus didn't want to kill the whores!'" SWOP readers would agree with the last statement about Jesus but it is Revelation and the prophetic whore metaphor that does the damage. Saying the reference is only a metaphor does not prevent the pervasive abuse of scripture. Kimberlee makes the emphatic point that, "the problem with this Bible text is that it is all metaphoric, none of it is reality, it is all like some crazy psycho babble nonsense, and the fundamentalists believe this shit and make laws out of it. The message is that you're a whore and unworthy and disrespectable." Robyn agreed: "It gives a lot of power, all of this, the Bible imagery and everything, it gives a lot of power to people that are against prostitution and against sex, and against women." Furthermore, "it isn't just against prostitutes. It is against women, to keep them in their place," added Gayle. Veronica clarifies why:

> What is the first thing a man does before he rapes or kills a woman? He starts calling her a whore. It doesn't matter if she has ever made a dime from sex, you're a whore if you're going down and you're going to get called a whore all the way down...Revelation doesn't just legitimate violence towards prostitutes, but it legitimates violence towards wives, towards all women.

Is the Whore Babylon a Prostitute? Does it Matter?

The dominant image in Revelation is of the powerful female abused. Liberationist readers claim that since we are dealing with a conventional biblical metaphor of the unjust political economy of an imperial city, that the text is not talking about prostitutes at all. This is something emphasized by commentators over and over. Babylon is really a statue of a pagan goddess, the personification of a city that is described.[52] The pagan goddess is dressed up like a respectable Roman matron. Or, the passage first describes this city personified as a statue but quickly shifts to a description of the military destruction of a city. SWOP readers discerned in Babylon multiple images of an aristocrat or queen, namely Jezebel, a goddess, a courtesan, all rich, powerful and sexual women. Such women are hated in misogynistic cultures, including our own. Veronica explains that:

> I feel that the reason that this passage is so hateful, and has so much energy, is because the whore was so powerful, and I am not just talking

---

52. See Adele Yarbro Collins, "Feminine Symbolism in the Book of Revelation," *Biblical Interpretation* 1(1993), pp. 20–33.

about a woman who exchanges sex for money, I am talking about a woman who is not owned by a man so she might be getting her money from a lot of different things. She might have become a widow and gone into his business, and I think they would still call her a whore because she is not legitimated sexually and I think that is a really important point...I don't think 'whore' as it is used in this verse is just about 'oh she gets paid for, you know, a half and half' I think it is about a much huger concept, which I think is why prostitutes are so vilified, and why people just want to focus on street prostitution. They don't want you to know there is so much money attached to it or power attached to it or anything else.

The reason for this hatred of independent prostitutes is because there is an overall cultural taboo on women getting paid for domestic or reproductive labour. Thus, what is threatening is the whore's independent power and money. If this secret were better known then "a lot more women would do it!" says Shemena, and that is why so much effort needs to go into maintaining the whore stigma. Veronica asserts that "since reproduction is the most powerful thing going on the planet earth, if we are in charge of our own reproduction, *then we are in charge*." This is what the fear and violence on the whore is about, because, as Shemena points out, "you don't want to give women that power." Shemena gave an even more concrete example of what she means:

Where I come from, which was really dire poverty, and you get that I used prostitution and dancing to get myself through college, that is how I got to college, that is how I got to the point where now I work now in the field that I love, in public health, and I am going to medical school, but you know what? The first thing that people say to me, now, when they find out that that is what I did, oh my god, it is like now everything that I have done since then is totally delegitimized. You remember at that one event, I had a professor from Berkeley come up to me and ask me 'now there are a lot of universities around this town, do you really mean Berkeley?'...Because you are such a dumb little stripper you don't even know what campus you are going to...This was during my final year I was graduating. Even now that I have a degree from Berkeley, even now that I am going to medical school, even now I have been doing all this other stuff, because I was busted, I can never actually rise above that status, *this is about power*, and its about keeping me from utilizing what I got out of it to even be in that part of the world.

So to SWOP readers, it is most natural to read against the grain in evaluating the Revelation passage because they find a woman like themselves, viciously punished for gaining power, money or sexual self sovereignty.

Jezebel was a biblical precedent of the whore imagery for Ms. Shiris. Despite my explanation that the whore was a metaphorical representation of personified Rome, Ms. Shiris insisted that:

> I think it is proper to talk about Jezebel as a whore especially because of her royal status, in many Mesopotamian societies coronation was done with a rite of sacred prostitution, and her having a religious position as a priestess and a queen, especially with the images of her decking herself up, it just screams an image of sacred prostitution. I will be blunt, it is rather painful to listen to, despite your rather poetic rendition of it, because I hear what is present in so many places in the Bible is condensed here, just the slam, slam pounding of fists upon the goddess image…I am not saying this figure is a sacred prostitute, I am saying that this image of her that is being picked up is the whore of Babylon, no author is going to pick that if it has a resonant image and if you look at Jezebel who is similarly this archetype of the luxuriously rich and powerful woman who was brought low by a society that just won't stand for this sort of thing and John is very much speaking the voice of the other Israelites there. The emotions are so similar; I can't just help seeing an echo of the earlier image.

I had to concede that since someone labelled "Jezebel" was denounced as a whore in Revelation 2, it was very appropriate to bring her into the discussion. Also, Jezebel and the Whore Babylon both have their bodies devoured.[53] Ms. Shiris is a Goddess worshiper and so the Revelation passage is blasphemous to her ears. On the other hand Veronica from her fundamentalist childhood recalled the effect on her the first time she read Revelation:

> As I read this part of the Bible, I was struck with what the Bible hates. And what I came away thinking is that the Bible hates a woman who is powerful, the Bible hates a woman that dresses in a way that is conspicuous, the Bible hates a woman who is carefree and a little obvious. I got it that the Bible hated a woman that was sexual. So she feels good about herself, she is powerful, she is not married to a particular man, and she is not owned by a man, all those things, sexually autonomous, all those things is what the Bible hated. And my feeling as a 12 year-old child was to feel immediately ashamed, and fearful, and the one thing I had to do was make myself smaller. So regardless of the historical resonance, I think the really important thing is what kind of cultural impact does this have, and I think the cultural impact has been to make women smaller.

53. Caroline Vander Stichele pointed out this similarity in "Just a Whore: The Annihilation of Babylon According to Revelation 17:16," *Lectio Difficilor* 1 (2000), p. 6, http://www.lectio.unibe.ch/00_1/1-2000-j.pdf.

Damienne Sin links the violence committed against the whore Babylon as related to men's fear of women's power especially as symbolized by a sex goddess:

> There is a deep symbolism here with woman, vagina, and death, and why men particularly, but women as well, want to squash that, why they want to kill prostitutes, kill the vagina, kill that which bore them and to which that they have to return. Because you *are* a goddess, you are absolutely a vector for all the love and the hatred that people hold around on sexuality, and that is God, God is that force, that creation, that creative force, that birth force and that is what a vagina is, and that is what women symbolize as prostitute, specifically as prostitutes, and it is very frightening for men to confront. A free vagina, does that make sense? A vagina in control of itself.

Since there was discussion of the whore Babylon's social class as a queen, we also spent some time discussing the significance of her attire. There is sometimes confusion over her description as lavishly dressed and the significance of the colours scarlet and purple. In a historical perspective, the image we are given in Revelation is not of the typical dress of a prostitute but instead of an upper class Roman matron.[54] This relates to a contemporary contested notion of what it means to be "dressed like a prostitute." Remember that Gary Ridgeway's mother too was accused of dressing like a hooker. SWOP readers laugh at such a notion when little girls dress in a manner more sexually provocative than the average sex worker. Kimberlee and Shemena have found that it is often non-prostitute women who dress in this manner. Says Kimberlee: "I really want to know what it means to dress up like a hooker! Because I keep getting 'what, you're a hooker? You can't be!'" And Shemena recalled a Halloween party she went to where everyone was "dressed like a hooker" and "I realized that the reason that all of them were dressed like hookers was that it was cheap and they all had the clothes already in their wardrobes. They just put on a little bit higher heels."

I gave the reasons that scholars thought a Roman matron was described not as a "garishly" or "gaudily" dressed hooker as many might impugn for women dressed nowadays in bright red colours. I explained that there were dress codes in Roman law in order for there to be clear markers of social status. Prostitutes, at least according to the Roman law, were expressly required to wear white togas while clothing of red and purple were

54. See Thomas McGinn, *Prostitution, Sexuality, and the Law in Ancient Rome*, pp. 160–63 for Roman laws proscribing dress codes.

expensive and the typical aristocratic dress. If it was a statue of the Goddess Roma being described then she would most likely be an image of respectability for the imperial propaganda to be understandable. Still, Veronica was insistent about the idea of the whore Babylon as a courtesan, not necessarily a Roman matron. She also contested my assumption that a powerful rich courtesan would not be respectable.

> I see her as a courtesan. I don't necessarily see her as somebody who is seeing a ton of men wearing her body out. I just see her as having 5 or 6 protectors and that she is at the top of her social hierarchy and that *is* what happens to courtesans. Even if she is wearing purple which was not allowed for sex workers. But from what I have studied about courtesans they have pretty well existed down throughout the millennia, and they were always in another category off from the regular prostitutes. They were allowed to be some of the most wealthy of women, visible women, celebrated women. Sometimes they would have parades to honor them. Statues made after them. So I have a hard time believing that all those celebrated courtesans were slaves wearing white togas.

She used the analogy of Pamela Harriman as someone who was reviled as a whore for her relations with powerful wealthy men and due to her attainment of great social power for herself. Veronica was expressly concerned that once again, prostitutes were being erased from history:

> Today there are courtesans. Pamela Harriman is considered a courtesan, by some. She actually married her money. But if you look at the art that travels around the world right now, the great Monet works of art, her name is at the bottom of that, an incredibly wealthy woman, she died a billionaire. But, most historians will not probably consider her a *whore*, and so it is not in the history books. And I am just saying that I have got a hunch that there were women that were like her all along and why not during Rome's time?

I myself was invested in the identification of Babylon as a respectable Roman matron because it was a necessary aspect of my reverse slander theory of countercultural speech in Revelation. Both of these tacks were rejected as liberating to prostitutes. The connection that SWOP readers feel towards the prostitute in the story was greater than the idea of potential solidarity with other disfranchised groups, now or in history. Since sex workers find it so difficult to get other resistance groups to ally themselves with their cause, due to stigma spillover, they do not automatically expect to be treated well by feminists, leftists, prison abolitionists, police monitoring groups, etc. So even if it is plausible to posit such a social matrix for the deployment of the whore metaphor, SWOP readers found it unlikely that people who talk in this way are true allies of prostitutes. Unless potential allies explicitly mention solidarity with prostitutes, it is the experience of SWOP readers that likely allies are not true allies even if it seems that their goals might be congruent. Too many potential allies have failed to publicly support sex workers because of the fear of stigma spill over. The stigma surrounding prostitution continues to hamper many closeted allies from being in overt solidarity with the rights cause. The fact that all current government funding to any advocacy agencies is contingent upon making an anti-prostitution pledge may be another factor.

One of the most consistent and interesting aspects of the reading was that SWOP women identified with Babylon, whoever she "really" was, simply because she is denounced as a "whore." The solidarity with "whores" whatever their place in the social hierarchy was stronger than class difference. If she is a rich matron, prostitutes are in solidarity. If she is a queen like Jezebel, they still identify with her. If she is a pagan goddess personifying Roman imperial might, they still identify with her. It is more difficult to identify with uncertain allies who used the social identities of prostitutes to name their enemies. As Kimberlee noted, "obviously they still thought of 'whore' as bad because that was the word that they used to describe this terrible power that was oppressing them."

Being Oppressed is No Excuse

This discussion of "whether the whore really is a whore" naturally led to an evaluation of whore metaphor in political and counter cultural language. The conclusion was that those who use the metaphor are not fully seeing prostitutes, or women, as part of the same struggle or as fully equal. I brought up the speech by Arundahti Roy, Tupac's slur on the Statue of Liberty and Dead Prez' expression of revolutionary culture: the "ho-lice." A long interesting comparison between Revelation and Hip-hop/Rap ensued. Many SWOP readers confessed to liking Hip-hop and Rap music, despite the talk of "bitches and hoes." But there was an equally strong concern about this language use. Both Robyn and Sweet were highly critical of this kind of talk. Said Robyn: "right now they are doing this whole thing around prostitution that is kind of bad. It is not *kind* of bad, it is tough, it is really bad." Sweet agreed "it is really pro pimp, pro pimps up, hoes down." Kimberlee explains it more fully:

> What is sad about the Hip-hop that I have heard, particularly with Tupac, was that there is all this yeah 'be powerful', and 'I respected my mom, even though she went through some hard shit' but then in other songs is still like 'fuck those bitches and slap those hos', and whatever,

so the real problem is that all these good messages that you talked about, where they are talking about their oppression and wanting it differently, but they are not seeing the women as part of their same struggle, they are saying 'this is the black man's struggle.'

In the same way, the authors of Revelation are held accountable for making the same kind of slight to sex workers, although there was certainly a more sympathetic hearing for them than for "the people who use our services and still say that we are bad people, the politicians, the sailors, you know who…they are the first person to get up on the podium and talk about what horrible and moral-less people we are," as Sweet characterized many customers. There is a difference between the criticism of these hypocritical types and when oppressed groups use the term "whore," but even then it is still criticized and belies a false or incomplete analysis of oppression. Kimberlee had the most empathy, and Sweet insisted on knowing the context of every political use of the metaphor. Says Kimberlee:

> If I had existed in their times I would have probably been on their side, I have a tendency to be on the side of the underdogs…I think that is how they were, in a really bad position and created this awful thing. I think that when we look back and read it, the term 'whore' means so much more to us than it did when they were writing it.

But it was Veronica that really brought the issue home for many in the group: "If we were in the Gay Liberation movement we would be beyond this conversation because it wouldn't be OK to be saying 'fag' for any political purpose." This turned around the discussion into a new direction. Everyone had to agree that no one would use slurs against other groups that have attained some measure of political power. Imagine if it were a slur against the disabled community or African Americans or Jews or Lesbian/Gay/Bisexual/Transgender people (LGBT). It would instead be called what it is, hate speech. People in the progressive community would not be accepting of the derision of the "Faggot of Babylon" as "just a metaphor." When there is homophobic language in rap music people rightly protest. While there is some measure of solidarity between the sex worker community and the LGBT movement it can still be difficult says Kimberlee:

> I did this panel for the queer women in the sex industry, I and I said 'Look'— a lot of the women there were like the anti's who were like 'this is so bad and your making things worse for all women' and whatever, and I said 'You know what? Look, you may not support prostitution and you may not like that I do it, but our enemies are the same. We may not have a lot in common but the people who want you dead are the same people who want me dead. And we are so much more powerful if

> we combine forces against these ignorant, Bible thumping, fundamentalist psychos.

Overall everyone agreed that the sex worker rights movement had a lot to learn from the Gay liberation movement and should use this struggle as a model, from the tactics of getting a sex worker sitcom or cartoon comic character to reclaiming the word "whore" in a manner similar to the word "queer." Veronica likes to say that she is an ex-prostitute and a "lifelong whore" in a deliberate strategy to defuse its stigmatizing power. In the Gay rights movement "the whole notion of queer was re-co-opted by the Gay community, they re-embraced it as their own. The same thing is happening with crazy people," argued Shemena. Robyn reminded everyone of history "I think that is what we started 30 years ago. With Margo St. James, we reclaimed the name of 'whore.' OK, we did! We started 'Whore Power.'" A problem with Rev. 17–19:10 is the metaphorical nature of its usage. Kimberlee points out: "Rome really was evil. What needs to be happening is, we need to be saying is 'Wait no, you can't take our name; we are the whores! You are not a whore, you are a scoundrel!'" The SWOP readers were cognizant of the critique of Rome and felt that it was a valid critique; it was the use of their identities as a negative that was the problem.

However, a pervasive misreading of whore metaphor continues unabated. There is a boomerang effect where this metaphor is hardly ever read clearly against its intended cities, people, or men. It is read not as metaphor but as literal reality. This violent rebounding is what I talked about at the third annual International Day to End Violence against Sex Workers on 17 December 2005. I spoke, along with many others, at the candlelight vigil for all the murdered prostitutes, in front of San Francisco City Hall. I took my lead from Yvonne Sherwood, a biblical scholar who wrote about the whore metaphor in Hosea. Sherwood's reception history of interpretation of Gomer in Hosea 1–3 charted a consistent trend of "resistant readers" when it came to the prostitute figure.[55] Male readers tend to refuse to see themselves feminized as "Gomer" and instead align themselves with Hosea. What she says applies to Revelation as well. This text is supposed to denounce leaders, politicians and the rich as corrupt and oppressive with this metaphor. However, most powerful people, like the rich or politicians, are generally resistant readers and can successfully scapegoat real whores for their crimes instead of engaging in reflection

---

55. Yvonne Sherwood, *The Prostitute and the Prophet: Hosea's Marriage in Literary-Theoretical Perspective* (Sheffield: Sheffield Academic Press, 1996), p. 262.

upon their own political ethics. The sex crime with much more resonance for such a group would be adultery (which used to garner the death penalty) but this transgression has been almost completely decriminalized by politicians, perhaps because they engage in it so frequently. California Assemblyman, Mark Leno, who spoke after me, laughingly said that I hit the nail on the head when it came to describing politicians. Other non-powerful people generally follow this resistant reading strategy and continue to scapegoat real women as whores for whatever ails society. Gary Ridgeway blamed his ex-wives for his killing sprees calling them "whores" as well as the prostitutes he killed. These are "metaphors he lives by." What Mieke Bal says about biblical rape is applicable to whore killers: "the best theory of metaphor is sublimation…behind the pervasiveness of the metaphor of war as rape lies repressed, the reality of rape as war."[56]

Prostitutes as Scapegoats

The Greek myth of the *pharmakos* who is a kind of human scapegoat[57] can be an instructive way of looking critically at the blame that prostitutes receive from society. I did my masters thesis on this *pharmakos* plot in order to explicate a feature of the Lukan text of 4:29: cliff hurling.[58] Many features of the characterization can apply to prostitutes just as well as to Jesus who is said to enact atonement for sins through his death. Sacrifice, substitution, status ambivalence from very high to the lowest of low, an ironic inversion of this unstable status from extreme sinner to sacred figure, and death by burning or ritual expulsion are all elements of this mythic person. While the sacrifice of Jesus is generally seen as a positive thing in conventional atonement theology, the *pharmakos mythos* can explicate some of the more negative implications of substitutionary or vicarious punishment, especially that experienced by marginalized groups like prostitutes.

56. Mieke Bal, "Metaphors He Lives By," *Semeia* 61 (1993), pp. 185–207, p. 205.

57. The *pharmakos* figure is often translated "scapegoat" because of the atonement ritual described in Leviticus 16 which features a goat who is laden with the sins of Israel and then driven out into the desert. What is more helpful about the *pharmakos* myth is that it features a human being in this role instead of an animal.

58. Avaren Ipsen, "The Influence of the *Pharmakos Mythos* on Chapter Four of the Gospel of Luke," unpublished MA thesis, Berkeley: Pacific School of Religion, May 1996.

The most common utilization of this myth is for male figures. However, there are several versions of the myth that survive antiquity that describe a male/female symbolic expulsion to purify Athens during the festival of *Thargalia*, or that display a solely female version of the myth. The first description is from the testimony of Istros as preserved by Harocration:[59]

> The Athenians used to lead out two men who would be a purification of the city during the Thargalia, one on behalf of the men, one on behalf of the women. Because *Pharmakos* is a proper name; he stole the Apollo's sacred bowls, was seized and stoned by the companions of Achilles, and the proceedings are a mimetic remembrance of this, according to Istros in *Epiphanies of Apollo, volume I.*

This text is from a first or second CE century grammarian, Harpocration, who is trying to explain the usage of the slur *pharmakos* in the speeches of the classical Athenian orators Lysias and Demosthenes. In order to explain the word he references the religious scapegoat ritual as described by the third BCE century historian Istros, whose works did not survive transmission from antiquity. The fourth century CE lexicographer Helladius gives a slightly different version:

> It was a custom in Athens to lead two *pharmakoi*, one for the men, one for the women, who were lead for the purpose of purification. The one for the men had black figs around his neck, and the other had white. They were also called συβακχοι. The purification was apotropaic against pestilential disease, taking its start from Androgeos the Cretan, who having died unjustly in Athens, the Athenians suffered a plague, and established the custom of always purifying the city with *pharmakoi*.[60]

The two passages describe different aspects of the same *pharmakos* ritual. The older version blames the vicarious victims as culpable for the theft of Apollo' sacred treasure. The second depicts a ritual to expiate the death of an innocent victim. The charge of temple robbery is one of the most common of the reasons given for the original *pharmakos* being put to death. However, in some versions the *pharmakos* is in truth innocent having been framed on false charges. The ritual is a way that the crime is purified, especially for a city experiencing a plague or famine or other type of misfortune. Whatever sin caused the city to experience disaster then is placed on the person of the *phamakos* who is ritually punished for the

---

59. *Harpocration: Lexeis of the Ten Orators*, ed., John J. Keaney (Amsterdam: Adolf Hakkeret, 1991), p. 258.

60. This passage is in Photius' *Bibliotheque*, tome VIII, ed., René Henry (Paris: 1977), 534a, p. 182.

crimes of the entire populace. It is generally a socially marginal figure who gets to enact this ritual role as shown in a fragment by the Latin author Petronius:

> *Sacred* means *accursed*. This expression is derived from a Gallic custom. For whenever the people of Massalia were burdened with pestilence, one of the poor would volunteer to be fed for an entire year out of public funds on foods of special purity. After this period he would be decked out with sacred herbs and sacred robes, and would be lead through the whole state while people cursed him, in order that the sufferings of the whole state might fall upon him and so he was cast out.[61]

In the accounts that directly describe the *pharmakos* ritual, it is figures of low status who undergo the scapegoat role on behalf of everyone else. However, in literary depictions where scholars detect the myth in the plot, it is more likely to be a higher status person who is to blame for the city's misfortune, like for example, Oedipus. Kings, in fact are often in a role reversal with marginal figures, like in the myth of King Codrus who was a legendary king of Athens who had an oracle that said the Athenians would not win a battle if the king did not die. Codrus therefore sacrificed himself by dressing as a poor person so that the Athenians would be victorious.[62] This role reversal goes in the opposite direction as is typical in these types of stories. The literary critic Northrup Frye sees the *phamakos* pattern as a good ironic vehicle in literature where the hero "gets isolated by society...if there is a reason for choosing him for catastrophe it is an inadequate reason and raises more objections than it answers."[63] The *pharmakos* figure is the typical victim recognizable "in stories of persecuted Jews or Negroes, in stories of artists whose genius makes them Ishmaels of a bourgeois society."[64] The *pharmakos* is inherently ambiguous, "neither guilty or innocent."[65]

A few examples of what scholars deem as female *pharmakoi* survive: Polycrite, Charila and Tarpia are mentioned by scholars as legendary women

---

61. In *Petronius* (Loeb Classical Library; London: Wm Heinemann, 1987), fragment 1, p. 387.

62. This story is preserved in Lycurgue, *Contra Leocrate: Fragments*, ed., F. Durrbach (Paris: 1932), pp. 84–89. Another version can be found in *Die fragmente der Griechischen Historiker* (FGrHist), ed., F. Jacoby (Berlin: Weidmannsche Buchhandlung, 1932), 3 Pherekydes fr. 154, p. 99.

63. Northrup Frye, *Anatomy of Criticism* (Princeton, NJ: Princeton University Press, 1957), p. 41.

64. Frye, *Anatomy of Criticism*, p. 41.

65. Frye, *Anatomy of Criticism*, p. 41.

194   *Sex Working and the Bible*

who conform to the mythical pattern but the element of *phthonos* (greed and envy) also is featured for Polycrite and Charila. Polycrite received cultic honors yearly during the Thargalia festival in Naxos at her tomb of "grudge" (βάσκανος) or "envy" (φθόνος). She had been a counterspy (a sort of inversion of Rahab) who saved her people but was then pelted to death with girdles upon her return home.[66] Charila was an orphan who instigated a Delphian ceremony when she hanged herself in shame due to her abusive treatment by the king. During a famine in her land she went to the king for a ration of food but he refused her because of her low status and further insulted her by throwing his shoe in her face. She committed suicide and it caused famine that needed to be expiated by ritually reenacting what happened to her with an effigy. In Plutarch's telling the ceremony was a "purification mixed with a sacrifice."[67] Seneca is the ancient source on the Roman figure Tarpia who is also the eponymous ancestress of the place where Romans were put to death by being pushed off a cliff, the Tarpian Rock. Walter Burkert lists Tarpia as a *phamakos* along with these other two Greek women. A Vestal Virgin, Tarpia was to be executed for unchastity but survived the fall and claimed that her survival proved her innocence.[68]

Scholars of the *pharmakos* myth like to emphasize that leaders such as monarchs are also marginal types, who along with women, criminals, the poor, etc. are easily blamable for the ills of society. Jan Bremmer writes that "where criminals are marginals at the bottom of society, the king is the lonely marginal at the top. The myth shows, however that high and low are interchangeable."[69] According to Robert Parker, "an obvious dichotomy among the scapegoats of myth and ritual is that between the socially elevated and debased. (In the legends of Oedipus and Codrus, it has been noted the one is transformed into the other). It is tempting to see here two conflicting diagnoses of public misfortune, corruption or incompetence

66. Ancient accounts of Polycrite can be found in F. Jacoby, *FGrHist*, (1932) 501 F 1, Parthenius 9=Andriskos or in Plutarch's *Bravery of Women*, in *Plutarch's Moralia*, (Loeb Classical Library: London: Wm Heinemann, 1918), 254b–f.

67. For the story of Charila, see Plutarch's *Greek Questions*, question 12, 293d–f in *Plutarch's Moralia*. Walter Burkert links the motif of *phthonos* to the *pharmakos* figure in *Structure and History in Greek Mythology and Ritual* (Berkeley, CA: University of California Press, 1979), pp. 72–79 and 173, note 1.

68. See *Controversiae I*, in *The Elder Seneca* (Loeb Classical Library; London: Wm Heineman, 1974), vol 1, 3.1ff and Burkert, *Structure and History*, pp. 76–77.

69. Jan Bremmer, "Scapegoat Rituals in Ancient Greece," *Harvard Studies in Classical Philology* 87 (1983), pp. 299–320, p. 304.

on high, and subversion and envy on the bottom."[70] Due to this pervasive pattern Walter Burkert has created a formula for the phenomenon: "the situation 'community endangered' versus 'individual distinguished' is turned into 'individual doomed' versus 'community saved'"[71] However, this formula does not evade a feeling of communal guilt that needs to be ritually expiated:

> Whatever the decision be in such a situation of despair, it is somehow immoral, unfair, but practicable. At the level of human consciousness, the troubling injustice must be reduced to overcome the trauma. There are two main possibilities for restoring good conscience to the survivors: either the victim must be termed subhuman, particularly guilty, or even 'offscourings' to be dumped—Greek legend makes '*pharmakos*' a 'temple-robber'; or else he is raised to superhuman level, to be honored forever. The extremes may even be seen to meet, deepest abasement turning into divinity.[72]

This last sentence reverberates with the death and torture of Jesus and how he "dies for our sins" and thus requires worship for undergoing this horrible punishment on behalf of humanity. However, as we see with the prostitute, when she is scapegoated it is also for crimes out of her control but she continues to be blamed, reviled and abused rather than revered. If women sacrifice their bodies to save their families, do they not offer their bodies for sacrifice in a manner just as noble as Jesus'? Why does this juxtaposition of the sacrifice of Jesus with that of a prostitute seem so different? Do we value the violent death of a man so much more than women who save their loved ones by having sex? Perhaps it is because in the Christian religious framework sex makes women inescapably impure and forever unclean however noble the intent of the act.

Some scholars contend that perhaps the problem is with the whole idea that punishment of one can expiate the sins of another. Perhaps the whole notion of vicarious atonement perpetuates the glorification and sanctification of abuse of the innocent and the justification of abuse for the marginalized who become demonized in the process. The problem that people have in comparing Jesus and prostitutes as scapegoats is that people do not see the problem with the doctrine of atonement wherein God is portrayed as a blood thirsty sadist who demands the death of his own child for the satisfaction of his own grandiose honour. This blindness to abuse is

70. Robert Parker, *Miasma: Pollution and Purification in Early Greek Religion* (Oxford: Clarendon Press, 1983), p. 260.
71. Burkert, *Structure and History*, p. 67.
72. Burkert, *Structure and History*, p. 72.

a manifestation of what Rita Nakashima Brock, Rebecca Parker and Joanne Brown call the "scapegoat syndrome" or "scapegoat projection" that is part and parcel of substitutionary atonement doctrine.[73] If the sacrificial death of Jesus were seen in a more critical manner, then the goal of Christians might shift towards ending state violence and behaviours of bloody coercion to obedience. Instead, these scapegoat mechanisms often encourage women to stay in abusive relationships so as to "redeem" their batterers through suffering. They likewise encourage the projection onto marginalized "others" all the hatred and resentment repressed towards abusers that needs to be displaced somewhere convenient and distant, as Gayle says: "It is a scapegoating. They need a scapegoat that they don't know personally. They have to take it away from their lives. It's too close, so you attack people that are *out there*." What needs to be seriously pondered is why such sacrifices are demanded in the first place and how they are built into the systems in which we all participate. The sacrifices of women are often institutionalized but still invisible and unappreciated.

Analysis of Differences between Biblical Scholars and SWOP Activists

Once again, sex worker activist readers insist on maintaining the identity of the prostitute in this story as in all the others. Metaphor or not, Babylon is still ever the whore and gets viciously punished for it. Whatever kind of whore Babylon is does not erase the fact SWOP readers tend to identify with any women labelled whore, whether they sell sex or not, whether they are aristocratic or divine or commoners, whether they are cities or statues or female bodies. The violence, metaphorical or not, still affects them. Feminist scholars often seem to distance themselves as much as possible from the label by making it a metaphor or by denying there is anything positive about the whore identity.

A sex worker reading does not invalidate the scathing critique of Rome that has been found in Revelation 17–18 by other liberation-oriented readers. Sex workers would have us consider if prostitutes are really part of the same struggle against colonial oppression as everyone else, and if so,

---

73. Joanne Carlson Brown and Rebecca Parker, "*For God so Loved the World?*" in Joanne Carlson Brown and Carole R. Bohn (eds.), *Christianity, Patriarchy and Abuse: A Feminist Critique* (New York: Pilgrim Press, 1989), pp. 1–30, p. 3, the concept "scapegoat" is there credited to Mary Daly. Rita Nakashima Brock's article is in the same volume: "And A Little Child Will Lead Us: Christology and Child Abuse," pp. 42–61, p. 53.

why people would continue to use their identity as a symbol of utter depravity. Thus, Revelation's figure of Babylon, as a symbolic critique of Rome is on par with a gangster rapper's critique of the Statue of Liberty as a lying "bitch" who cannot guarantee constitutional rights to black Americans. Both are derisive critiques of imperial propaganda couched in very offensive language. The offensive language is quite possibly a very effective rhetorical strategy designed to provoke important necessary realizations.[74] The vision of imperial Rome's demise ultimately might very well be good news to Rome's large population of prostitutes, but the offensive metaphor makes that outcome uncertain.

SWOP readers have no difficulty in lifting the veil of polemical appearance to see an innocent scapegoat somewhere in the vicinity of the vision. What is constantly being obscured and distorted is the cold, hard reality of institutional structures that put women in certain status categories based on sex roles such as legitimate wife, concubine, prostitute, slave woman. This economic hierarchy has been over-moralized in order to divert attention onto certain scapegoated groups of sexual outlaws from the utter systematicity of it all. SWOP readers have the ability to empathize with Babylon because people like to blame prostitutes for all kinds of social ills past and present. SWOP readers know to de-demonize negative portraits of the whore figure because it is already part of the tool kit for their own survival and self-esteem.

SWOP Commentary on the Whore Babylon (Rev. 17–19:4)

In conclusion to the section on the Whore Babylon, we explain the story by threading quotes by speakers: *Avaren*, Sweet, Gayle, Robyn, Veronica, Damienne Sin, Kimberlee and Ms. Shiris:

> I just have to say that this text reminds me of being blamed for everything, for whatever is going on: serial killers, drugs, crime, bad neighborhoods, drug problems, moral decay of the family, husbands cheating on their wives; that's all laid at the feet of the whore. Spread of STDs, we're blamed for everything. Plagues, a lot of this is about disease. It is a scapegoating. They need a scapegoat that they don't know personally. They have to take it away from their lives. It's too close, so you attack

---

74. For an example of a hermeneutic that deals squarely with the violence of prophetic sexual metaphors but nevertheless still endeavors to affirm the positive aspects of its critique, see the work of Renita Weems, *Battered Love: Marriage, Sex and Violence in the Hebrew Prophets* (Minneapolis, MN: Fortress Press, 1995).

people that are *out there*. And they talk about how dangerous sex work is. Then acknowledge the fact that if you are a woman between the ages of 25 and 45, and you get murdered, it is probably from your husband or boyfriend. But it is like, a 'whore' is bad, you know what I mean. A whore is a nasty woman who doesn't deserve to mix with the likes of anybody.

And it says in here they strip and beat her, or something? She is burned like a sacrifice, that's what it always reminds me of, she is the sacrificial lamb who is burnt forever and ever and ever. *They eat her. Eat her flesh.* Her demise is within, what, one hour? She is done, this powerfully huge, powerful woman is undone within a matter of moments. Because God judges her. Because it starts out 'come to see God's judgment on the whore of Babylon.' And it is so violent because we justify all violence with God, right? That is because, if God says it, let it be so, get out the ax and chop somebody's head off!

If you were Gary Leon Ridgeway (the Green River Killer) and you were reading this, you'd feel like you were on a holy mission of God wouldn't you? Well there are right wing religious fanatics who send me and other sex workers hate mail every month. And they have the nerve to say prostitutes and whoremongers are all going to burn. And then at the bottom they ask me for money... 'and if you want to help us send our message please send money to ministry blah blah blah.'

When I was on Fox News two years ago and a congressman asked me, 'Veronica, have you read the Bible?' I said 'yes, I have read it cover to cover, have you?' And he said 'well what does your Bible tell you?' And I said, 'It says, kill the whore.' And he and the other woman who was representing this right wing organization said 'Oh no, Jesus didn't want to kill the whores!'

The problem with this Bible text is that it is all metaphoric, none of it is reality, it is all like some crazy psycho babble nonsense, and the fundamentalists believe this shit and make laws out of it. The message is that you're a whore and unworthy and disrespectable. It gives a lot of power, all of this, the Bible imagery and everything, it gives a lot of power to people that are against prostitution and against sex, and against women. It isn't just against prostitutes. It is against women, to keep them in their place. What is the first thing a man does before he rapes or kills a woman? He starts calling her a whore. It doesn't matter if she has ever made a dime from sex, you're a whore if you're going down and you're going to get called a whore all the way down. Revelation doesn't just legitimate violence towards prostitutes, but it legitimates violence towards wives, towards all women. Yes it does. Just ask Gary Leon Ridgeway. How did he vindicate himself every day when he went to bed? He read it in the Bible that it was OK to kill some whores.

I mean, I can see clearly how somebody was trying to be poetic and create it as a metaphor, I can see that so clearly but then when you bring up the point that these people were slaves, they actually did live terrible lives, and if I had existed in their times I would have probably been on their side. I have a tendency to be on the side of the underdogs. But there is a psychology that happens when reality is not going to get you out of your slavery, but things are the way they are and there is absolute force and violence keeping you where you are at, like people who have had sexual assault when they are children, like, you just go somewhere else and you create a different reality for yourself, so I can, like, I think that is how they were, in a really bad position and created this awful thing. I think that when we look back and read it the term 'whore' means so much more to us than it did when they were writing it. But obviously they still thought of 'whore' as bad because that was the word that they used to describe this terrible power that was oppressing them.

Even though scholars may identify the whore as being a Roman matron, not a real sex worker, but an upper class woman, the statue Roma who is a personification of all the good values of Rome, I see her as a courtesan. I don't necessarily see her as somebody who is seeing a ton of men wearing her body out. I just see her as having 5 or 6 protectors and that she is at the top of her social hierarchy and that *is* what happens to courtesans. Even if she is wearing purple which was not allowed for sex workers. But from what I have studied about courtesans they have pretty well existed down throughout the millennia, and they were always in another category off from the regular prostitutes. They were allowed to be some of the most wealthy of women, visible women, celebrated women. Sometimes they would have parades to honor them. Statues made after them. So I have a hard time believing that all those celebrated courtesans were slaves wearing white togas.

Speaking of clothing, one of the things that you were talking about, I'd like to go back to, thinking about the way that she was dressed, and the kind of power she has over all these different aspects of commerce, and like the height of luxury, and you are talking about why you want to do sex work when I talk about why I did it, money was part of it but money wasn't all of it, and that is certainly how it is being portrayed here, it is this very focused on trade, let's not talk about anything else, so the whore herself, Babylon, is not any whore I have ever met. I can tell you that much. I've never met her.

I really want to know what it means to dress like a hooker! Because I keep getting 'what, you're a hooker? You can't be!' You know, when you go out you realize and all the little girls are dressed like hookers and you're not. The last Halloween party that I went to about five years ago all the women were dressed like hookers and I realized the reason that all of them were dressed like hookers was that it was cheap and they all had the clothes already in their wardrobes. They just put on a little bit higher heels. This is a party at my husband's boss' house and you know all the wives came dressed like whores and you know what I came dressed as? A 1940s Red Cross nurse. That was probably the only one in a real hooker's outfit that was there.

Today there are courtesans. Pamela Harriman is considered a courtesan, by some. She actually married her money. But if you look at the art that travels around the world right now, the great Monet works of art, her name is at the bottom of that, an incredibly wealthy woman, she died a billionaire. But, most historians will not probably consider her a whore, and so it is not in the history books. And I am just saying that I have got a hunch that there were women that were like her all along and why not during Rome's time?

I feel that we get written out of history. I feel that the reason that this passage is so hateful, and has so much energy, is because the whore was so powerful, and I am not just talking about a woman who exchanges sex for money, I am talking about a woman who is not owned by a man so she might be getting her money from a lot of different things. She might have become a widow and gone into his business, and I think they would still call her a whore because she is not legitimated sexually and I think that is a really important point. I think one of the reasons that Pamela Harriman was considered a whore is not because she wasn't doing some thing that other women have not done which is like, marry for money, but because she did it with so much self interest. <u>That</u> people really hated. They wanted her to be suffering for her kids and suffering for her husband. And she was interested in her own advancement. So I don't think 'whore' as it is used in this verse isn't just about 'oh she gets paid for, you know, a half and half' I think it is about a much huger concept, which I think is why prostitutes are so vilified, and why people just want to focus on street prostitution. They don't want you to know there is so much money attached to it or power attached to it or anything else. Because a lot more women would do it! Since reproduction is the most powerful thing going on the planet earth, if we are in charge of our own reproduction, <u>then we are in charge.</u>

I have a photo that a client brought me printed off the internet, it is a real photo, and you may have seen it, and I have it up in my closet and it is a woman who has a pair of black bikini panties on and across it says. 'I have the pussy, so I make the rules' I think if enough women realized that, we would run the world. We would say OK make your choice, are you guys going to fight, are you going to make a war or you going to have pussy?

You don't want to give women that power. Where I come from, which was really dire poverty, and you get that I used prostitution and dancing to get myself through college, that is how I got to college, that is how I got to the point where now where I work now in the field that I love, in public health, and I am going to medical school, but you know what? The first thing that people say to me, now, when they find out that that is what I did, oh my god, it is like now everything that I have done since then is totally delegitimized, you remember at that one thing, I had a professor from Berkeley come up to me and ask me 'now there are a lot of universities around this town, do you really mean Berkeley?' Because you are such a dumb little stripper you don't even know what campus you are going to! This was during my final year I was graduating. Even now that I have a degree from Berkeley, even now that I am going to medical school, even now I have been doing all this other stuff, because I was busted, I can never actually rise above that status, <u>this is about power</u>, and its about keeping me from utilizing what I got out of it to even be in that part of the world.

When I was 12 years old and I got physically ill, reading it. I didn't have any concept that there had been sacred Goddesses, I knew nothing about sacred prostitution; I knew nothing about any of that at all. I was just into the Bible and I thought it was the inspired word of God. But as I read this part of the Bible I was struck with what the Bible hates. And what I came away thinking is that the Bible hates a woman who is powerful, the Bible hates a woman that dresses in a way that is conspicuous, the Bible hates a woman who is carefree and a little obvious. I got it that the Bible hated a woman that was sexual. So she feels good about herself, she is powerful, she is not married to a particular man, and she is not owned by a man, all those things, sexually autonomous, all those things is what the Bible hated. And my feeling as a 12 year-old child was to feel immediately ashamed, and fearful, and the one thing I had to do was make myself smaller. So regardless of the historical resonance I think the really important thing is what kind of cultural impact does this have, and I think the cultural impact has been to make women smaller.

And if you take the name 'whore of Babylon' yes there is no doubt that that is an image of Roma, for all the reasons that this is a sea city and Babylon ain't on the ocean. But the whore of Babylon is chosen both because Babylon is an archetypical rich and powerful city, the same thing you get with Cecil B. de Mille on Egypt in contrast to the heroes. The image of the whore Babylon is one that echoes over and over in the Bible, both in the Old and New Testament, although it is not presented in that name. The figure is obvious because the whore Babylon is literally the prostitute Goddess.

There is a deep symbolism here with woman, vagina, and death, and why men particularly, but women as well, want to squash that, why they want to kill prostitutes, kill the vagina, kill that which bore them and to which that they have to return. Because you *are* a Goddess, you are absolutely a vector for all the love and the hatred that people hold around on sexuality, and that is God, God is that force, that creation, that creative force, that birth force and that is what a vagina is, and that is what women symbolize as prostitute, specifically as prostitutes and it is very frightening for men to confront. A free vagina, does that make sense, a vagina in control of itself. Look any culture that oppresses women in that way specifically, the most blatant examples are those which will put women under blankets and shove them in a room and shut the door and paint the windows black, oh my god! Kill, kill it, kill it!

I think it is proper to talk about Jezebel as a whore especially because of her royal status, in many Mesopotamian societies coronation was done with a rite of sacred prostitution, and her having a religious position as a priestess and a queen, especially with the images of her decking herself up, it just screams an image of sacred prostitution. I hear what is present in so many places in the Bible is condensed here, just the slam, slam pounding of fists upon the Goddess image. I am not saying this figure is a sacred prostitute, I am saying that this image of her that is being picked up, is the whore of Babylon, no author is going to pick that if it has a resonant image and if you look at Jezebel who is similarly this archetype of the luxuriously rich and powerful woman who was brought low by a society that just won't stand for this sort of thing and John very much speaking the voice of the other Israelites there. The emotions are so similar; I can't just help seeing an echo of the earlier image.

Soon after joining sex work I found myself worshiping the Goddess, I had been an atheist my entire life. I am endlessly confused by the metaphysics of it all. I know, I can't help it, when looking at the Goddess, I am staring into my mother's face because I know she sacrificed herself for me and for my sister. I wonder. I may have found happiness there but why is it I couldn't find happiness in that life? Yeah, I had a choice, I had a choice, I have been shouting that so loud. So, I am finally out, I finally put myself in a place beyond all possible doubt that I am a rebel against society and not part of its power structure. But I don't know, I think there was a part of me deep down inside that knew there was no other place for me. I just, nothing else in life could be working. And I have being shouting loud and proud to be a part of SWOP.

One of the reasons why doing this interpretation it is important to me is because when you are caught up in it and it is not so much a choice for you, and then you are raised with all these beliefs in terms of it already being bad, because I too experienced the Bible, it is like it compounds the fact if you have got any biblical beliefs going on, it compounds like how you must be a really bad person for having anything to do with sex work. I know that I am not a bad person and I know now that as my adult self with my experiences behind me that I might make a conscious decision to do sex work in an empowering way. But it is a whole different world than when you need a little extra time and do sex work to feed your kids, it is totally different than to feed your man or feed your habit. When you're doing it through fear, and that is how I started too, I did it through fear, I was starving to death.

I am worried about the Hip-hop culture and what is going on through Rap. I don't think Hip-hop is the only musical culture that is doing it though. But right now they are doing this whole thing around prostitution and that is kind of bad. It is not kind of bad, it is tough, it is really bad, it is really really really bad, it is really pro pimp, pro pimps up, hos down. What is sad about the Hip-hop that I have heard was that there is all this yeah 'be powerful,' and 'I respected my mom, even though she went through some hard shit' but then in other songs is still like 'fuck those bitches and slap those hos,' and whatever, so the real problem is that all these good messages that you talked about, where they are talking about their oppression and wanting it different, but they are not seeing the women as part of their same struggle, they are saying 'this is the black man's struggle.' *That is what a lot of people say about Revelation, they say that it is written by men who are oppressed but they can't necessarily see women as allies*, because you got to be above somebody right? You gotta be better than somebody. *So that it is not a perfect liberation message and you can't squeeze a perfect liberation message out of it because oppressed people sometime don't have a perfect liberation message, only a partial one.* You know, I have to say I like Hip-hop, even though I hear the 'ho' and 'bitches' and what ever, but I like the music. What do I think of the use of the metaphor? For example the 'holice'? It is the whore metaphor, they are using the whore metaphor to talk about the police. I think it is the same thing as saying 'you're a pussy, you're nothing but a pussy man,' every time you want to put somebody down you refer them back to a woman…either you're talking about a woman of ill repute or you're talking about a woman's genitals. One of the worst things you can say. But are they using it in a political sense? Everybody uses it to talk about politics but are they justified? Is it just perpetuating the problem or is it making a statement? If it is making a statement, I don't think it is necessarily an anti-prostitute statement. But if we were in the Gay Liberation movement we would be beyond this conversation. Because it wouldn't be OK to be saying 'fag' for any political purpose. We could learn a lot from the Gay movement. We need to get our own sitcom dammit!

I was at the women's rights conference and I did this panel for the queer women in the sex industry and a lot of the women there were like the anti's who were like 'this is so bad and you're making things worse for all women' and whatever, and I said 'You know what? Look, you may not support prostitution and you may not like that I do it, but our enemies are the same. We may not have a lot in common but the people who want you dead are the same people who want me dead.

And we are so much more powerful if we combine forces against these ignorant, Bible thumping, fundamentalist psychos. Colgate can use tits to sell toothpaste but we can't sell our own bodies, heaven forbid we have control over it ourselves, you know! But they can use it anyway they want.'

I just have to reiterate what I said, about the other passage too, that I am not going to find any of this liberating until she says 'fuck you motherfuckers' and starts fighting. I haven't seen any prostitutes fighting yet, I haven't seen prostitutes standing up for themselves, everything we did just got written out of history. We need a Zena or something. But I bet we had a Zena! It is just like she said, but that is not going to be written because women didn't write this book. We need a comic book character; you know Annie Sprinkle was a comic book character for a while. 'The whore of Babylon fights back.' On the other hand, when we think about the metaphor, Rome was fighting back and Rome really was evil. What needs to be happening is, we need to be saying is 'Wait, no, you can't take our name; we are the whores! You are not a whore, you are a scoundrel!' Stop co-opting! The whole notion of queer was re-co-opted by the gay community, they re-embraced it.

If you realize that the whore of Babylon is so powerful, that the God of Israel was intimidated into acting petty and vengeful, then you can take solace in the fact that she is the object of his hatred and jealousy, not the perpetrator; she remains innocent even as she is reviled. You need to put something in there about the little scared men who were penning Revelation. They were so overwhelmed by this self owned woman. Like 'you got the power' you can imagine, she must have been like fire! Can you imagine? They have got this religion that tries to tell them that by God's power they are in charge of women and they go to Rome and they see these powerful women. When she walks down the road, they had to part like the Red Sea, it probably just made them burn, burn. They go home and probably beat their wives some more. Whore of Babylon has to be like 'oh yeah, exactly, you are petty and insecure, you want to fight? Let's go.' He is probably like, 'you're a woman, move to the side and she is like, what, I am a woman, <u>you</u> move to the side! And not because I am servile and so much more delicate than you' she is probably like Zena. I am a loudmouthed woman, but because it is a man's world, 'you: women, be down, you fucking women!'

Chapter 7

CONCLUSIONS: AMENDMENTS TO LIBERATION HERMENEUTICS

> The *ekklēsia of women* as the new model of church can only be sustained if we overcome the structural patriarchal dualisms between Jewish and Christian women, laywomen and nun-women, homemakers and career women, between active and contemplative, between Protestant and Roman Catholic women, between married and single women, between spiritual and physical mothers, between heterosexual and lesbian women, between church and the world, the sacral and the secular...*Solidarity in the struggle with poor women, Third-World women, lesbian women, welfare mothers, or older and disabled women spells out our primary spiritual commitment and accountability.*[1]

At the end of her groundbreaking work, *In Memory of Her*, Elisabeth Schüssler Fiorenza articulated a very attractive conception of an *"ekklēsia of women,"* as an historical reconstruction and as an unrealized future. She has also advocated this concept as a theoretical space for feminist scholarship:

> Within the logic of radical equality one can theorize the *ekklēsia* of women as a site of feminist struggles for transforming societal and religious institutions. Such a theoretical frame can displace the feminist alterity-construct *woman* as the theoretical space from which to struggle and replace it with the democratic construct of the *ekklēsia* of women, which is at once an historical and an imagined reality, already partially realized but still to be struggled for. Historically and politically the image of the *ekklēsia* of women, in the sense of the democratic assembly or the congress of women is an oxymoron, a combination of contradictory terms for the purpose of articulating a feminist political alterity.[2]

This vision has inspired me in my activist work and in my academic work to become a biblical scholar. The problem sex workers most frequently

---

1. Schüssler Fiorenza, *In Memory of Her*, p. 349, emphasis mine.
2. Elisabeth Schüssler Fiorenza, *But She Said: Feminist Practices of Biblical Interpretation* (Boston, MA: Beacon Press, 1992), p. 130.

encounter is that people assert these wonderful visions but then ultimately exclude sex workers in actual practice. Thus, liberation and feminist scholars have a way to go when it comes to articulating readings that are fully liberating to prostitutes. The utilization of the standpoint of sex worker activists has disclosed an ongoing commitment to respectability on the part of those who supposedly profess a commitment to poor women, even my own work which is trying to be so explicitly on the side of prostitutes, can at times unwittingly betray this commitment. The extent to which biblical scholars maintain these standards of in/decency encourages the ability of repressive institutions to police the bodies of poor women with legitimacy. In/decency is a key component in many ideological justifications for the poverty of women. It interferes with a true preferential option for poor women. If we wish to be truly liberating for all women, it behooves us to reflect and act otherwise.

Such an "assembly of women" is not an utterly new notion; the ancient Greek comedian, Aristophanes, wrote a play called the *Ecclesiazusae* where women take over the city state of classical Athens and institute a quasi-communist society where marriage and private property are abolished. However, a man making fun of these women and such crazy egalitarian notions wrote the play. One of the specific ways that Aristophanes ridicules citizen women of Athens is for their sexual jealousy that causes them to not have a relationship of solidarity with prostitutes. One of the laws they pass makes it a crime to have sex with prostitutes, who can henceforth only have intercourse with slaves.[3] Such a law shows who was excluded from this parodied *ekklēsia* of women, the lack of solidarity among women somewhat explains it as a failed utopia. This vision of a democracy of women is something a modern day *ekklēsia* of women may want to study as a warning.

The problem of omission of prostitutes exists in many academic disciplines. Our sex worker activists reading the Bible urge scholars seriously to ponder the surplus value of in/decency as a possible reason for this omission. What sectors of the economic hierarchy overall benefit monetarily from that lack of wages garnered by decent women? The taboo on paying for women's work and the sexual mode of reproduction helps to keep the economy afloat. The surplus value of this labour generally does not accrue to women. A repressive state apparatus enforces compliance by refusing to extend equal protection against violence to indecent women and by criminalizing sex for pay. Until very recently, most states implicitly extended

---

3. Aristophanes, Vol III (LCL 180) line 719ff, pp. 314–16.

police power to husbands to personally discipline their women. This keeps wages low or non-existent for the domestic and reproductive labour done by most women, especially the "decent" ones. Differential legal treatment and penalties for violence against black women today parallels the way non-Israelite women were treated under Deuteronomic Laws.[4] This constructs violence at an institutional level. Even though biblical arguments used against prostitutes do not have much merit, religious institutions continue to play a very important role in providing the ideological justification to repressive institutions interested in controlling the bodies of women, especially poor, non-white women. We must decide whether to choose a real *ekklēsia* of women or Aristophanes' parody version, *Ecclesiazusae.*

SWOP readers have brought rich interpretive insights to our passages of biblical prostitution. The story of Rahab was given a novel twist by sex workers who can explain her "treason" in that she is perhaps not treated as a full citizen. Comparison of the plot of the passage with Robyn's arrest by John Ashcroft is compelling. That sex workers are often abused as "snitches" gives a coherent explanation of why sex workers often see their needs at odds with those of the state. The story of Solomon's Judgment discloses the violence of the court of Solomon and the unequal treatment of sex workers before the law. The story of anointing woman is where SWOP readers come into their own and demand a full re-evaluation of how sex is deemed spiritually inferior or sinful, especially commercial sex. Finally, the reading of ideological violence in the whore metaphor of Revelation 17–19 underscores the urgency of struggle of sex worker activists to end scapegoating and violence against women and to redirect our attention to what really matters, the gendered division of labour in economies that are bad for women. The inclusion of prostitutes is mandatory for an adequate feminism.

None of the SWOP readings should be understood as superseding other valid liberation readings of these texts. While sex workers could understand Rahab's behaviour as a prostitute pre-existing the invasion of Jericho, this does not eliminate the equally legitimate understanding of Rahab a puppet for post-colonial propaganda. The historical example of Korean women who were taken and used as "comfort women" by invading Japanese soldiers shows a very different but historically repeating reality where women are conscripted into forced sexual labour by a military power and then named

---

4. See Traci West, *Wounds of the Spirit*, p. 145 and Cheryl Anderson, *Women, Ideology and Violence*, pp. 71, 75.

whores afterward.[5] Fanciful popular stories of colonized women, such as Pocahontas and La Malinche, who are depicted as loving their colonial invaders, still exist and function as imperial propaganda.

In the case of Mary Magdalene and the Whore Babylon, other equally valid understandings of what is libratory are also operational. Veronica Monet, for example, can fully understand how a non-prostitute, first apostle, Mary Magdalene could be a very empowering image for the majority of women, and especially for children raised in the church who aspire to leadership. Sex workers know better than anyone how the whore stigma functions to silence women. What sex workers want is more solidarity and great care with how their identity is used as effective slander. They would prefer that the whore slander be defused of its damaging power. That the violence that prostitutes experience has been legitimated by literalized images of violence against the biblical whore Babylon should make any liberation oriented scholar give pause. However, as a bitterly ironic portrayal of the grand matron Roma, a symbol of Rome, liberation scholars and readers are right to demand we continue to hear that critique of empire. SWOP readers do not object to the critique of empire but to their identities being used as poetic vehicles for all that is depraved and perverted in the unjust world we all inhabit. Literalized sexual metaphors can obfuscate the identity of real villains.

For those interested in including prostitutes into the *ekklēsia* of women, SWOP readers have suggestions toward a more liberating hermeneutic. The first and most important advice is to not erase the identity of prostitutes in the biblical text. This seems to be a very common strategy of mainstream scholars, as well as liberation oriented scholars, with many texts of prostitution. Yvonne Sherwood, in her study of Hosea scholarship, calls this phenomenon "The Strange Case of the Missing Prostitute."[6] With this disappearance, some hard issues of prostitution politics are evaded. At the 2005 SBL panel review of her book, *Postcolonial Feminist Interpretation of the Bible*, Musa Dube told me that she does not characterize Rahab as a prostitute in her post-colonial feminist hermeneutic "because in my context

---

5. See Yani Yoo, "*Han*-Laden Women: Korean 'Comfort Women' and Women in Judges 19–21," *Semeia* 78 (1997), pp. 37–46 and Chung Hyun Kyung, "Your Comfort Vs. My Death," in Mary John Mananzan, Mercy Amba Oduyoye, Elsa Tamez, J. Shannon Clarkson, Mary C. Grey, Letty Russell (eds.), *Women Resisting Violence: Spirituality for Life* (Maryknoll, NY: Orbis Books, 1996), pp. 129–40.

6. This is the title of Chapter 1, Sherwood, *The Prostitute and the Prophet*, pp. 17–82.

women don't choose to be prostitutes." The issue of agency is incredibly urgent however for an adequate theory of women and globalization, especially regarding migrant women. Laura Agustín argues, "Granting agency to migrating individuals does not mean denying the vast structural changes that push and pull them. On the other hand, it does not mean making them over-responsible for situations largely not of their own making."[7] SWOP prostitutes want their stories told and whatever agency they do have to be respected and acknowledged. They want their contributions to the economy, their families and liberation movements to be remembered. Prostitutes' rights activists want their stories visible whether they chose their profession as a first choice or not. The prostitution aspect of the text is an opportunity to look at the structural role of sex and prostitution in various political economies and analyze its connection to female oppression in general. Failure to include prostitute theorizing on prostitution bodes failure for any strategy for liberation.

Second, liberation oriented scholars need to make visible women's participation in the economy, whether paid or not, including sex work. Prostitutes urge that reproductive labour be a part of all economic models, including non-procreative sexual labour because such sex still contributes to the rejuvenation of the work force. Mainstream economics, Marxist criticism and even liberation theology fall short in this regard. Abolitionist feminists refuse to acknowledge that sex work is work. If it is a source of capital accumulation, then it needs to be assessed as part of the overall economy so that we know realistically how people without living wages manage to live and support their families.

Third, scholars need to question conventional mores of sexual decency that clouds vision when it comes to studies of sex work. Martha Roth and other scholars of Ancient Near Eastern law argue that the laws around prostitution were not promulgated for moral reasons but instead for economic reasons: to reproduce propertied social classes via legitimate heirs born by legitimate wives, not concubines, mistresses or prostitutes.[8] The laws were designed to avoid inheritance disputes. We also should not confuse the morality of modern day sex workers with their professional

7. Laura Agustín, "The Disappearing of a Migration Category: Migrants who Sell Sex," *Journal of Ethnic and Migration Studies* 32.1 (2006), pp. 29–47, or http://www.nodo50.org/conexiones/Laura_Agustin/LAgustin_Disappearing.pdf. I use the online PDF version's pagination: p. 11.

8. Martha Roth, "Marriage, Divorce and the Prostitute in Ancient Mesopotamia," in *Prostitutes and Courtesans*, pp. 21–39, p. 34.

choices. Women do not generally choose sex work because they are "promiscuous," (although promiscuity is a male construct reflecting male anxiety about women who control their own sexuality) but because of the socioeconomic sexual hierarchy that exists which doles out "decency" for upper class women and "indecency" for the underclass majority. This structural reality has gotten to be highly moralized in every branch of discourse on prostitutes. In terms of the modern day dramatic rise in prostitution globally, Laura Agustín argues that migrant sex workers be researched in a manner similar to all other migrants: "I argue that a diversity of projects and experiences granted to other migrants must be granted to these as well, allowing them to be studied as transnational migrants, as members of diasporas, as entrepreneurial women, and as flexible workers and as active agents participating in globalisation. Not to do so is to further stigmatise people using sex for instrumental ends and perpetuate a tendency to view commercial sex as the end of virtue and dignity."[9] In/decency keeps prostitution in a special exceptional category which fails to squarely face the fact that there is a current burgeoning demand for sexual labour worldwide and a very sizable population of workers who prefer sexual labour to other kinds of labour that pays less.

Given the economic social hierarchy of in/decency, the repentance of whores in particular is a big smokescreen for a deeper more endemic injustice. "Repentance" becomes a way to make individual prostitutes somehow responsible for social structures they did not create, nor could they change them, individually. The text of Luke's Gospel in chapter 3:12–14 gives insight into what repentance meant for the tax collectors and soldiers (that is to say: male sinners) who followed John the Baptist: "even tax collectors came to be baptized, and they asked him, 'Teacher, what should we do?' He said to them, 'Collect no more than the amount proscribed for you.' And soldiers also asked him, 'And we, what should we do?' He said to them, 'Do not extort money from anyone by threats or false accusation, and be satisfied with your wages.'" These men were not asked to quit their jobs as a condition of repentance. Why does everyone assume that the repentant woman sinner of Luke 7, often thought a prostitute, needs to quit her job to repent? How would it be possible under these adverse economic conditions for poor women to lose their one source of livelihood? Since tax-collectors are usually paired with sinners, women sinners who happen to be prostitutes should be held to similar standards as tax-collectors and soldiers especially when quitting one's "immoral"

9. Agustín, "The Disappearing of a Migration Category," p. 16.

profession is not a viable option due to the systematicity of oppressive institutions.

Fourthly, biblical scholars are asked to take great care to not re-inscribe the pejorative valence of "whore" as slander either by denouncing or denying the slander. This can be a strategy of respectability and keeps women weak and divided. Instead, scholars need to try to identify with prostitutes since the whore stigma affects and is used to control all women. Sexual violence against women should always be wrong no matter who women have sex with, how frequently or whatever the terms of consent. Furthermore, criminal abuse of sex workers is just that: abuse, not necessarily intrinsic to the sex work itself. Sex worker activists are in a struggle against the violence and abuse that they experience on the job but not necessarily the sexual work itself. Ms. Shiris writes that "only I get to call me a whore" and furthermore:

> I'm not certain about 'most prostitutes', but this sex worker personally feels uncomfortable with the term 'whore' when used to casually associate prostitution with ill-defined evil, or specifically with a lack of integrity. Using the term 'nigger' as a derogatory reference to a non-black person still draws power from racist views about the world and reinforces them. The use of the term 'whore' does the same, if and when the word is used as a disparaging reference. (I've no objection to the term being used in a reclaiming sense of cultural pride, but one should be as careful as when similarly using the term 'dyke' to refer to a lesbian. Generally, it's a bad idea unless you're another whore or best friends with one.)[10]

Finally, biblical scholars who profess a liberation project need to get comfortable with the idea of sex workers as agents with ideas and strategies that are different from that of the non-prostitute experts on prostitution. Sex worker rights activists are pragmatists, just as standpoint theory is a materialist method. The starting point for rights activists and materialists is precisely where sex workers are currently located in their struggles to survive, now. The attainment of the survival needs of sex workers is primary, as is equal protection before the law and the attainment of basic human rights. The opposing abolitionist position is idealist: it opposes even acceptance of the *idea* of prostitution in the present and thus sees the elimination of prostitution as both primary goal and starting point.[11] Many

10. Ms. Shiris has a Blog called Lady Aster where this quote can be found at http://www.swop-usa.org/Asterblog.html
11. The idealist orientation is apparent in the book title of a prominent abolitionist, Sheila Jefferys' *The Idea of Prostitution.*

of these feminists refuse to concede any validity to the rights view or to stay in respectful dialogue making their discourse very modernist in its claims to truth. Sex worker activists need to be honestly heard. Such respect is the ethical way of doing other kinds of research unrelated to sex. Laura Agustín points this out well with respect to migrant sex workers: "Despite the fact that ethical research must never originate from a claim that subjects investigated do not know their own minds, many that write about the sale of sex disqualify the stated desires of women and transsexuals, as well as men, to travel, see the world, make a lot of money, and do whatever work is available along the way. This is research that begins from a moralizing position."[12] This is a problem of in/decency; sex worker activists have solutions.

12. Agustín, "The Disappearing of a Migration Category," p. 16.

Discussion Questions

Instructions for respondents: Please read the Bible texts carefully and then answer the questions below. If you do not find a question meaningful, feel free to skip it. The main point is to read these texts in light of your own experiences. You can use the other sides of these pages to write and add pages as needed.

Rahab Questions (Joshua 2 and 6):

1. In what ways does the depiction of prostitution in this story overlap with what you experience and know about prostitution?
2. To your knowledge, in general, what relation exists between the military and prostitution?
3. What ethnic and class conflicts can you identify in this story?
4. What do you think about Rahab's help to the invading Israelites? How do you explain her behavior? Is this what you would do?
5. Why do you think Rahab is considered a heroine in Jewish and Christian tradition?
6. Is this a liberating story for prostitutes?

Questions on Solomon and the two prostitutes (I Kgs 3:16–28):

1. What aspects of this story overlap with your experiences with prostitution?
2. Do you think Solomon is a good judge? Would you want to be in his courtroom?
3. Why do you think the writer depicts these mothers as prostitutes?
4. Do the mothers get justice?
5. Where is the violence in this story? Who is violent?
6. Is there a way to read this story so as to not disparage either mother?
7. Does Solomon have to be the hero?
8. Is this story liberating to prostitutes?

Anointing Woman Questions (Jn 12:1–8/Mk 14:3–9/Mt. 26:6–13/Lk. 7:36–50)

1. What aspects of this story intersect or overlap with your experiences in prostitution?
2. How would you characterize the behavior of the anointing woman?
3. How would you describe the other characters' attitude towards the anointing woman?
4. Why do you think that so many readers think that anointing woman is a prostitute? Do you think she is a prostitute?
5. Many readers also have considered this story to be about Mary Magdalene. What do you think about this?
6. How do you feel about a Mary Magdalene who is not a prostitute but instead a wealthy female disciple of Jesus?
7. Do you think this is a story that is liberating to prostitutes? Why or why not?
8. How do you reconcile the differences in the 4 versions of the story?
9. Do you feel that some versions of this story are more or less liberating or harmful to prostitutes that the others? Which ones and why?
10. How do you interpret the story's assertion that the "poor are always with you"?
11. Do you see a conflict between the woman's actions and the needs of the poor?
12. Are there any other things about this story that strike you as important that I have not asked about?

Questions on the Whore Babylon (Rev. 17–19:4):

1. What story elements relate to your experience of prostitution?
2. How would you characterize the whore Babylon?
3. Who is Babylon a metaphor for? Who are her clients?
4. Why do you think she is so luxuriously dressed? Do most prostitutes live so luxuriously?
5. Why is she punished so violently?
6. Does this story legitimate violence against prostitutes?
7. Even if Babylon is really a metaphor, is this image of a prostitute still harmful for sex workers?
8. What prostitution stereotypes do you see in this story?
9. How do you feel about the use of prostitution as a political metaphor (that is to say, "the white house is a whore house" or the "ho-lice" for police in rap music)?
10. Do you know of a way to read this story in a way that is liberating for prostitutes?

BIBLIOGRAPHY

Abad, Angelita, Marena Briones, Tatiana Cordero, Rosa Manzo and Marta
    Marchan, "The Association of Autonomous Women Workers, Ecuador,
    '22nd June'" in Kamala Kempadoo and Jo Doezema (eds.), *Global Sex
    Workers: Rights, Resistance, and Redefinition* (New York: Routledge, 1998),
    pp. 172–77.
Aelian, *Historical Miscellany* (trans. N.G. Wilson; Loeb Classical Library,
    Cambridge, MA: Harvard University Press, 1997).
Agustín, Laura María, "Helping Women Who Sell Sex: The Construction of
    Benevolent Identities," *Rhizomes* 10 (2005), http://www.rhizomes.net/
    issue10/agustin.htm
_____ "Migrants in the Mistress's House: Other Voices in the Trafficking Debate,"
    Social Politics 12. 1, (2005b), pp. 96–117
_____ "The Disappearing of a Migration Category: Migrants who Sell Sex," *Journal
    of Ethnic and Migration Studies* 32(1), (2006), pp. 29–47, or http://www.
    nodo50.org/conexiones/Laura_Agustin/LAgustin_Disappearing.pdf
Albert, Alexa, *Brothel: Mustang Ranch and Its Women* (New York: Ballentine
    Books, 2001).
Alciphron, *The Letters of the Courtesans* (trans. Allen Benner and Francis Fobes;
    Loeb Classical Library, Cambridge, MA: Harvard University Press, 1959).
Almodovar, Norma Jean, *From Cop to Call Girl* (New York: Avon Books, 1993).
Althaus-Reid, Marcella, *Indecent Theology: Theological Perversions in Sex, Gender
    and Politics* (London and New York: Routledge, 2000).
_____ "On Wearing Skirts Without Underwear: 'Indecent Theology Challenging
    the Liberation Theology of the Pueblo'. Poor Women Contesting Christ,"
    Feminist Theology 20 (January 1999), pp. 39–51.
Althusser, Louis, "Ideology and Ideological State Apparatus (Notes Towards an
    Investigation)," Lenin and Philosophy and Other Essays (New York: Monthly
    Review Press, 2001), pp. 85–126, p. 97.
Anderson, Cheryl, *Women, Ideology and Violence: Critical Theory and the
    Construction of Gender in the Book of the Covenant and the Deuteronomic
    Law* (New York and London: T &T Clark, 2004).
Applegate, Judith, "'And she wet his feet with her tears': A Feminist Interpretation
    of Luke 7:36–50," in Harold Washington, Susan Lochrie Graham and Pamela
    Thimmes (eds.), *Escaping Eden: New Feminist Perspectives on the Bible* (New
    York: New York University Press, 1999), pp. 69–90.

Aquino, Maria Pilar, *Our Cry for Life: Feminist Theology from Latin America*, (Maryknoll, NY: Orbis Books, 1993).

Aristophanes, *Lysistrata*, vol. III (trans. B.B. Rodgers; Loeb Classical Library, Cambridge, MA: Harvard University Press, 1996).

_____ *Acharnians*, vol. I (trans. B.B. Rodgers; Loeb Classical Library; Cambridge: Harvard University Press, 1992).

Ashbury, Herbert, *The Barbary Coast: An Informal History of the San Francisco Underground* (New York: Thunder's Mouth Press, 1933).

Assante, Julia, "The kar.kid/*harimtu*, Prostitute or Single Woman? A Reconsideration of the Evidence," in *Ugarit-Forschungen* Band 30 (1998), pp. 31–96.

Ateek, Naim Stifan, "A Palestinian Perspective: The Bible and Liberation," in R.S. Sugirtharajah (ed.), *Voices from the Margin: Interpreting the Bible in the Third World* (Maryknoll, NY: Orbis Books, 1991), pp. 280–86.

Athenaeus, *Deipnosophists* (trans. Charles Gulick; Loeb Classical Library, Cambridge, MA: Harvard University Press, vols. v and vi, 1957 and 1959).

Bagnall, Roger, "Missing Females in Roman Egypt," *Scripta Classica Israelica* 16 (1997), pp. 121–38.

Bal, Mieke, "Metaphors He Lives By," *Semeia* 61 (1993), pp. 185–207.

Barr, David, "Towards an Ethical Reading of the Apocalypse: Reflections on John's Use of Power, Violence and Misogyny," in *SBL Seminar Papers* (1997), pp. 358–73.

_____ *Tales of the End: A Narrative Commentary on the Book of Revelation* (Santa Rosa, CA: Polebridge Press, 1998).

Barry, Kathleen, *Female Sexual Slavery* (New York: New York University Press, 1984).

_____ *The Prostitution of Sexuality* (New York: New York University Press, 1995).

Bauckham, Richard, "Economic Critique of Rome in Revelation 18," in Alexander Loveday (ed.), *Images of Empire* (Sheffield: JSOT Press, 1991), pp. 47–90.

Beal, Timothy, "Ideology and Intertextuality: Surplus of Meaning and Controlling the Means of Production," in Danna Nolan Fewell (ed.), *Reading Between Texts* (Louisville, KY: Westminster John Knox Press, 1992).

Beard, Mary and John Henderson, "With This Body, I Thee Worship, Sacred Prostitution in Antiquity," in Maria Wyke (ed.), *Gender and the Body in the Ancient Mediterranean* (Oxford: Blackwell Publishers, 1998), pp. 56–79.

Bell, Laurie, *Good Girls/Bad Girls: Sex Trade Workers and Feminists Face to Face* (Toronto: Women's Press, 1987).

Bell, Shannon, *Reading, Writing, and Rewriting the Prostitute Body* (Indianapolis, IN: Indiana University Press, 1994).

_____ *Whore Carnival* (Brooklyn, NY: Autonomedia, 1995).

Bellevie, Lesa, *The Complete Idiot's Guide to Mary Magdalene* (New York: Alpha Books, 2005).

Bennett, Harold, *Injustice Made Legal: Deuteronomic Law and the Plight of Widows, Strangers, and Orphans in Ancient Israel* (Grand Rapids, MI: Eerdmans, 2002).

Betz, Hans Dieter (ed.), *The Greek Magical Papyri in Translation: Including the Demotic Spells* (Chicago, IL: University of Chicago Press, 1992).

The Bible and Culture Collective, *The Post-modern Bible* (New Haven, CT: Yale University Press, 1995).

Bird, Phyllis, "Harlot as Heroine: Narrative Art and Social Presupposition in Three Old Testament Texts," *Semeia* 46 (1989), pp. 119–39.

_____ *Missing Persons and Mistaken Identities: Women and Gender in Ancient Israel* (Minneapolis, MN: Fortress Press, 1997a).

_____ "The End of the Male Cult Prostitute: A Literary-Historical and Sociological Analysis of Hebrew *qadesh-qedeshim*," in *Supplements to Vetus Testamentum* 66 (1997b), pp. 37–80.

_____ "Prostitution in the Social World and the Religious Rhetoric of Ancient Israel," in Christopher Faraone and Laura McClure (eds.), *Prostitutes and Courtesans in the Ancient World* (Madison, WI: University of Wisconsin Press, 2006), pp. 40–58.

Bishop, Ryan and Lillian S. Robinson, *Night Market: Sexual Cultures and the Thai Economic Miracle* (New York: Routledge, 1998).

Boer, Roland, "King Solomon Meets Annie Sprinkle," *Semeia* 82 (1998), pp. 151–82.

Boling, Robert, *Joshua* (Garden City, NY: Doubleday, Anchor Bible; 1982).

Bremmer, Jan, "Scapegoat Rituals in Ancient Greece," *Harvard Studies in Classical Philology* 87 (1983), pp. 299–320.

Brenner, Athalya, *The Intercourse of Knowledge: On Gendering Desire and "Sexuality" in the Hebrew Bible* (Leiden: Brill, 1997).

_____ "I am Rahab, the Broad," in *I am...Biblical Women Tell Their Own Stories* (Minneapolis, MN: Fortress Press, 2005), pp. 82–98.

Bright, Susie, *Sexual State of the Union* (New York: Simon and Schuster, 1997).

Brock, Rita Nakashima, "And A Little Child Will Lead Us: Christology and Child Abuse," in Joanne Carlson Brown and Carole R. Bohn (eds.), *Christianity, Patriarchy and Abuse: A Feminist Critique* (New York: Pilgrim Press, 1989), pp. 42–61.

_____ *Journeys by Heart: A Christology of Erotic Power* (New York: Crossroad, 1995).

_____ "Politicians, Pastors and Pimps: Christianity and Prostitution Policies," in Kathleen Sands (ed.), *God Forbid: Religion and Sex in American Public Life* (Oxford: Oxford University Press, 2000), pp. 245–61.

Brock, Rita Nakashima and Susan Brooks Thistlethwaite, *Casting Stones: Prostitution and Liberation in Asia and the United States* (Minneapolis, MN: Fortress Press, 1996).

Brown, Joanne Carlson and Rebecca Parker, "*For God so Loved the World?*" in Joanne Carlson Brown and Carole R. Bohn (eds.), *Christianity, Patriarchy and Abuse: A Feminist Critique* (New York: Pilgrim Press, 1989), pp. 1–30.

Budin, Stephanie, "Sacred Prostitution in the First Person," in Christopher Faraone and Laura McClure (eds.), *Prostitutes and Courtesans in the Ancient World* (Madison, WI: University of Wisconsin Press, 2006), pp. 77–92.

_____ *The Origin of Aphrodite* (Bethesda, MD: CDL Press, 2002).

Bullough, Vern and Bonnie Bullough, *Prostitution: An Illustrated Social History* (New York: Crown Publishers, 1978).

_____ *Women and Prostitution: A Social History* (Buffalo: Prometheus Books, 1987).

Burkert, Walter, *Structure and History in Greek Mythology and Ritual* (Berkeley, CA: University of California Press, 1979).

Burns, John Barclay, "*qades* and *qadesa*: Did they Live off Immoral Earnings?" *Proceedings: Eastern Great Lakes and Midwest Biblical Societies* 15 (1995), pp. 157–68.

Butler, Judith, *The Psychic Life of Power: Theories in Subjection* (Stanford, CT: Stanford University Press, 1997).

Cameron, Alan, "Asclepiades' Girlfriends," in Helene Foley (ed.), *Reflections of Women in Antiquity* (New York: Gordon and Breach Science Publishers, 1981), pp. 275–302.

Camp, Claudia, "1 and 2 Kings," in Carol Newsom and Sharon Ringe (eds.), *The Women's Bible Commentary* (Louisville, KY: Westminster/John Knox Press, 1992), pp. 96–109.

_____ *Wise, Strange, and Holy: Strange Woman and the Making of the Bible* (Sheffield: Sheffield Academic Press, 2000).

Campbell, K.M., "Rahab's Covenant: A Short Note on Joshua ii 9–21," *Vestus Testamentum* 22 (1972), pp. 243–44.

Catullus, *Catullus, Tibillus, and Pervigilium Veneris* (Loeb Classical Library; Cambridge, MA: Harvard University Press, 1956).

Chacon, Jennifer, "Misery and Myopia: Understanding the Failures of U.S. Efforts to Stop Human Trafficking," *Fordham Law Review* 74: 6 (2006), pp. 2977–3040.

Chapkis, Wendy, *Live Sex Acts: Women Performing Erotic Labor* (New York: Routledge, 1997).

Charles, R.H., *A Critical and Exegetical Commentary on the Revelation of St. John* (Edinburgh: T &T. Clark, 1920, 2 vols.).

Childs, Bevard, A Study of the Formula,' Until This Day," *JBL* 82 (1963), pp. 279–92.

Coakley, J.F., "The Anointing at Bethany and the Priority of John," *JBL* 107 (1988), pp. 241–56.

Cohen, Edward, "Free and Unfree Sexual Work: An Economic Analysis of Athenian Prostitution," in Christopher Faraone and Laura McClure (eds.), *Prostitutes and Courtesans in the Ancient World* (Madison, WI: University of Wisconsin Press, 2006), pp. 95–124.

Collins, Patricia Hill, *Fighting Words: Black Women and the Search for Justice* (Minneapolis, MN: University of Minnesota Press, 1998).

_____ *Black Feminist Thought: Knowledge, Consciousness, and the Politics of Empowerment* (New York: Routledge, 2000).

_____ *Black Sexual Politics: African Americans, Gender and the New Racism* (New York: Routledge, 2004).

Cordova Quero, Martin Hugo, "The Prostitutes also Go into the Kingdom of God: A Queer Reading of Mary of Magdala," in Marcella Althaus-Reid (ed.),

Liberation Theology and Sexuality: The New Radicalism from Latin America (Aldershot: Ashgate Publishing).

Corley, Kathleen, "Were the Women around Jesus Really Prostitutes? Women in the Context of Greco-Roman Meals," in David J. Lull (ed.), *Society of Biblical Literature 1989 Seminar Papers* (Society of Biblical Literature, 1989), pp. 487–521.

_____ *Private Women, Public Meals: Social Conflict in the Synoptic Tradition* (Peabody, MA: Hendrickson Publishers, 1993).

_____ "The Anointing of Jesus in the Synoptic Tradition: An Argument for Authenticity," *JSHJ* 1.1(2003), pp. 61–72.

Corrington Streete, Gail, *The Strange Woman: Power and Sex in the Bible* (Louisville, KY: Westminster John Knox Press, 1997).

Cross, Frank Moore, "A Response to Zakovitch," in Susan Niditch (ed.), *Text and Tradition* (Atlanta, GA: Scholars Press, 1990), pp. 99–104.

Dalla Costa, M.R. and Selma James, *The Power of Women and the Subversion of the Community* (Bristol: Falling Wall Press, 1972).

Daniel, Robert W. and Franco Maltomini (eds.), *Supplementum Magicum*, Vol. II (Opladen: Westdeutscher Verlag GmbH, 1992).

Davies, Margaret, "On Prostitution," in M. Daniel, R. Carroll, David A. Clines and Phillip R. Davies (eds.), *The Bible in Human Society: Essays in Honor of John Rogerson* (Sheffield: Sheffield Academic Press, 1995), pp. 225–48.

Delacoste, Frederique and Priscilla Alexander (eds.), *Sex Work: Writings by Women in the Sex Industry* (San Francisco, CA: Cleis Press, 1998, 2nd edn).

Demosthenes, *In Neaeram*, Vol. IV (trans. A.T. Murray; Loeb Classical Library; Cambridge, MA: Harvard University Press, 1988).

Derrett, J.D., "The Anointing at Bethany and the Story of Zacchaeus," in *Law and the New Testament* (London: Darton, Longmann & Todd, 1970), pp. 266–78.

Detienne, Marcel, *The Gardens of Adonis: Spices in Greek Mythology* (trans. Janet Lloyd; Princeton, NJ: Princeton University Press, 1994 [1972]).

Dio Chrysostom, *Euboean Discourse*, Vol. I (trans. J.W. Cohoon; Loeb Classical Library; Cambridge: Harvard University Press, 1971).

Donaldson, Laura, "The Sign of Orpah: Reading Ruth through Native Eyes," in R.S. Sugirtharajah (ed.), *Vernacular Hermeneutics* (Sheffield: Sheffield Academic Press, 1999), pp. 20–36.

Donohue, John, "Tax Collectors and Sinners: An Attempt at Identification," *CBQ* 33 (1971), pp. 39–61.

Douris, Athena, "The Sounds of Silence," *Alice Magazine*, January 2000.

Dreher, Carlos, "Solomon and the Workers," *Subversive Scriptures: Revolutionary Readings of the Christian Bible in Latin America* (ed. and trans. Leif Vaage; Valley Forge, PA: Trinity Press International, 1997), pp. 25–38.

Dube, Musa, *Postcolonial Feminist Interpretation of the Bible* (St. Louis, MO: Chalice Press, 2000).

_____ "Rahab Says Hello to Judith: A Decolonizing Feminist Reading," in *Toward a New Heaven and a New Earth: Essays in Honor of Elisabeth Schüssler Fiorenza* (Maryknoll, NY: Orbis Books, 2003), pp. 54–72.

Dussel, Enrique, "Theology of Liberation and Marxism," in Ignacia Ellacuria and Jon Sobrino (eds.), *Mysterium Liberationis: Fundemental Concepts of Liberation Theology* (Maryknoll, NY: Orbis Books, 1993), pp. 85–102.

Eagleton, Terry, *Ideology: An Introduction* (New York: Verso, 1991).

Ehrenreich, Barbara and Arlie Hochschild (eds.), *Global Women: Nannies, Maids, and Sex Workers in the New Economy* (New York: Metropolitan Books, 2002).

Elliott, J.K. "The Anointing of Jesus," *Expository Times* 85 (1973–74), pp. 105–107.

Engels, Fredrick, "The Origin of the Family, Private Property, and the State," in Robert Tucker (ed.), *The Marx-Engels Reader* (New York: W.W. Norton, 1978), pp. 734–59.

Enloe, Cynthia, *Bananas, Beaches, & Bases: Making Feminist Sense of International Politics* (Berkeley, CA: University of California Press, 1990).

Evans, Hilary, *Harlots, Whores & Hookers: A History of Prostitution* (New York: Dorset Press, 1979).

Exum, Cheryl, *Plotted, Shot and Painted: Cultural Representations of Biblical Women* (Sheffield: Sheffield Academic Press, 1996).

_____ "Pornoprophetics" in Athalya Brenner, *The Intercourse of Knowledge: On Gendering Desire and "Sexuality" in the Hebrew Bible* (Leiden: Brill, 1997), pp. 153–74.

Faraone, Christopher, "Aphrodite's KESTOS and Apples for Atalanta: Aphrodisiacs in Early Greek Myth and Ritual," *Phoenix* 44 (1990), pp. 224–43.

_____ *Ancient Greek Love Magic* (Cambridge, MA: Harvard University Press, 1999).

_____ "Priestess and Courtesan: The Ambivalence of Leadership in Arisophanes' Lysistrata," in Christopher Faraone and Laura McClure (eds.), *Prostitutes and Courtesans in the Ancient World* (Madison, WI: University of Wisconsin Press, 2006), pp. 207–23.

Faraone, Christopher and Dirk Obbink, *Magika Hiera: Ancient Greek Magic & Religion* (Oxford: Oxford University Press, 1991).

Farley, Margaret, Serene Jones (eds.), *Liberating Eschatology: Essays in Honor of Letty M. Russell* (Louisville, KY: Westminster John Knox Press, 1999).

Farley, Melissa (ed.), *Prostitution, Trafficking and Traumatic Stress* (New York: Haworth Press, 2003).

Fekkes, Jan, *Isaiah and Prophetic Traditions in the Book of Revelation* (JSNTSup 93; Sheffield: Sheffield Academic Press, 1994).

Fernandez, Dagoberto Ramirez, "The Judgment of God on the Multinationals: Revelation 18," in Leif Vaage, ed., and trans; *Subversive Scriptures: Revolutionary Readings of the Christian Bible in Latin America* (Valley Forge, PA: Trinity Press International, 1997), pp. 75–100.

Fewell, Danna, "Joshua," in Carol Newsom and Sharon Ringe (eds.), *The Women's Bible Commentary* (Louisville, KY: Westminster/John Knox Press, 1992a), pp. 63–66.

_____ (ed), Reading Between Texts: Intertextuality and the Hebrew Bible (Louisville, KY: Westminster/John Knox Press, 1992b), pp. 189–97.

Fewell, Danna and David Gunn, *Gender, Power & Promise: The Subject of the Bible's First Story* (Nashville, TN: Abingdon Press, 1993).

Fisher, Eugene J., "Cultic Prostitution in the Ancient Near East? A Reassessment," *BTB* 6 (1976), pp. 223–36.

Flemming, Rebecca, "*Quae Corpore Quaestum Facit:* The Sexual Economy of Female Prostitution in the Roman Empire," *Journal of Roman Studies*: 89 (1999), pp. 38–61.

Fontaine, Carole, "The Bearing of Wisdom on the Shape of 2 Samuel 11–12 and 1 Kings 3," in Athalya Brenner (ed.), *A Feminist's Companion to Samuel and Kings* (Sheffield: Sheffield Academic Press, 1994), pp. 143–67.

Ford, J. Massyngbaerde, *Revelation* (Anchor Bible; Garden City, NY: Doubleday, 1975).

_____ "The 'Call girl' in Antiquity and her Potential for Mission," in *Proceedings: Eastern Great Lakes and Midwest Biblical Societies*, Volume XII: 1992 (Grand Rapids, MI: The Societies, 1992), pp. 105–16.

_____ "BTB Readers Guide: Prostitution in the Ancient Mediterranean World," *BTB* 23:3 (1993), pp. 128–34.

Foucault, Michel, *The History of Sexuality: An Introduction*, Vol.I (New York:Vintage, 1990).

Frazer, James, *Adonis, Attis, Osiris: Studies in the History of Oriental Religion* (Hyde Park, New York: University Books, 1961).

Frye, Northrup, *Anatomy of Criticism* (Princeton, NJ: Princeton University Press, 1957).

Frymer-Kensky, Tikva, *In the Wake of the Goddess: Women, Culture and the Transfomation of Pagan Myth* (New York: Fawcett Columbine, 1992).

Gager, John, *Curse Tablets and Binding Spells From the Ancient World* (Oxford: Oxford University Press, 1992).

Garrett, Susan, "Revelation," in Carol Newsom and Sharon Ringe (eds.), *A Woman's Bible Commentary* (Louisville, KY: Westminster John Knox, 1992), pp. 469–74.

Gaster, Theodor H., *Myth, Legend and Custom in the Old Testament, Vol. 2* (Gloucester: Peter Smith, 1981).

Gateley, Edwina, *I Hear a Seed Growing: God of the Forests, God of the Streets* (Trabuco Canyon, CA: Source Books, 1990).

Giblin, Charles Homer, "Mary's Anointing for Jesus' Burial-Resurrection (John 12:1–8)," *Biblica* 73 (1992), pp. 560–64.

Gibson, J., "*Hoi Telônai kai Hai Pornai*," *JTS* 32 (1981), pp. 429–33.

Gonzalez, Catherine Gunsalus and Justo Gonzalez, *Revelation* (Louisville, KY: Westminster John Knox Press, 1997).

Goodfriend, Elaine, "Prostitution," *Anchor Bible Dictionary* (New York: Doubleday, 1992), vol. V, pp. 505–10.

Gottwald, Norman, *The Tribes of Yahweh: A Sociology of the Religion of Liberated Israel, 1250–1050 BCE* (Maryknoll, NY: Orbis Books, 1979).

Grabbe, Lester, *Wisdom of Solomon* (Sheffield: Sheffield Academic Press, 1997).

Sex Working and the Bible

Graf, Fritz, *Magic in The Ancient World* (Cambridge, MA: Harvard University Press, 1997).

Gray, John, *Joshua, Judges and Ruth*, New Century Bible (London and Edinburgh: Nelson and Sons Ltd, 1967).

_____ *I & II Kings: A Commentary* (Philadelphia, PA: Westminster Press, 1970).

Greek Anthology, Volumes I–V (trans. W.R. Paton; Loeb Classical Library; Cambridge, MA: Harvard University Press, 1960).

The Greek Bucolic Poets (trans. J.M. Edmonds; Loeb Classical Library: London: Wm. Heinemann, 1923).

Gruber, Mayer I., "Hebrew *Qedesah* and Her Canaanite and Akkadian Cognates," *Ugarit-Forschungen* Band 18 (1986), pp. 133–48.

Gudorf, Christine, *Victimization: Examining Christian Complicity* (Philadelphia, PA: Trinity Press, 1992).

Guider, Margaret, *The Daughters of Rahab: Prostitution and the Church of Liberation in Brazil* (Minneapolis, MN: Fortress Press, 1995).

Gutierrez, Gustavo, "Option for the Poor," in Jon Sobrino and Ignacio Ellacuria (eds.), *Systematic Theology: Perspectives from Liberation Theology* (Maryknoll, NY: Orbis Books, 1993), pp. 22–37.

_____ *A Theology of Liberation* (Maryknoll: Orbis Books, 1994).

Harding, Sandra, *Is Science Multicultural? Postcolonialisms, Feminisms and Epistemologies* (Indianapolis, IN: Indiana University Press, 1998).

_____ *Whose Science? Whose Knowledge? Thinking from Women's Lives* (Ithaca, NY: Cornell University Press, 1991).

Harding, Sandra (ed.), *Feminism and Methodology: Social Science Issues* (Indianapolis, IN: Indiana University Press, 1987).

Harris, W.V., "Demography, Geography and the Source of Roman Slaves," *Journal of Roman Studies* 89 (1999), pp. 62–75.

Harstock, Nancy, *Money, Sex and Power: Toward a Feminist Historical Materialism* (New York: Longman Inc, 1983).

Hawk, L. Daniel, "Strange Houseguests: Rahab, Lot and the Dynamics of Deliverance," in Danna Nolan Fewell (ed.), *Reading Between Texts: Intertextuality and the Hebrew Bible* (Louisville, KY: Westminster/John Knox Press, 1992), pp. 89–97.

Heijst, Annelies van, "Beyond Divided Thinking: Solomon's Judgment and the Wisdom-Traditions of Women," *Louvain Studies* 19 (1994), pp. 99–117.

Henderson, Jeffrey, *The Maculate Muse: Obscene Language in Attic Comedy* (Oxford: Oxford University Press 1991).

Hens-Piazza, Gina, *Of Methods, Monarchs and Meanings: A Sociorhetorical Approach to Exegesis* (Macon, GA: Mercer University Press, 1996).

Hesiod, *Hesiod, the Homeric Hymns and Homerica* (trans. Hugh G. Evelyn-White; Loeb Classical Library; Cambridge, MA: Harvard University Press, 1970).

Heyward, Carter, *Touching our Strength: The Erotic as Power and the Love of God* (San Francisco, CA: Harper and Row, 1989).

Hinkelammert, Franz, "Taking Stock of Latin American Liberation Theology," *COELI*, winter (1996), pp. 17–31.

Hobson, Barbara Meil, *Uneasy Virtue: The Politics of Prostitution and the American Reform Tradition* (New York: Basic Books, 1987).

Holst, Robert, "The One Anointing of Jesus: Another Application of the Form-Critical Method," *JBL* 95.3 (1976), pp. 435–46.

Horkheimer, Max, "Authority and the Family," from *Critical Theory: Selected Essays* (New York: Continuum, 1999).

Hornsby, Teresa, "Why is She Crying? A Feminist Interpretation of Luke 7.36–50," in Harold Washington, Susan Lochrie Graham and Pamela Thimmes (eds.), *Escaping Eden: New Feminist Perspectives on the Bible* (New York: New York University Press, 1999), pp. 91–104.

Horsley, Richard, *Jesus and the Spiral of Violence: Popular Jewish Resistance in Roman Palestine* (Minneapolis, MN: Fortress Press, 1993).

Howard-Brook, Wes and Anthony Gwyther, *Unveiling Empire: Reading Revelation Then and Now* (Maryknoll, NY: Orbis Books, 1999).

Ilan, Tal, *Jewish Women in Greco-Roman Palestine* (Peabody, Mass: Hendrickson, Publishers, 1996).

International Prostitute's Collective, *Some Mother's Daughter: The Hidden Movement of Prostitute Women against Violence* (London: Crossroads Books, 1999).

Ipsen, Avaren, "The Influence of the *Pharmakos Mythos* on Chapter Four of the Gospel of Luke," unpublished MA thesis, Berkeley: Pacific School of Religion, May 1996.

_____ "Political Economy, Prostitution, and the *Eschaton* of the Whore Babylon: A Feminist Integration of Sex into an Economic Analysis of Revelation 17–19," in Frank Crusemann, Marlene Crusemann, Claudia Janssen, Rainer Kessler and Beate When (eds.), *Dem Tod Nicht Glauben: Sozialgeschichte der Bibel* (Gutersloher: Gutersloher Verlagshaus GmbH, 2004), pp. 504–27.

Isasi-Díaz, María, "Economic Violence Against Minority Women in the USA," in Mary John Mananzan, Mercy Amba Oduyoye, Elsa Tamez, J. Shannon Clarkson, Mary C. Grey, and Letty Russell (eds.), *Women Resisting Violence: Spirituality for Life* (Maryknoll, NY: Orbis Books, 1996), pp. 89–99.

Jacoby, F. (ed.), *Die fragmente der Griechischen Historiker* (FGrHist), (Berlin: Weidmannsche Buchhandlung, 1932).

Jaget, Claude (ed.), *Prostitutes—Our Life* (Bristol: Falling Wall Press, 1980).

James, Selma, *Marx and Feminism* (London: Crossroads Books, 1986).

Jeffreys, Sheila, *The Idea of Prostitution* (Melbourne: Spinifex, 1997).

Jobling, David, "'Forced Labor': Solomon's Golden Age and the Question of Literary Representation," *Semeia* 54 (1992), pp. 57–76.

Jones, G.H., *1 and 2 Kings, Vol. 1* (Grand Rapids, MI: Eerdmans, 1984).

Josephus, *Jewish Antiquities, Vol. IX* (trans. Louis Feldman; Loeb Classical Library; Cambridge, MA: Harvard University Press, 1965).

Kai Ma, "Taking Sides on Prostitution," *In the Fray*, 7 February 2005, p. 11.

Keaney, John J., (ed.), *Harpocration: Lexeis of the Ten Orators* (Amsterdam: Adolf Hakkeret, 1991), p. 258.

Kempadoo, Kamala, and Jo Doezema (eds.), *Global Sex Workers: Rights, Resistance and Redefinition* (New York: Routledge, 1998).

Keuls, Eva, *The Reign of the Phallus: Sexual Politics in Ancient Athens* (New York: Harper and Row, 1985).

Kim, Jean, "'Uncovering her Wickedness': An Inter(con)textual Reading of Revelation 17 from a Postcolonial Feminist Perspective," *JSNT* 73 (1999) pp. 61–81.

King County Journal Staff, *Gary Ridgeway: The Green River Killer* (Seattle, WA: King County Journal, 2003).

Kitzberger, Ingrid Rosa, "Love and Foot Washing: John 13:1–20 and Luke 7:36–50 Read Intertextually," *Biblical Interpretation* 2 (1994), pp. 190–206.

Kollontai, Alexandra, *Selected Speeches and Articles* (New York: International Publishers, 1984).

Kramer, Phyllis Silverman, "Rahab: From Peshat to Pedagogy, or: The Many Faces of a Heroine," in George Aichele (ed.), *Culture, Entertainment, and the Bible* (Sheffield: Sheffield Academic Press, 2000), pp. 156–72.

Kraybill, J.N., *Imperial Cults and Commerce in John's Apocalypse* (Sheffield: Sheffield Academic Press, JSNTSup 132; 1996).

Kyung, Chung Hyun, "Your Comfort Vs. My Death," in Mary John Mananzan, Mercy Amba Oduyoye, Elsa Tamez, J. Shannon Clarkson, Mary C. Grey, Letty Russell (eds.), *Women Resisting Violence: Spirituality for Life* (Maryknoll, NY: Orbis Books, 1996), pp. 129–40.

Lamb, Regene and Claudia Jansen, "Zoellnerinnen und Prostituierte gelangen eher in das Reich Gottes als ihr (Mt. 21, 31)" in Kuno Fuessel and Franz Segbers Hgs, *So lernen die Voelker des erdkreises Gerechtigkeit: ein Arbeitsbuch zu Bibel und Oekonomie* (Salzburg: Verlag Anton Pustet, 1995), pp. 275–84.

Lasine, Stuart, "The Riddle of Solomon's Judgment and the Riddle of Human Nature in the Hebrew Bible," *JSOT* 45 (1989), pp. 61–86.

_____ "The Ups and Downs of Monarchical Justice: Solomon and Jehoram in an Intertextual World," *JSOT* 59 (1993), pp. 37–53.

_____ "The King of Desire: Indeterminacy, Audience, and the Solomon Narrative," *Semeia* 71 (1995), pp. 85–118.

Leigh, Carol, *Unrepentant Whore: Collected Works of Scarlot Harlot* (San Francisco, CA: Last Gasp, 2004).

Leite, Gabriela, *Eu, Mulher da Vida* (Rio de Janeiro: Rosa dos Tempos, 1992).

_____ "Women of the Life, We Must Speak," in Gail Pheterson (ed.), *A Vindication of the Rights of Whores* (Seattle: Seal Press, 1989), pp. 288–93.

_____ "The Prostitute Movement in Brazil: Culture and Religiosity," in *International Review of Mission* 85:338 (1996), pp. 417–26.

Lewis, Nantawan Boonprasat, and Marie Fortune (eds.), *Remembering Conquest: Feminist/Womanist Perspectives on Religion, Colonization, and Sexual Violence* (New York: Haworth Press, 1999).

Lewis, Nantawan Boonprasat, "Toward an Ethic of Feminist Liberation and Empowerment: A Case Study of Prostitution In Thailand," in S.Chiba, G. Hunsberger and L.E.J. Ruiz (eds.), *Christian Ethics in Ecumenical Context: Theology, Culture, and Politics in Dialogue* (Grand Rapids, MI: Eerdmans, 1995), pp. 219–30.

Licht, Hans, *Sexual Life in Ancient Greece* (New York: Dorset Press, 1993).

Long, Burke, *1 Kings: With an Introduction to Historical Literature* (Grand Rapids, MI: Eerdmans, 1984).

Lorde, Audre, "Uses of the Erotic: The Erotic as Power*," from *Sister Outsider* (Freedom, CA: Crossing Press, 2000), pp. 53–58.

Lucian, *The Dialogues of the Courtesans, Vol. VII* (trans. M.D. MacLeod; Loeb Classical Library; Cambridge, MA: Harvard University Press, 1961).

_____ *The Syrian Goddess, Vol. IV* (trans. A.M. Harmon; Loeb Classical Library; Cambridge, MA: Harvard University Press, 1925).

Lycurgue, *Contra Leocrate: Fragments*, ed. F. Durrbach (Paris: Societe d'edition "Les belles letters", 1932).

Mack, Burton, *A Myth of Innocence* (Philadelphia, PA: Fortress Press, 1988).

MacMullen, Ramsay, *Enemies of the Roman Order: Treason, Unrest, and Alienation in the Empire* (London: Routledge, 1992).

Maisch, Ingrid, *Mary Magdalene: The Image of a Woman Through the Centuries* (trans. Linda Maloney; Collegeville, MN: Liturgical Press, 1998).

Maldonado, R., "Reading Malinche Reading Ruth: Towards a Hermeneutics of Betrayal," *Semeia* 72 (1995), pp. 91–109.

Marcuse, Herbert, *Eros and Civilization: A Philosophical Inquiry into Freud* (Boston, MA: Beacon Press, 1966).

Marinatos, Nanno, "Striding across Boundaries: Hermes and Aphrodite as Gods of Initiation" in David Dodd and Christopher Faraone (eds.), *Initiation in Ancient Greek Rituals and Narratives: New Critical Perspctives* (London and New York: Routledge, 2003), pp. 130–51.

Marx, Karl, *The Marx-Engels Reader* (Robert Tucker [ed.]; New York: W.W. Norton, 1978).

McCarter, P. Kyle, *1 Samuel*, Anchor Bible; (Garden City, New York: Doubleday, 1980).

McGinn, Thomas, *Prostitution, Sexuality, and the Law in Ancient Rome* (Oxford: Oxford University Press, 1998).

_____ *The Economy of Prostitution in the Roman World: A Study of Social History and the Brothel* (Ann Arbor, MI: University of Michigan Press, 2004).

_____ "Zoning Shame in the Roman City," in Christopher Faraone and Laura McClure (eds.), *Prostitutes and Courtesans in the Ancient World* (Madison, WI: University of Wisconsin Press, 2006), pp. 161–76.

McKinlay, Judith, "Rahab: A Hero/ine?" *Biblical Interpretation* 7:1 (1999), pp. 45–57.

_____ *Reframing Her: Biblical Women in Postcolonial Focus* (Sheffield: Sheffield Phoenix Press, 2004).

Mehlman, Bernard, "Rahab as a Model of Human Redemption," in Blumberg, Herman J. Benjamin, Braude, Bernard H. Mehlman (eds.), *"Open Thou Mine Eyes...": Essays on Aggadah and Judaica Presented to Rabbi William G. Braude on His Eightieth Birthday and Dedicated to His Memory* (Hoboken, NJ: KTAV Publishing, 1992), pp. 133–48.

Metzger, Bruce, *Breaking the Code: Understanding the Book of Revelation* (Nashville, TN: Abingdon Press, 1993).

Meyers, Carol, "The Israelite Empire: In Defence of King Solomon," *Michigan Quarterly Review* 22:3 (1983), pp. 412–28.

_____ *Discovering Eve: Ancient Israelite Women in Context* (Oxford: Oxford University Press, 1988).

Meyer, Marvin and Richard Smith (eds.), *Ancient Christian Magic: Coptic Texts of Power* (Princeton, NJ: Princeton University Press, 1999).

Mies, Maria, *Patriarchy and Accumulation on a World Scale: Women in the International Division of Labor* (New York: Zed Books, 1998).

Miguez, Nestor, "Apocalyptic and the Economy: A Reading of Revelation 18 from the Experience of Economic Exclusion," in Fernando Segovia and Mary Ann Tolbert (eds.), *Reading From This Place: Social Location and Biblical Interpretation in a Global Perspective, Vol. 2* (Minneapolis, MN: Fortress Press, 1995), pp. 250–62.

Miller, Alice, *For Your own Good: Hidden Cruelty in Child-rearing and the Roots of Violence* (New York: Farrar, Straus, Giroux, 1983).

Millet, Kate, *The Prostitution Papers: A Candid Dialogue* (New York: Avon Books, 1973).

Monet, Veronica, *Veronica Monet's Sex Secrets of Escorts: What Men Really Want* (New York: Penguin, 2005).

Nagle, Jill (ed.), *Whores and Other Feminists* (New York: Routlege, 1997).

Nelson, James B., and Sandra P. Longfellow, *Sexuality and the Sacred: Sources for Theological Reflection* (Louisville, KY: Westminster/John Knox Press, 1994).

Nelson, Richard, *First and Second Kings* (Atlanta, GA: John Knox Press, 1987).

Newing, Edward, "Rhetorical Art of the Deuteronomist: Lampooning Solomon in First Kings," *Old Testament Essays* 7 (1994), pp. 247–60.

Newman, Murray, "Rahab and the Conquest," in James T. Butler, Edgar W. Conrad and Ben C. Ollenburger (eds.), *Understanding the Word: Essays in Honor of Bernhard W. Anderson* (Sheffield: Sheffield Academic Press, JSOT Press, 1985), pp. 167–84.

Newton, Judith and Deborah Rosenfelt (eds.), *Feminist Criticism and Social Change: Sex, Class, and Race in Literature and Culture* (New York: Methuen, 1985).

Noth, Martin, *The Deuteronomistic History* (Sheffield: Sheffield Academic Press, 2001).

Nygren, Anders, *Agape and Eros* (trans. Philip Watson; London: SPCK, 1953).

Oakman, Douglas, "Jesus and Agrarian Palestine: The Factor of Debt," *Society of Biblical Literature 1985 Seminar Papers* (Society of Biblical Literature, 1985), pp. 57–73.

Oakman, Douglas, *The Economic Aspect in the Words and Ministry of Jesus* (Berkeley, CA: Graduate Theological Union, Thesis Ph.D, 1986).

Olsen, Kelly, "*Matrona* and Whore: Clothing and Definition in Roman Antiquity," in Christopher Faraone and Laura McClure (eds.), *Prostitutes and Courtesans in the Ancient World* (Madison, WI: University of Wisconsin Press, 2006), pp. 186–204.

Osiek, Carolyn and David Balch, *Families in the New Testament World* (Louisville, KY: Westminster/John Knox Press, 1997).

Parker, Kim, "Solomon as Philosopher King? The Nexus of Law and Wisdom in 1 Kings 1–11," *JSOT* 53 (1992), pp. 75–91.

Parker, Robert, *Miasma: Pollution and Purification in Early Greek Religion* (Oxford: Clarendon Press, 1983).

Penchansky, David, "Up for Grabs: A Tentative Proposal for Doing Ideological Criticism" *Semeia* 59 (1992), pp. 35–41.

Petronius (Loeb Classical Library; London: Wm. Heinemann, 1987).

Petzer, Shane A., and Gordon M. Issacs, "SWEAT: The Development and Implementation of a Sex Worker Advocacy and Intervention Program in Post-Apartheid South Africa (with Special Reference to the Western City of Cape Town)," in Kamala Kempadoo and Jo Doezema (eds.), *Global Sex Workers: Rights, Resistance, and Redefinition*(New York: Routledge, 1998), pp. 192–96.

Pheterson, Gail, *The Prostitution Prism* (Amsterdam: Amsterdam University Press, 1996).

Pheterson, Gail (ed.), *A Vindication of the Rights of Whores* (Seattle, WA: Seal Press, 1989).

Photius, *Bibliotheque*, tome VIII, ed., René Henry (Paris: Societe d'edition Les Belles Lettres, 1977).

Pippin, Tina, *Death and Desire: The Rhetoric of Gender in the Apocalypse of John* (Louisville, KY: Westminster John Knox Press, 1992).

Plato, *Republic, Vol. 1* (trans. Paul Shorey; Loeb Classical Library; London: Wm. Heinemann, 1924).

Plutarch, *Plutarch's Moralia* (Loeb Classical Library; London: Wm. Heinemann, 1918).

Polzin, Robert, *Moses and the Deuteronomist: A Literary Study of the Deuteronomic History* (New York: Seabury Press, 1980).

Pomeroy, Sarah, *Goddesses, Whores, Wives and Slaves: Women in Classical Antiquity* (New York: Schocken Books, 1975).

Pyper, Hugh, "Judging the Wisdom of Solomon: The Two-Way Effect of Intertextuality" *JSOT* 59 (1993), pp. 25–36.

Queen, Carol, *Real Live Nude Girl: Chronicles of Sex-Positive Culture* (San Francisco, CA: Cleis Press, 2002).

Reich, Wilhelm, *The Mass Psychology of Fascism* (New York: Noonday Press, 1970).

Reichert, David, *Chasing the Devil: My Twenty Year Quest to Capture the Green River Killer* (New York: Little, Brown and Co, 2004).

Richard, Pablo, *Apocalypse: A People's Commentary* (Maryknoll, NY: Orbis Books, 1995).

Robbins, Vernon, "Using a Socio-Rhetorical Poetics to Develop a Unified Method: The Woman who Anointed Jesus as a Test Case," in Eugene H. Lovering Jr. (ed.), *Society of Biblical Literature 1992 Seminar Papers* (Society of Biblical Literature, 1992), pp. 302–19.

Roberts, Nickie, *Whores in History: Prostitution in Western Society* (London: Grafton, 1992).

Robinson, Bernard, "The Anointing by Mary of Bethany (John 12)," *Downside Review* 115 (April 1997), pp. 99–111.

Rosen, Ruth, *The Lost Sisterhood: Prostitution in America, 1900–1918* (Baltimore, MD: John Hopkins Press, 1982).

Rossing, Barbara, *The Choice Between Two Cities: Whore, Bride, and Empire in the Apocalypse*, Harvard Theological Studies 48 (Harrisburg, PA: Trinity Press, 1999).

Rostovtzeff, Mikhail, *The Social and Economic History of the Roman Empire* (Oxford: Clarendon, 1926).

Roth, Martha, "The Priestess and the Tavern: LH 110," in Barbara Bock, Eva Cancik-Kirschbaum and Thomas Richter (eds.), *Munuscula Mesopotamica: Festschrift fur Johannes Renger* (Munster: Ugarit-Verlag, 1999), pp. 445–64.

_____ "Marriage, Divorce and the Prostitute in Ancient Mesopotamia," in Christopher Faraone and Laura McClure (eds.), *Prostitutes and Courtesans in the Ancient World* (Madison, WI: University of Wisconsin Press, 2006), pp. 21–39.

Royalty, Robert, *Streets of Heaven: The Ideology of Wealth in the Apocalypse of John* (Macon, GA: Mercer University Press, 1998).

Ruiz, Jean-Pierre, *Ezekiel in the Apocalypse: The Transformation of Prophetic Language in Revelation 16, 17–19, 10* (Frankfurt am Main: Verlag Peter Lang, 1989).

Sabbe, M., "The Anointing of Jesus in John 12, 1–8 and its Synoptic Parallels," in F. Van Segbroeck, C.M. Tuckett, G. Van Belle and J. Verheyden (eds.), *The Four Gospels 1992: Festschrift Frans Neirynck* (Leuven: University Press, 1992), pp. 2051–82.

Schaberg, Jane, "How Mary Magdalene Became a Whore," *Bible Review* 8:5 (October 1992), pp. 31–52.

_____ *The Resurrection of Mary Magdalene: Legends, Apocrypha and the Christian Testament* (New York: Continuum, 2003).

Schottroff, Luise, *Let the Oppressed Go Free: Feminist Perspectives on the New Testament* (trans. Ann Marie Kidder; Louisville, KY: Westminster/John Knox Press, 1993).

_____ *Lydia's Impatient Sisters: A Feminist Social History of Early Christianity* (trans. Barbara and Martin Rumscheidt; Louisville, KY: Westminster/John Knox Press, 1995).

_____ "Through German and Feminist Eyes: a Liberationist Reading of Luke 7:36–50," in Athalya Brenner (ed.), *The Feminist Companion to the Hebrew Bible in the New Testament* (Sheffield: Sheffield Academic Press, 1996), pp. 332–41.

Schottroff, Luise and Wolfgang Stegemann, *Jesus and the Hope of the Poor* (Maryknoll, NY: Orbis Books, 1986).

Schroer, Silvia, *Wisdom has Built her House: Studies on the Figure of Sophia in the Bible* (Collegeville, MN: Liturgical Press, 2000).

Schüssler Fiorenza, Elisabeth, *In Memory of Her: A Feminist Theological Reconstruction of Christian Origins* (New York: Crossroad, 1985).

_____ *Revelation: Vision of a Just World*, Proclamation Commentaries (Minneapolis, MN: Fortress Press, 1991).

_____ *The Book of Revelation: Justice and Judgment* (Minneapolis, MN: Fortress Press, 1998).

Scott, James, *Domination and the Arts of Resistance: Hidden Transcripts* (New Haven, CT: Yale University Press, 1990).

Scott, Martin, *Sophia and the Johannine Jesus* (Sheffield: Sheffield Academic Press, 1992).

Segovia, Fernando, "Cultural Studies and Contemporary Biblical Studies," in Fernando Segovia and M.A. Tolbert (eds.), *Reading from this Place, Vol. 2* (Minneapolis, MN: Fortress Press, 1995).

Selvidge, Marla, "Reflections on Violence and Pornography: Misogyny in the Apocalypse and Ancient Hebrew Prophesy," in Athalya Brenner (ed.), *A Feminist Companion to the Hebrew Bible in the New Testament* (Sheffield: Sheffield Academic Press, 1996), pp. 274–85.

Seneca, *The Elder Seneca* (Loeb Classical Library; London: Wm. Heinemann, 1974).

Sherwood, Yvonne, *The Prostitute and the Prophet: Hosea's Marriage in Literary-Theoretical Perspective* (Sheffield: Sheffield Academic Press, 1996).

Shrage, Laurie, *Moral Dilemmas of Feminism* (New York: Routledge, 1994).

Skinner, Marilyn, "Nossis *Thelyglossos*: The Private Text and the Public Book," in Sarah Pomeroy (ed.), *Women's History and Ancient History* (Chapel Hill, NC: University of North Carolina Press, 1991), pp. 20–46.

Smith, Dorothy, *The Everyday World as Problematic: A Feminist Sociology* (Boston, MA: Northeastern University Press, 1987).

_____ *Writing the Social: Critique, Theory and Investigations* (Toronto: University of Toronto Press, 1999).

Soggin, J. Alberto, *Joshua* (Philadelphia, PA: Westminster Press, 1972).

Steinberg, Naomi, *Kinship and Marriage in Genesis: A Household Economics Perspective* (Minneapolis, MN: Fortress Press, 1993).

Stewart, Andrew, "Reflections," in Natalie Kampen (ed.), *Sexuality in Ancient Art: Near East, Egypt, Greece and Italy* (Cambridge: Cambridge University Press, 1996), pp. 136–54.

Stichele, Caroline Vander, "Just a Whore: The Annihilation of Babylon According to Revelation 17:16," *Lectio Difficilor* 1 (2000), http://www.lectio.unibe.ch/00_1/1-2000-j.pdf.

Stubbs, Kenneth Ray (ed.), *The New Sexual Healers: Women of the Light* (Larkspur CA: Secret Garden, 1994).

Stumpp, Eva, *Prostitution in der romischen Antike* (Berlin: Akademie Verlag, 1998).

Sturdevant, Saundra Polluck and Brenda Stoltzfus, *Let the Good Times Roll: Prostitution and the U.S. Military in Asia* (New York: New York Press, 1992).

Sugirtharajah, R.S., "'For you always have the poor with you,': An Example of a Hermeneutics of Suspicion,' *Asia Journal of Theology* 4 (April 1990), pp. 102–107.

Sutter, Luzia Rehmann, *Vom Mut, genau hinzusehen: Feministisch-befreiungstheologische Interpretationen zur Apokalyptik* (Luzern: Edition Exodus, 1998).

Theophrastus, *Enquiry into Plants and Minor Works on Odours and Weather Signs, Vol. II* (trans. Sir Arthur Hort; Loeb Classical Library; Cambridge, MA: Harvard University Press, 1949).

Thompson, Leonard, *The Book of Revelation: Apocalypse and Empire* (Oxford: Oxford University Press, 1990).

_____ *Revelation* (Nashville, TN: Abingdon Press, 1998).

Truong, Thanh Dam, *Sex, Money, and Morality: The Political Economy of Prostitution and Tourism in Southeast Asia* (London: Zed Books, 1990).

Van Der Toorn, Karel, "Female Prostitution in Payment of Vows in Ancient Israel," *JBL* 108 (1989), pp. 193–205.

Tucker, Gene, "The Rahab Saga," in James M. Efrid (ed.), *The Use of the Old Testament in the New and Other Essays: Studies in Honor of William Franklin Stinespring* (Durham, NC: Duke University Press, 1972), pp. 66–86.

Valentino, Margaret and Mavis Johnson, "On the Game and On the Move," in Claude Jaget (ed.), *Our Life* (Bristol: Falling Wall Press, 1980).

Volosinov, V.I., *Marxism and the Philosophy of Language* (trans. I.R. Titunik; New York: Academic Press, 1973).

Vuola, Elina, *Limits of Liberation: Feminist Theology and the Ethics of Poverty and Reproduction* (New York and London: Sheffield Academic Press, 2002).

Walkowitz, Judith, *Prostitution and Victorian Society: Women, Class and the State* (Cambridge: Cambridge University Press, 1980).

Walkowitz, Judith, *City of Dreadful Delight: Narratives of Sexual Danger in Late-Victorian London* (Chicago, IL: University of Chicago Press, 1992).

Walsh, Jerome, *1 Kings* (Collegeville, MN: Liturgical Press, 1996).

Ward, Roy Bowen, "*Porneia* and Paul," *Proceedings: Eastern Great Lakes and Midwest Biblical Societies, Vol. VI* (1986), pp. 219–29.

Waring, Marilyn, *If Women Counted: A New Feminist Economics* (San Francisco, CA: Harper and Row, 1988).

Warrior, Robert, "A Native American Perspective: Canaanites, Cowboys, and Indians," in R.S. Sugirtharajah (ed.), *Voices from the Margin: Interpreting the Bible in the Third World* (Maryknoll, NY: Orbis Books, 1991), pp. 287–95.

Wengst, Klaus, *Pax Romana and the Peace of Christ* (Philadelphia, PA: Fortress Press, 1987).

_____ "Babylon the Great and New Jerusalem: The Visionary View of Political Reality in the Revelation of John," in Henning Graf Reventlow; Yair Hoffman; Benjamin Uffenheimer (eds.), *Politics and Theopolitcs in the Bible and Postbiblical Literature*, JSOT Supplemental Series 171 (Sheffield: JSOT Press, 1994), pp. 189–202.

West, Gerald, *Biblical Hermeneutics of Liberation: Modes of Reading the Bible in the South African Context* (Maryknoll, NY: Orbis Books, 1991).

_____ *The Academy of the Poor: Towards a Dialogical Reading of the Bible* (Sheffield: Sheffield Academic Press, 1999).

West, Gerald and Musa Dube (eds.), *The Bible in Africa: Transactions, Trajectories and Trends* (Boston, MA: Brill, 2001).

West, Traci, *Wounds of the Spirit: Black Women, Ethics and Resistance Ethics* (New York: New York University Press, 1999).

White, Luise, "Prostitution, Identity, and Class Consciousness in Nairobi during World War II," *Signs* 2:1 (1985), pp. 255–73.

_____ *The Comforts of Home: Prostitution in Colonial Nairobi* (Chicago, IL: University of Chicago Press, 1990).

Winsor, Ann Roberts, *A King is Bound in the Tresses: Allusions to the Song of Songs in the Fourth Gospel* (New York: Peter Lang, 1999).

Wu, Rose, "Women on the Boundary: Prostitution Contemporary and in the Bible," *Feminist Theology* 28 (2001), pp. 69–81.

Yarbro Collins, A., "Revelation 18: Taunt-song or Dirge?" in Jan Lembrecht (ed.), *L'Apocalypse johannique et l'Apocalyptique dans le Nouveau Testament* (Bibliotheca Ephemeridum Theologicarum Lovaniensium LIII; Louvain: Leuven University Press, 1980), pp.185–204.

_____ *Crisis and Catharsis: The Power of the Apocalypse* (Philadelphia, PA: Westminster, 1984).

_____ "Persecution and Vengeance in the Book of Revelation," in *Apocalypticism in the Mediterranean World and the Near East. Proceedings of the International Colloquium on Apocalpticism, Uppsala 1979*, ed., David Hellholm (Tubingen: Mohr, 1989).

_____ "Feminine Symbolism in the Book of Revelation," *Biblical Interpretation* 1(1993), pp. 20–33.

Yee, Gale, "Ideological Criticism: Judges 17–21 and the Dismembered Body," in Gale Yee (ed.), *Judges and Method: New Approaches in Biblical Studies* (Minneapolis, MN: Fortress Press, 1995), pp. 146–70.

_____ *Poor Banished Children of Eve: Women as Evil in the Hebrew Bible* (Minneapolis, MN: Fortress Press, 2003).

Yoo, Yani, "*Han*-Laden Women: Korean 'Comfort Women' and Women in Judges 19–21," *Semeia* 78 (1997), pp. 37–46.

Zakovitch, Yair, "Humor and Theology or the Successful Failure of Israelite Intelligence: A Literary-Folkloric Approach to Joshua 2," in Susan Niditch (ed.), *Text and Tradition* (Atlanta: Scholars Press, 1990), pp. 75–98.

Zamora, Jim Herron, "Suspect's Sex Charges Date to Mid-60s", *San Francisco Examiner*, 17 October 1997.

Index of References

Index of Names

Farley, Melissa 47, 50–1, 53, 106–7
Fernandez, D.R. 172
Fewell, D. 61, 66–7, 69–70
Fisher, E.J. 67
Flemming, R. 126–7, 175
Fontaine, C. 91, 108
Ford, J.M. 42
Foucault, M. 136–7
Frazer, J. 159
Frye, N. 193
Frymer-Kensky, T. 155

G
Gaster, T.H. 93
Gay, P. 136
Goodfriend, E. 101
Gottwald, N. 57, 60, 62, 64, 73, 78
Grabbe, L. 155
Gray, J. 37–8, 64
Gressman, H. 93
Gruber, M.I. 67
Gudorf, C. 27
Guider, M.E. 5–6, 13, 17–25, 27, 29, 56, 58, 61, 69, 71, 74, 122–3
Gunn, D. 61, 66–7, 69–70
Gutierrez, G. 13–21, 25, 28
Gwyther, A. 171–2

H
Harding, S. 8, 30, 32, 34
Harris, W.V. 127–8
Harrison, A. 52
Harstock, N. 6, 8, 30, 32–3
Hawk, L.D. 66–7
Heijst, A. van 91, 108
Henderson, J. 67, 141, 144
Hens-Piazza, G. 105–6
Heyward, C. 160
Hinchberger, B. 24
Hinkelammert, F. 28
Horkheimer, M. 136
Hornsby, T. 125, 132, 135–6
Horsley, R. 125
Howard-Brook. W. 171–2
Hughes, S. 42, 122

I
Ilan, T. 128
International Prostitute's Collective 34, 42, 179

Ipsen, A. 173, 191
Isasi-Díaz, M. 53
Issacs, G.M. 45

J
Jacoby, F. 194
Jaget, C. 34, 46, 99, 101, 103
Jansen, C. 125, 127
Jeffreys, S. 47, 58, 66, 72, 153, 211
Jobling, D. 95–6, 107
Johnson, M. 44, 47, 99
Jones, G.H. 93

K
Kampen, N. 129
Keaney, J.J. 192
Keesling, C. 154
Kempadoo, K. 21, 34, 94, 100
Keuls, E. 127, 129, 138–9, 144–5
Kim, J. 173, 174
King County Journal Staff 179–80, 182
Kitzberger, I.R. 132–3
Kraybill, J.N. 172
Kyung, C.H. 122, 173, 208

L
Lamb, R. 125, 127
Lasine, S. 90–2, 105–6, 109
Leigh, C. 39, 73, 133, 147
Leite, G. 1, 5–6, 10, 13, 20–25, 39–40, 42, 44, 46, 101, 122
Lewis, N.B. 11
Linafelt, T. 90
Long, B.O. 93
Longfellow, S.P. 134
Lorde, A. 136–7, 160

M
Ma, K. 54
Mack, B. 131–2
Maisch, I. 122
Maldonado, R. 84
Maltomini, F. 158
Manzo, R. 44
Marchan, M. 44
Marcuse, H. 136
Marinatos, N. 153
Marosi, R. 42, 122
Marx, K. 8, 26, 30, 32
McCarter, P.K. 110